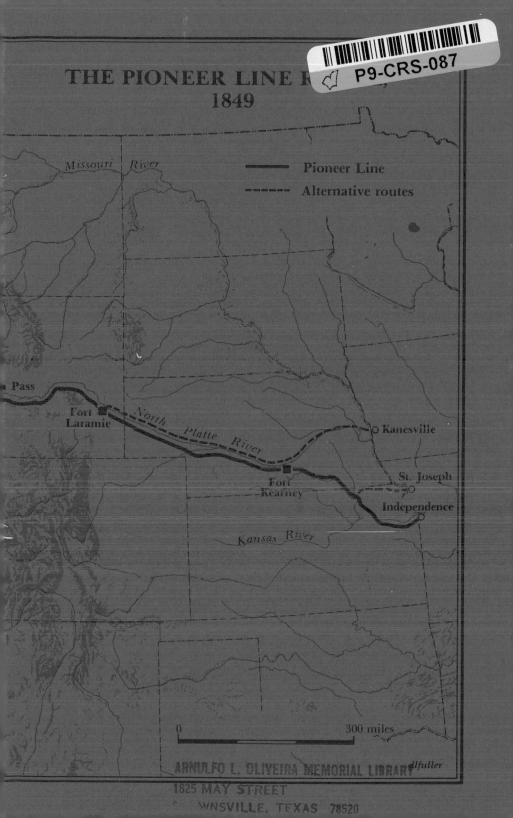

THE PIONEER LINE
1849

Pioneer Line

Alternative routes

Missouri River

Pass

Fort Laramie

North Platte River

Kanesville

Fort Kearney

St. Joseph

Independence

Kansas River

0   300 miles

dlfuller

Overland to California with the Pioneer Line

Overland to California
with the Pioneer Line

THE GOLD RUSH DIARY OF BERNARD J. REID

Edited by Mary McDougall Gordon

STANFORD UNIVERSITY PRESS
Stanford, California 1983

Stanford University Press, Stanford, California
© 1983 by the Board of Trustees of the
Leland Stanford Junior University
Printed in the United States of America
ISBN 0-8047-1192-5   LC 82-62450

Maps on pp. 42, 54, 72, 90, 114, and 132 by
courtesy of J. S. Holliday. From *The World Rushed
In: The California Gold Rush Experience* (New
York: Simon and Schuster, 1981). With alterations
by the original cartographer, D. L. Fuller.

Published with the assistance of the
Andrew W. Mellon Foundation.

For my beloved daughters
ALEXANDRA and EVE

Preface

The publication of Bernard J. Reid's overland diary is the result of the interest and perseverance of Alfred D. Reid, Jr., of Pittsburgh, Pennsylvania. Alfred Reid grew up hearing about his great-grandfather, a forty-niner who reputedly had written a diary of his overland journey to California in 1849, though no one knew where the diary was or whether it still existed. The only evidence of Bernard Reid's western adventure was a diary he had kept in California in 1850, published in 1937 in the *Pony Express Courier*. His eldest son, Ambrose, Alfred Reid's grandfather, had sent the diary to the *Courier*.

In 1953 an uncle of Alfred Reid's discovered in the attic of his house in Pittsburgh a typed journal obviously based on the long-lost 1849 diary, and copies were circulated within the family. Presumably written by Bernard Reid, it included in addition to an introduction recounting the events that led to his decision to join the gold rush, a copy of a letter written home in October 1849 after his arrival in San Francisco. In 1961 James D. Van Trump and Alfred D. Reid, Jr., edited and published the letter in the *Western Pennsylvania Historical Magazine*, and Alfred Reid placed a copy of the typed journal in the library of the Western Pennsylvania Historical Society.

The eventual discovery of a lifetime of records preserved by Bernard Reid is such a breathtaking example of serendipity that it deserves to be told in some detail. In a letter sent to Marguerite Major of the University of Santa Clara on August 25, 1978, a copy of which is in my possession, Alfred Reid writes:

Then a hiatus occurred until 1966 when a cousin directed me to a
"junk" shop in Pittsburgh where she had discovered some articles re-
lated to my family. She reported that the proprietor of the shop pro-
fessed some knowledge of the Reid history that bore investigation. I followed up this lead some weeks later and found that the proprietor had
in his possession three packing crates full of material which he had
picked up from a residential sidewalk where they had been set out for
an annual clean-up campaign pick-up by the City refuse collection
department.

My surmise is that the "papers" were in the possession of my grand-
parents and when my grandmother died in 1935 they were packed up
for storage and eventually ended up in my uncle's garage, unlabeled
and forgotten. In a fit of tidiness he set them out for the refuse collec-
tor, and the junk shop proprietor on a scavenger hunt picked them up
out of curiosity. When he opened the crates he became fascinated with
the contents and kept them at his home rather than offering them for
sale, except for a few old photographs and textbooks. I acquired from
him everything he had and rescued from burning were the "papers,"
which upon examination contained not only the long-lost manuscript of
the 1849 diary but a wealth of other material. . . .

A footnote event occurred in 1974 when I found in an antique store a
collection of several dozen letters written by members of my family, included in which was a letter written by B.J.R. two weeks prior to his
death. These letters had been purchased from the "junk" shop proprietor in 1970 when he had gone out of business. They had been separated
from the other material because of the value of the stamps on the enve-
lopes and were overlooked when I acquired the mother lode. In both
instances I paid a "reward" to the dealers for discovering and preserv-
ing what I felt was really my own.

In what Alfred Reid calls another "outrageous coincidence," I
met him in 1975 as I was preparing to leave Carnegie-Mellon
University in Pittsburgh for the University of Santa Clara. A colleague of mine, David Fowler, told me that a neighbor of his was
the grandson of a forty-niner who had taught at Santa Clara in
1852, the year following its founding as Santa Clara College, the
first institution of higher learning to open in California. I met
David Fowler's neighbors, the Reids, who introduced me to their
son Alfred. He had graduated from the University of Santa
Clara in 1955, received a degree in architecture from Carnegie-
Mellon, and practiced in an architectural firm with his father.
Alfred told me about the provenance of the Reid Papers, and
subsequently gave me copies of Bernard Reid's 1849 diary, the
typed journal based on the diary, and another diary kept by his
great-grandfather from 1846 to 1847.

It is difficult to describe my excitement on first reading those copies. The typed journal, then of dubious authenticity, was easy to read in its narrative form, included an excellent and informative introduction, and explained some puzzling or terse entries in the 1849 diary. But after comparison with the 1849 diary, it was clear that there were omissions in the journal and that it contained some inaccurate recollections of people or events, flights of imagination, and descriptive passages that owed something to Bernard Reid's familiarity with Parkman and other nineteenth-century Western writers. Moreover, these passages were written in a self-conscious "literary" style marred by sentimental excess. The 1849 diary on which the journal was based provoked none of these reservations. I thought it one of the most engrossing accounts of an overland journey that I had ever read. From the moment I finished it, I wanted to edit the diary. Reid was an observant eyewitness, and his daily entries, filled with vivid imagery, mount in interest and poignancy as his wagon train pursues its memorable journey. The years spent in preparing the diary for publication have increased my respect for Bernard Reid's accuracy, good sense, and ability to convey in an admirable "plain style" the epic struggle to reach California.

Alfred Reid gave me the publishing rights to the Reid Papers in 1978 and at that time directed that their ownership pass from him to the University of Santa Clara. By 1980 all the material had been transferred to the University's archives, which already contained some of Reid's correspondence, written when he taught there in 1852. Much of the collection had never been opened and was covered with decades of grime and soot. It proved to be even more of a treasure trove than I expected. Included in the Papers were letters Reid had written home from the West; correspondence with other passengers on the Pioneer Line, the commercial wagon train on which he traveled across the plains; Reid's "ticket" for the trip and a passenger list; other diaries; memorabilia; family records; and a lifetime of correspondence. In the last crate, unpacked in 1980, I found the manuscript of the typed journal based on the 1849 diary, written in Reid's hand in 1904. My comparison revealed that the typed journal is not a verbatim copy of the manuscript. Reid's son Ambrose had edited his father's manuscript, mainly for stylistic reasons, before having it typed in 1931.

The "long-lost" manuscript of the 1849 diary which Alfred Reid discovered in 1966 and later showed to me is not Bernard Reid's original overland diary but a copy made in his hand in 1903. When copying the original diary, by then probably in tatters, Reid left errors intact. When writing the journal based on the diary in 1904, however, Reid carefully corrected spelling, punctuation, and grammatical errors in passages taken from the diary. In a roundabout way, therefore, the manuscript of the journal confirmed the authenticity of his copy of the 1849 diary. The copy reproduced in this volume assuredly is a fair copy. The original diary unfortunately remains lost.

In this volume I include the introduction to the journal Bernard Reid wrote in 1904 as a prologue to the 1849 diary. He undoubtedly consulted his records in order to refresh his memory, but there are some faulty recollections that I indicate in footnotes. To flesh out the diary, I also include excerpts from the 1904 journal; from letters Reid wrote home about the journey; from the diary of Niles Searls, another passenger on the Pioneer Line; and from diaries or newspaper accounts written by others who observed the Pioneer Line along the trail. The actual editing of the diary, and my reconstruction of Bernard Reid's life in the Introduction and Afterword, have benefited immeasurably from my access to the rich Reid collection in the archives of the University of Santa Clara.

I have let the diary stand much as it is in order to preserve textual integrity. In some instances, and without notice to the reader, I have corrected inconsistencies in spelling (where Reid spells a word in two different ways), changed punctuation to modern usage, and deleted or added punctuation marks in the interest of clarity. In excerpts from Reid's letters, omissions in the text are indicated by ellipsis points. Because so many proper names are mentioned by Reid, or are significant in the unfolding saga of the Pioneer Line, I have avoided forbidding additions to the footnotes by including in this volume an appendix with biographical information on persons mentioned in the text. Additional explanations about editorial method are provided when necessary in the footnotes.

It is with deep pleasure that I acknowledge the assistance of those who made this book possible. My greatest debt, of course, is to Alfred D. Reid, Jr., who collected and safeguarded the Reid Papers, generously granted me the publishing rights, and gave the Papers to the University of Santa Clara, where ease of access has lightened the burden of research. Alfred has remained from the outset an enthusiastic and helpful supporter of this endeavor. To his parents, Mr. and Mrs. Alfred D. Reid, to Mr. A. C. Reid of Louisville, and to Mrs. Russell Dunholter of Cincinnati, I also owe thanks for answering some queries about the family. I hope that Alfred and all members of the Reid family will feel that I have done justice to the diary written by the admirable man I have come to know so well.

I am indebted to Gerald McKevitt, colleague, friend, and archivist at the University of Santa Clara, whose help and support have been unstinting, and I appreciate the many kindnesses of Julia O'Keefe, the assistant archivist. Alice Whistler, reference librarian at the Orradre Library of the University, has been, as always, of invaluable help to me. The staffs at the Bancroft Library, University of California, Berkeley, the Beinecke Rare Book and Manuscript Library, Yale University, the Henry E. Huntington Library, San Marino, California, the Lovejoy Library, University of Southern Illinois, Edwardsville, and the Stanford University libraries have been unfailingly helpful. I would like to thank particularly James Hart, William Roberts, and Estelle Rebec of the Bancroft, and John Neal Hoover of the Lovejoy. I wish to acknowledge here the permission of the Bancroft Library to quote from the diary of Niles Searls, the Beinecke Library to quote from the letters of James Lyne and William Wilson, and the diary of Joseph Hamelin, the Huntington Library to quote from the diary of Israel Shipman Pelton Lord (ms., HM19408), and the Missouri Historical Society to quote from the journal of Henry Atkinson Stine.

A number of colleagues have given up valuable time to advise me or to read parts of the manuscript. With gratitude I thank Gerald Alexanderson, the late Ray Billington, Don Dodson, Frank Duggan, Norris Hundley, Howard Lamar, Matt Meier, Kathryn Kish Sklar, and Thomas Turley. I want to add a special note of thanks to William Stanton, a long-time mentor. My work profited from his learning, fine sense of style, and acerb wit. None, of course, is responsible for any errors. I must express, too, a debt of gratitude to the late Frederick Merk, who first introduced me to the westward movement when I arrived in this country as an Australian graduate student. I thank the editor of the *Pacific Historical Review* for permission to incorporate, in the Introduction and Afterword, parts of my article, "Overland to California in 1849: A Neglected Commercial Enterprise," and the editor of the *Western Pennsylvania Historical Magazine* for permission to quote from Bernard Reid's "California Gold Rush Letter."

I could not wish for more congenial editors than those at Stanford University Press. My thanks to the Director, Leon Seltzer, for legal advice, and to John Feneron for ably supervising production. Ellen Hershey has been an ideal copy editor—meticulous, tactful, and intelligent. I cannot thank Ellen enough for her total immersion in the text, and for an interest that went far beyond the call of duty. Jess Bell, my editor, was enthusiastic about the diary from the beginning, and has been extraordinarily helpful during the time spent revising and editing.

Linda Campbell, my department's valued secretary, has typed many drafts of the manuscript with her usual patience and good humor, and Candace Lambrecht in innumerable ways helped me to meet my deadlines. I also owe thanks to Marguerite Major, Joan Murphy, and Nancy Miller of the University of Santa Clara, Kathryn Kumler and Charles Schweizer of the University of Southern Illinois at Edwardsville, Todd Webb of Bath, Maine, Michael McIntyre of San José State University, and Rosamond and Harold Bacon of Stanford, for past favors.

I am grateful for the grants-in-aid from the University of Santa Clara and the Sourisseau Academy of San José State University that enabled me to work at the Beinecke and Huntington libraries. I especially appreciate the encouragement and support of former and present administrators at Santa Clara: William Donnelly; Timothy O'Keefe; Joseph Subbiondo; Paul Locatelli; and the President, William Rewak, who hand-carried all of Bernard Reid's diaries from Pittsburgh to the University's archives.

Close friends and family, many far away, gave no direct assistance during the preparation of this work, but provided me with warm and loving support. To the two most dear I dedicate this book.

Saratoga, California   M. McD. G.

Contents

Maps and Illustrations

Note on Citation

Full authors' names, titles, and publication data for works cited in this volume will be found in the Bibliography, pp. 227–36. Overland diaries and journals are cited by the authors' last names and relevant dates or page numbers; unless otherwise noted, the year is 1849. All cited correspondence to and from Bernard Reid or other members of the Reid family is in the Reid Papers unless otherwise noted.

Editor's Introduction

Editor's Introduction

One of the great adventures in American history was the gold rush to California. In the first year of that epic folk experience, when forty-niners set out for the goldfields by sea and land, the most popular route was along the California Trail. Looking back at an "unending stream" of wagons crossing the prairie, it seemed to one gold seeker as if the whole family of man had set its face westward.[1]

Before the news of the gold strike reached "the States" in the fall of 1848, the majority of overlanders were restless groups of farming people moving westward in search of Eden. Between 1844—the year when wagons first crossed the Sierra Nevada—and 1848, about 2,700 settlers emigrated to California. But as "gold mania" swept the country, the nature of emigration changed. The number of overlanders surged in 1849 to some 35,000, and most were not settlers but gold seekers planning to rush to the goldfields, make their fortunes, and return home as men of substance. Among those now sweeping westward along the California Trail were many from small towns and cities— veritable greenhorns who knew little about the rigors of over- land travel. Misadventures like wagon breakdowns, gunshot wounds, and drownings (accounts of which form litanies in gold rush diaries) caused far more deaths than Indians, who were no- tably peaceable in 1849.

Yet such misfortunes were minor compared with the problems

---

[1] Notes to the Editor's Introduction are on pp. 209–14.

caused by heavily laden wagons. Overloading was almost universal, and the majority of emigrants clung to their possessions until forced to accept the inevitable. Accounts of the 1849 emigration are replete with descriptions of the extraordinary amount of debris that littered the western landscape. An even more calamitous result of overloading was the strain on draft animals—lifelines on the trail, as any experienced plainsman knew. Overburdened stock, already faltering early in the journey, were in poor condition to face mounting hazards. On the trail beyond Fort Laramie diarists repeatedly noted the numbers and stench of dead beasts of burden, and many animals that survived the rough terrain of the Rocky Mountains gave out on the fearsome Humboldt desert or in the Sierra Nevada. A "great army of tramps" struggled to the goldfields on foot, and only the dispatch of relief expeditions from California saved them from more terrible fatalities.[2]

Unforeseen circumstances further complicated westward travel in 1849. A late spring delayed the forty-niners' departure from frontier towns, intensifying their fears by raising the spectre of the Donner party, trapped in the Sierra Nevada by the early autumn snows of 1846. Even the easiest stage of the journey, along the relatively smooth trail across the prairie to Fort Laramie, proved arduous. Gales, hailstorms, and incessant rain brought discomfort and more delay as emigrants struggled with a muddy trail, swollen rivers, stampedes, and damage to wagons and supplies. Worse, Asiatic cholera moved up the rivers from New Orleans and traveled along the trail with the caravans. Euphoric forty-niners quickly sobered when faced with the prospect of a sudden death and lonely burial on the desolate prairie.[3]

In the vast literature on this westward saga, the most vivid and dependable sources are the diaries kept by the forty-niners themselves. As the historian David Potter has written, their daily accounts are "the only perfectly contemporaneous and authentic records" of a major historical event—they are to the gold rush what "the sagas were to the Vikings, or the *Chansons* to the Age of Chivalry."[4] This volume contains the text of one of those diaries, written by Bernard J. Reid as he crossed the plains along the California Trail.

Born on April 24, 1823, Bernard Joseph Reid grew up in western Pennsylvania, in the township of Youngstown, about forty miles from Pittsburgh. His parents, Meredith and Eleanor Hanlon Reid, had emigrated from Ireland in 1818 with an infant son, James Vincent. Accompanying them were Meredith Reid's brother Simon and his parents. The family followed James Reid, another of Meredith's brothers, who had settled near Youngstown the year before.

Except for their devout Catholicism, the Reids were not the stereotypical Irish immigrants who would arrive in waves a few decades hence after the devastating potato famine. The family had the means to travel west from the port of entry and build a house on several acres of land, and the three brothers had received a sound basic education in Ireland. After arriving in advance of his family, James had taught school near Youngstown. A few years later he opened a private school in Butler, a township outside Pittsburgh, and in 1822 he began studying for the priesthood. Simon's occupation remains obscure, but he became relatively prosperous. Bernard Reid's father was a surveyor who during the slack winter seasons taught in schools as far away as western Virginia in order to make his family "comfortable at home."[5]

Four children were born to Meredith and Eleanor Reid in Youngstown. In addition to James Vincent, the son born in Ireland, the family eventually included Mary, John, Bernard, Catharine (Kate), and a foster child, Ellen Findley. Meredith Reid never became affluent, and during the depression that followed the Panic of 1837 he had "bare enough to live." He died of dysentery in 1844, leaving no money but two houses with a combined value of 1,250 dollars and some prized possessions—surveying instruments, a watch, and a staff. Yet despite the family's straitened circumstances, the daughters received some private tuition designed to fit them for teaching in elementary schools, and the sons studied the classics with their Uncle James at academies he founded in his various parishes. Meredith Reid taught the boys advanced mathematics and surveying.[6]

Young Bernard attended an academy near Fayetteville, Ohio, and "fixed [his] heart" on a college education. Although his father was sympathetic to his goal, the family means were too slender; before his sixteenth birthday Bernard Reid began teaching school near Youngstown. A year later he left for Pittsburgh, determined to "do anything else rather than teach school." For a time the youth worked in a dry goods store, but he lost the job in the lean times that reduced his father's income. Reluctantly he returned to teaching in a succession of schools near that city. In 1842, the year his mother died, Reid followed his brother John to the new town of Clarion, about 65 miles north of Pittsburgh, where he taught in a private school. Before the year was out the two brothers had borrowed money to found a Clarion newspaper, the *Iron County Democrat*, with Bernard serving as its editor. Three years later they sold the paper, apparently receiving only enough money to settle their debt. John resumed working in a store and Bernard became the county surveyor, appointed for a three-year term.[7]

The Reid family was close-knit. After their father's death the three dependent daughters moved to Clarion to live with their brothers; Bernard was fond of "the girls," especially Kate, "a treasure of a sister." James, now married, lived nearby in Freeport, a river town on the way from Clarion to Pittsburgh. The two uncles visited from time to time, and the Reverend James Reid regarded himself as a surrogate father to his orphaned nieces and nephews.[8]

But the youngest son was restless. For a more acute understanding of the conflicts Bernard Reid experienced as a young man, theories advanced by Daniel J. Levinson in *The Seasons of a Man's Life* seem remarkably pertinent. In his succinct summary of a well-recognized stage in male development, Levinson observes that the "season" he calls "Entering the Adult World" occurs roughly between the ages of twenty-two and twenty-eight. This stage, he writes, creates turmoil for many young men because they face two contradictory tasks: the free exploration of the external world with its multiple possibilities, and the assumption of adult responsibilities that fulfill desires for stability, roots, and "membership in the tribe."[9] There is ample evidence that Bernard Reid was unable to achieve a balance between these conflicting tasks.

At the age of twenty-four, Reid left his home in Clarion to live and work in St. Louis. As an old man he would recollect that in 1846, on the spur of the moment, he wrote to surveyors-general in frontier districts offering his services as an experienced surveyor. Months later, he received an offer from the surveyor-general based in St. Louis, which he immediately accepted.[10] The decision to leave home, however, had been germinating for some time.

To a casual observer, Bernard Reid might have appeared old for his years. Self-supporting from the age of sixteen, he was frugal, industrious, religious, and a "total abstainer" (having taken the pledge at seventeen). He held a responsible job and was dedicated to self-improvement, over the years studying German and "Mnemonics," and joining a "literary institute."[11]

Yet he never had left home. After moving from his parents' household, the youth had lived in Pittsburgh with his brother James, and in Clarion with his brother John and their sisters. Unlike the two older brothers, Bernard was eager to "explore the external world." And any desires for stability, roots, and membership in the tribe were frustrated by lack of a satisfying occupation or a romantic attachment that might have encouraged him to establish his own household.

For some time Bernard Reid had harbored romantic feelings toward Letitia Farran, the daughter of an Irish-Catholic family he visited frequently when in Pittsburgh. The young man received no heartening response from the nineteen-year-old Letitia. Following an afternoon spent with her in 1846, he mourned privately that "no look or tone was there—other than those of *friendship*. And though friendship is a treasure of purest gold, yet mere *gold* is esteemed as dross by one who has set his heart on *rubies*."[12]

He was equally disconsolate about finding work that would give direction to his life. Schoolteaching had been irksome and newspaper publishing unprofitable. The priesthood appeared a likely calling to a number of his pastors. Dependent for services in Clarion on a circuit-riding priest, Reid frequented St. Paul's Cathedral on regular visits to Pittsburgh and was a familiar guest at the bishop's residence, where the clergy were friends of his Uncle James. But devout as he was, the young man concluded that he had "no vocation," and his days "must be spent in the world . . . without losing sight of [an] eternal interest in the next."[13] Nor did he regard surveying as a life's work. In intervals between field work, Reid began reading law with a Clarion attorney, since it promised a better livelihood; in Clarion County, he observed, there were five Catholic congregations, "few if any *good* lawyers and *not one Catholic lawyer.*" Yet he felt an "aversion" to the profession that was difficult to overcome.[14]

Having thus avoided those decisions about marriage and work that typically mark the transition from early to mature adulthood, in January 1847 Reid began his first attempt to explore the external world. During the slack winter season he set out on a tour of towns in Ohio and western Virginia (now West Virginia) to teach a system of mnemonics, or memory training. Reid had learned to memorize long lists of facts, even the day of the week of any given date, "however remote"; he planned to teach his method for a charge of one dollar a person.[15] For nearly three months he traveled up and down the rivers to towns like Parkersburg and Charleston in Virginia, and Marietta and Gallipolis in Ohio. Reid religiously kept a diary of the trip, begun when he left Clarion on December 23, 1846.

From his diary it is clear that the wanderer enjoyed traveling on steamboats, exploring the countryside, sight-seeing in the more interesting towns like Marietta, and observing the characters he met on steamboats and in wayside taverns. Joining happily in singing and dancing parties held in neighborhood houses or hotel parlors, he betrayed some interest in young women met at these gatherings by embellishing a number of entries in the diary with decorous but appreciative sketches of those who caught his fancy.[16]

The diary reveals other facets of Reid's character. Always sober and responsible, he kept methodical accounts and refrained from drinking or gambling in the convivial atmosphere of riverboats and taverns. Dressing conservatively in a frock coat, he moved easily in local circles of established lawyers, physicians, clergymen, and politicians. Since the weather was persistently bad, Reid spent a good deal of time confined to his lodgings. Occasionally grumbling about the loneliness and tedium, he nevertheless seems to have been remarkably self-contained; many contented hours were spent reading, writing letters, and playing his flute.[17]

Yet there was more than a dash of Victorian romanticism beneath the sobriety and self-control. Reid relished popular poetry of the day like the lachrymose poems of the English sentimentalist, Mrs. Felicia Hemans, wrote a long narrative of his trip in effusive verse, admired the wonders of untouched nature, and pressed flowers for keepsakes. The ties to home remained close despite his wandering urge, and he wrote long, affectionate letters to the family in Clarion.[18]

What Reid did not enjoy were the classes in mnemonics that paid for the new experiences. He cringed in embarrassment when giving showman-like presentations in order to attract customers, and found the poor attendance discouraging, never gathering more than twenty "scholars" for any session. Delighted to teach his last class on April 1, 1847, Reid arrived back in Pittsburgh with only a small profit and the knowledge that teaching mnemonics was no way to underwrite any future travels.[19]

Returning to "compass and chain," Reid received the offer from St. Louis on June 8. The bewildered family, who had known nothing of his applications for a surveying post on the frontier, nevertheless seemed pleased with his "good fortune" (the salary of 900 dollars a year certainly exceeded Reid's previous earnings). His brother James and "Reverend Uncle" arrived for a family farewell, and Reid left on June 23, writing in his diary that Clarion had "never felt so much like home" as when he was leaving it. A week later he departed from Pittsburgh's "dusky shore," and on July 6, 1847, arrived in St. Louis.[20]

Thus Bernard Reid was living close to the western frontier when news of the gold strike in California reached "the States." Only rumors about gold had spread by the fall of 1848, yet the excitement was feverish enough to affect hundreds of men, who quickly set sail for El Dorado. After the arrival of a positive report from Richard Mason, California's first territorial governor, followed by President Polk's confirmation of the rich discovery

The St. Louis riverfront as Bernard Reid saw it in 1847. Note the domes and spires in the background. In his diary on July 6 of that year, Reid wrote that the city "looked very well from the river, rising with a gradual slope, spreading out to a great extent, and crowned by so many domes and spires glittering in the evening sun." *Courtesy: Missouri Historical Society.*

in December, the fever became a "mania" raging with "intense vigor" and carrying men off to the goldfields by every available ship.[21]

As the news circulated by the nation's press penetrated every corner of the nation, thousands of other emigrants began preparations for the overland journey. The best-known route at the time was the California Trail. It followed the well-used Oregon Trail across the prairie to Fort Laramie, and crossed the Rockies at South Pass. The trail diverged from the Oregon route at Fort Hall (in present-day Idaho), and moved southwest along creeks and rivers to follow the Humboldt River through what is now Nevada. After reaching the "Sink" or terminus of the river, the trail crossed a forbidding desert and the Sierra Nevada before reaching the valleys of northern California. The distance was roughly two thousand miles, and an "ideal" wagon trip took four months. Because the use of animal power shaped emigration in the preindustrial West, wagons were confined to the frontier until spring grass was high enough for forage, and emigrants traveled always with the knowledge that they must cross the Sierra before the first snowfall. The trail perforce stayed close to water and vegetation, regardless of additional mileage or aggravated hardship from steep grades, and the unavoidable deserts were terrible tests of endurance.[22]

Thousands of forty-niners eager to reach the goldfields formed large joint-stock wagon companies during the winter months. The preparations were time-consuming. Members organized their companies along military lines and formed committees to buy equipment and supplies. Many elected officers of their trains, and solemnly framed constitutions and by-laws to protect property and preserve social order after they left the bounds of "civilization." Others joined faster and cheaper pack trains, or formed partnerships to travel in smaller groups. Only a few hardy souls dared to travel alone.[23]

But what of those who wanted no part of laborious preparation, and could afford to travel in comparative style? Until the gold rush there was no incentive to provide commercial transportation to California. With the emergence of a different kind of emigrant population in 1849, however, a few enterprising men sensed a new clientele seeking faster and more comfortable passage by land. Early in that year, advertisements for commercial transportation overland to the goldfields began appearing in newspapers up and down the country.

These promoters of overland transportation were not alone in detecting windfalls as national hysteria about gold intensified. Ships were pressed into service for the voyage to San Francisco, and the cost of passage rose sharply. Merchants and stock dealers began competing energetically for unprecedented trade, and prices climbed when the supply of wagons and animals failed to meet demand. Gambling dens, taverns, brothels, and enterprising hucksters did a brisk business in such "outfitting" towns as Independence and St. Joseph, where hordes of forty-niners began collecting in the spring.[24] Along the overland trail,

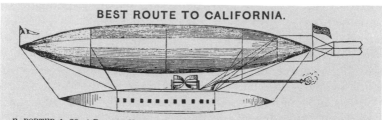

BEST ROUTE TO CALIFORNIA.

R. PORTER & CO., (office, room No. 40 in the Sun Buildings,—entrance 128 Fulton-street, New-York,) are making active progress in the construction of an Aerial Transport, for the express purpose of carrying passengers between New York and California. This transport will have a capacity to carry from 50 to 100 passengers, at a speed of 60 to 100 miles per hour. It is expected to put this machine in operation about the 1st of April, 1849. It is proposed to carry a limited number of passengers—not exceedihg 300—for $50, including board, and the transport is expected to make a trip to the gold region and back in seven days. The price of passage to California is fixed at $200, with the exception above mentioned. Upwards of 200 passage tickets at $50 each have been engaged prior to Feb. 15. Books open for subscribers as above.

Rufus Porter's "aerial locomotive," as advertised in a promotional circular, 1849. *Courtesy: Bancroft Library.*

travel assumed an "expensive dimension." Transient trading posts, blacksmiths' shops, and gambling "lodges" sprang up in anticipation of an exceptional season. Traders raised their prices at the infrequent government forts and well-established outposts as hapless emigrants clamored for goods and services. Rival ferry operators competed for profits at dangerous river crossings.[25]

The most breathtaking scheme for overland service was passage by "aerial locomotive," initiated by Rufus Porter, a versatile if eccentric inventor who in 1845 had founded *Scientific American*. Porter's proposed airship was a balloon driven by steam-powered propellers (a model on exhibit in New York City looked somewhat like a future dirigible). His company allegedly sold 200 tickets for the maiden flight to California at a special rate of 50 dollars each, including meals served with wines. But Porter abandoned his scheme—in order, he announced, to prepare for the Second Coming.[26]

More conservative ventures were advertised in Missouri papers early in 1849. A number of promoters from St. Louis and towns along the Missouri River announced plans to take passengers overland by wagon for prices ranging from 100 to 300 dollars a person.[27] But only one such company actually crossed the plains. This was the Pioneer Line.

Unlike other local ventures, the Pioneer Line secured testimonials from prominent citizens and enthusiastic endorsement by the *Missouri Republican*, the most influential St. Louis newspaper. Its proprietors were Thomas Turner and a man known as Allen, whose first name has been lost; they formerly had transported army supplies to Santa Fe and Chihuahua during the Mexican War. Evidently having sufficient capital to free them from dependence on an immediate sale of tickets, Turner and Allen ordered equipment and supplies in advance; they also began advertising in newspapers outside Missouri. The owners announced that their train consisted of specially built "carriages" (a euphemism for lightweight wagons), each drawn by four mules and providing sleeping quarters for three of six passengers who formed a mess, taking their meals together; others would sleep in tents belonging to the Pioneer Line. Heavier wagons, a few equipped with pontoons for fording rivers, would carry baggage and supplies. Each passenger could take one hundred pounds of baggage, with any excess costing twenty cents a pound. The fare from Independence to San Francisco was 200 dollars, and the proprietors, surely for promotional purposes, estimated the time of travel at a mind-boggling 55 to 60 days.[28]

The *Missouri Republican* indefatigably promoted this St. Louis venture, claiming it was the best scheme yet devised to reach California and that the proprietors ("we know them well") were capable of performing all they proposed. By March 9 the company had 100 passengers. Turner and Allen announced that on April 15 the train would be in camp eight miles from Independence, on the Santa Fe Trail.[29]

When the Pioneer Line assembled on its campground, enthusiasm for such a "magnificent enterprise" seemed justified. An "enormous" herd of "remarkably fine" mules, twenty-two massive freight wagons, and twenty handsome carriages marked in "staring letters" with the name of the Pioneer Line made "quite a show." The captain and co-owner of the train, Thomas Turner, headed a small personal staff and a crew of some forty teamsters and herders. As an added attraction, Turner and Allen had hired a noted mountain man and overland guide, Moses "Black" Harris, to act as "pilot" of the train.[30] Confident newspaper reports of the Pioneer Line's "superior advantage" over other wagon trains, "flaming advertisements" displayed conspicuously in Independence, and rumors that "skillful *valets*" would attend its "gay and festive" passengers proved too enticing for many emigrants. They sold off their wagons and animals and "almost forced themselves into the Pioneer Line."[31] Turner and Allen increased the number of passengers to at least 125, ordered additional equipment, and announced that a second train with 75 passengers would leave Independence in June. Moreover, the gratified proprietors promised to establish a trading post near the goldfields and provide regular passenger service to and from California.[32]

The passengers who so eagerly joined the Pioneer Line were all men, and they came from towns and cities throughout the nation. The largest contingent, of approximately 48, was from the Midwest. At least 27 were Southerners, 22 came from the Middle Atlantic states, and 22 from New England.[33] Among them were lawyers, hotelkeepers, merchants, sea captains, surveyors, clerks, a sprinkling of gamblers and speculators, and physicians. The physicians numbered ten, in fact, prompting one passenger to write that "if any suffer from sickness it will not be for the want of medical advisers."[34]

Some in this assorted group were middle-aged or elderly. David T. McCollum was fifty years old, Dr. C. H. Swift had left grown children in Alabama, and Walter Hawxhurst of Iowa, like two other passengers, had brought along his son. One of the "Pioneers" believed Walter Hawxhurst, at fifty-five, to be the oldest man on the train, but Augustus O. Garrett (who lived to return to Illinois) was sixty-five. The majority, however, were young and single. Most likely the youngest was Robert Hawxhurst, only fifteen years old.[35]

The Pioneers, therefore, were urban, middle-class, Anglo-American men, like so many emigrants of 1849. One former officer had traveled along the Santa Fe Trail during the Mexican War.[36] But the rest were inexperienced frontiersmen, reluctant enough about facing the rigors of conventional travel that they were willing to pay for services to deliver them to California. As one remarked, they rejoiced at the comforts in store and the prospect of a speedy arrival, and set out "elated in spirit, only pitying those less fortunate in their choice of conveyance."[37]

Among the "gay and festive" passengers on this enviable wagon train was Bernard Reid. Upon arriving in St. Louis in 1847 he had settled in as an examiner of surveys and found the work "light and pleasant." Joining a "gentlemen's" sodality, a fellowship group sponsored by Father Arnold Damen, the Dutch pastor of the Jesuit church he faithfully attended, and lodging in a superior boarding house, Reid acquired a "little circle" of agreeable friends. As part of his continuing dedication to self-improvement, he began studying French and bought William Blackstone's *Commentaries on the Laws of England* to refresh his memory on the common law. Yet Reid thought of his life in St. Louis as an interlude, and missed his family and friends in Clarion.[38]

Unsettled as he was, Reid seized the opportunity to join thousands of other young men in the adventure of a lifetime. Living in St. Louis, an important base in the gold rush, he was at the center of the exuberant preparations. Certainly he had an interest in gold seeking, enough to enroll in classes on "the searching, testing and smelting of gold" offered in the city by J. H. Tooke, a charlatan quick to exploit the innocents who were heading for El Dorado.[39] But the journey itself was the lodestar. A passenger train appealed to Reid because he could buy a pony to explore the wilderness, study French and the common law at his leisure, and continue working to earn money until the late spring, an impossibility if he joined a joint-stock wagon train.

Bernard Reid began his overland diary on May 24, 1849, nine days after the Pioneer Line set out across the prairie. He made daily entries until September 23, two days after arriving at the goldfields, and concluded the diary on October 7 while panning gold at Weber Creek, in the Sacramento Valley. Shortly before his death in 1904, Reid wrote a journal based on his overland diary. In an introduction he recalled his preparations to join the gold rush and his experiences during the early days of travel across the prairie. The introduction is included in this volume as a prologue to the diary.

One of the diary's claims upon our interest is its ability to convey a lively sense of the moment as the Pioneers struggled on to California. Reid was a keen observer and a faithful recorder of daily events. The rhythm and energy of his prose seem the more remarkable because the diary was written in haste and under conditions of hardship. Unlike so many overland diaries, Reid's becomes more eloquent as the journey assumed nightmarish proportions. There are few better descriptions than Reid's of Soda Springs, the "City of Rocks," or the desolate Sink of the Humboldt River. His account of the dust that maddened emigrants as they plodded along the upper reaches of the Humboldt is only one example of his ability to capture a moment with striking imagery. "Towards sundown" on August 25, he tells us, "the air becalms and the dust after rising a few feet high overspreads the plain like a lake of smooth muddy water. Along our line of wagons some are completely submerged in it. Others show only their tops, which seem to go floating along like little boats in the water. Here and there the heads of the men on foot stick up and glide along in rows and groups like ducks on a pond."

The diary has a still better claim upon our interest because it provides such a rich account of passage on the first commercial wagon train to set out across the plains. Scattered information on the Pioneer Line has been available for decades, yet scholars have given it only glancing attention.[40] The train received extensive newspaper publicity, and a good number of observers commented on its progress along the trail. Moreover, four other passengers left records of their journey. Niles Searls, a sober young lawyer born in New York state, kept a diary of the trip. He remained in California and later served as chief justice of the state supreme court. Lell H. Woolley, another gold seeker born in New York, also stayed in California, where he prospered in business and wrote his memoirs in old age. In 1849 he was a fledgling merchant and an ardent Mason. David T. McCollum wrote letters about the journey that were published in an Ann Arbor, Michigan, newspaper. By 1849 McCollum, who returned to Ann Arbor in 1851, was an established businessman, local Whig politician, and Methodist lay leader active in the temperance and abolition movements. Richard H. McDonald provided reminiscences for a biography written by his son in 1891. A physician born in Kentucky and a pious Congregationalist, McDonald abandoned medicine in California to become president of the Pacific Bank in San Francisco. He ran as candidate for governor of California in 1882 on the Prohibition party ticket.

The records of all these men are less substantial than those left by Bernard Reid. Woolley's and McDonald's contributions are the reminiscences of old men, and McCollum filled two letters with despairing commentary about his recurrent sickness, the deaths of young companions, and the desolation of a land of "Graves and Drought."[41] The most informative source, the diary of Niles Searls, contains only seven entries between July 28 and October 1, the day when a remnant of the Pioneer Line crossed the Sierra Nevada. In addition to his overland diary and the journal written in 1904, Bernard Reid preserved long letters written to his family from California, diaries kept during his western exile, and a lifetime of correspondence and memorabilia containing nuggets of information about the Pioneer Line. Combined with the sources formerly available to scholars, the Reid collection provides the records necessary for a comprehensive history of a distinctive wagon train.

Yet Bernard Reid's diary is more than a "contemporaneous and authentic" chronicle of a distinctive wagon train's memorable journey. The Pioneer Line carried what one observer described as an "incongruous" mixture of gold seekers. Other forty-niners who joined large wagon trains were united by family or regional ties, worked together to organize their joint-stock companies, and elected officers of their trains. Passengers on the Pioneer Line came from all parts of the Union and were "tumbled in together" to form a company.[42] They were dependent on the captain and crew of a profit-making enterprise, and owned only their baggage. Sharing in "the perpetual vexations and hardships" of life on the overland trail,[43] the Pioneers faced problems unlike those of emigrants traveling in more conventional trains. The passengers' responses to their situation shed light on the social behavior and cultural attitudes of a diverse group of white American men, thrown together in unusual circumstances for months of grueling travel across the plains. In the following pages we can relive their experiences as the Pioneer Line struggled along the trail to California.

Overland to California with the Pioneer Line

The opening page of Bernard Reid's overland journal, written in 1904 and based on his 1849 diary. *Courtesy: Archives, Univ. of Santa Clara.*

Prologue

"No pen can adequately describe our start"

In 1904 Bernard J. Reid, then nearly eighty-one, wrote a journal based on the diary he had kept on the overland trail in 1849. The journal opens with an introduction, describing Reid's move from Pennsylvania to Missouri in 1847, his preparations to join the gold rush to California, and his early experiences as a passenger on the Pioneer Line. Reid concluded the introduction after recalling the wagon train's journey from Independence, Missouri, to the Kansas River.

The first entry in Reid's overland diary is dated May 24, 1849, nine days after the Pioneer Line had set out across the plains. Since the introduction to the journal covers the preceding events as Reid remembered them in 1904, it serves here as a prologue to his overland diary.

Overland to California in '49

St. Louis was my residence when I started on the journey indicated by the title, but I was a Pennsylvanian. My sojourn in Missouri came about in an odd way that may be fitly recorded here as a preface to my trip. In the Fall of 1838 I began to teach school and followed that employment for three years. I had previously mastered the science and to some extent the practice of surveying. In the spring of 1842, at the age of 19, I emigrated from Westmoreland county, Pa., to the new town of Clarion in the new county of the same name, where for three years I edited and published a county newspaper. In the Spring of 1845 I was appointed county surveyor, and the next Spring began to read law in the intervals between jobs of field work. In November of that year, while feeling blue in a spell of rainy weather, I happened on the Annual Report of the Commissioner of the General Land Office, containing the reports made to him by the Surveyor Generals of U.S. public lands in the various districts. These showed the operations of their several offices for the preceding year, including the work of deputy surveyors in the field and clerks and draughtsmen in their offices. Here was a chance, it occurred to me, of "going west and growing up with the country," although Horace Greely had not yet made that expression famous.[1] Under the spur of the moment, without realizing how quixotical the idea was, I wrote to the surveyor generals at Detroit, Dubuque, St. Louis, Little Rock and Jackson, describing my qualifications with due (but not excessive) modesty and offering my services as a deputy surveyor or clerk. I was of course a total stranger to all of them and did not know a single soul in any of their cities to refer them to, and had no political or other "pull" to employ in my interest. In a day or two, when returning sunshine had dispelled the blues, I laughed at my folly of supposing that I could obtain a public employment at long range and by so un-heard of a method. In due course of mail I received courteous but unfavorable replies from four of the parties addressed, but none from St. Louis, and before spring came all thoughts of my western chimera were dismissed from my mind.[2] Early in June, however, I was surprised to receive a letter from Gen. Frederick R. Conway, surveyor general for the District of Illinois and Missouri, at St. Louis, offering me the position of examining clerk in his office,[3] which was accepted and the Fourth of July found me on a steamboat from Pittsburgh, ploughing up the Mississippi river between Cairo [Illinois] and St. Louis. On the evening before two other Pennsylvanians, Brewster and Simpson, and myself, had planned an old fashioned Fourth of July celebration on the steamer, the Captain

[1] Horace Greeley (not Greely), the renowned newspaper editor and exponent of westward emigration, took his famous slogan "Go West, young man, and grow up with the country" from an article written by John Soule (1851). His enthusiasm did not extend to emigration beyond the Mississippi, however. See Smith, *Virgin Land*, pp. 234–35; and Unruh, *The Plains Across*, pp. 36–40.

[2] Reid, diary, 1846–47, Jan. 3, 5, 1847. Letters to Reid from surveyors-general in Detroit, Michigan (Dec. 1, 1846), Jackson, Mississippi (Dec. 8, 1846), and Dubuque, Iowa (Dec. 10, 1846), are in the Reid Papers.

[3] Reid, diary, 1846–47, June 8, 1847; F. R. Conway to Bernard Reid, May 29, 1847. Upon receiving Conway's letter, Reid wrote: "Bountiful God! how thankful I should be. . . . How unexpected—how undeserved this good fortune is!" Conway was not a military man; his title was a shortened form of surveyor-general.

kindly consenting to furnish a special dinner for the occasion. We had constituted ourselves a committee of arrangements and had selected Mr. L., a St. Louis lawyer, of good appearance, to deliver a suitable oration. I was to read the declaration of independence, and Brewster and Simpson were to prepare and distribute toasts to be read after the removal of the cloth. The dinner was a splendid one and everything passed off well, including the oration, notwithstanding the fact that after his acceptance of the role assigned him Mr. L. had come to me to ask whether it was July 4th, 1796, that the declaration of independence was adopted.[4]

I found Gen. Conway a perfect gentleman of the old school, for whose memory I shall always have a high regard, and my confreres in the office were pleasant gentlemen. I was fortunate in happening on a private boarding house kept by Captain [Jonas] Newman and his estimable wife, who belonged to one of the leading French families of the city. My fellow boarders were a refined, agreeable and, in general, a superior class of people. One of them afterwards became Chief Justice of California, another a judge of a county court in California, another attorney-general and another surveyor general of the same state, two others became Jesuit Priests, another became Gen. Rosecrans' Chief of Staff in the civil war and was killed at the battle of Stone River, and still another, whose manners were as gentle and refined as any of the rest, became a duellist and killed his man in California and was afterwards himself killed, with his whole party, in a filibustering expedition to Nicaragua.[5]

When the news of the discovery of gold in California reached

[4] Reid, diary, 1846–47, June 29–July 6, 1847. Reid describes this trip, from Pittsburgh to Cincinnati on the *Hibernia* and from Cincinnati to St. Louis on the *Colorado*, at some length in his diary. He first met John A. Brewster and Thomas Simpson (who practiced law in Lexington, Missouri) in Cincinnati. Mr. L. is A. W. Lewis. This celebration, mentioning Lewis, Brewster, Simpson, and Reid was reported in the *Missouri Republican*, July 8, 1847; the paper stated that Reid gave the toast to the Union. For details on Brewster and other significant figures, see Appendix A, pp. 187–207.

[5] The future chief justice of California is Robert F. Morrison, the judge of the county court is W. J. Graves, the attorney-general is Edward J. C. Kewen, and the surveyor-general is Reid's friend from Philadelphia, John A. Brewster. The two Jesuits are J. M. Hayes and S. P. Lalumière, and General Rosecrans's aide is Lt. Col. Julius Garesché. The freebooter killed in the irregular military adventure or filibustering expedition to Nicaragua is Edward Kewen's brother, Achilles Kewen.

"the states," it naturally caused a great stir. Through the winter of 1848−9 the subject of overland excursions to the gold regions in the Spring was much discussed. St. Louis, being the nearest large city to the frontier of civilization, became the center of activity in the way of preparation for the journey. From almost every state west of the Alleghenies companies were being organized and equipped to start across the plains as soon as the opening of Spring would admit, mostly with ox teams to haul the canvas-covered wagons or prairie schooners, some with mules and a few with horses.

During that winter Captain (afterwards General) Fremont's journal of his explorations on the plains, the Rocky Mountains and California fell into my hands, and its perusal gave me a strong desire to see for myself the interesting countries he described.[6] Without however giving up my position some weeks in advance, I could not well have given the necessary attention to the selection of a company to travel with, and my part in procuring the means of transportation and the necessary equipment for such a journey. Just then, in March 1849, a circular was issued by Turner, Allen & Company, of St. Louis, who claimed to have had experience in transporting army supplies to New Mexico and Chihuahua in the war just ended, and proposing to organize a "Pioneer Train" to carry passengers across the plains in 55 days. In their prospectus they said "elliptic spring wagons, covered and fitted up comfortably for carrying six passengers each, will be provided. Price of passage, including rations, $200. 100 pounds baggage per man,—extra baggage 20 cents per pound. We expect to make the trip in 55 or 60 days, but we take provisions for 100 days. We have taken much pains to select the kind of mules best adapted for the trip. We start for a quick trip and all that the best kind of mule teams, the most complete outfit and experienced conductors can accomplish, we promise to do."[7] One hundred passengers was the limit mentioned. So ra-

[6] John C. Frémont's *Report of the Exploring Expedition to the Rocky Mountains in the Year 1842, and to Oregon and North California in the Years 1843−'44* had been published in 1845. For the book's importance in stimulating interest in the West, see Potter's introduction to Geiger and Bryarly, pp. 20, 22.

[7] Reid is quoting from the circular, not preserved in the Reid Papers. The Pioneer Line's first advertisement appeared in the *Missouri Republican*, Feb. 6, 1849, with similar wording.

pid was to be the transit that a return trip from California was to be made by the train the same season. How far these promises were fulfilled will appear in the sequel. Suffice it to say here that the journey lasted 165 days[8] and the train was more than decimated by sickness and deaths on the way, and most of the delay and much of the sickness was the direct result of bad faith and mismanagement on the part of the proprietors. Names of prominent business men of St. Louis were given as references, and so attractive was the scheme that before the end of April 120 tickets were sold,—and so were the purchasers, myself among them.[9]

To be able to scout on all sides in hunting game and seeing the countries described by Fremont, I bought a mustang pony from a soldier returned from Chihuahua. On account of his Mexican origin I named him Don, and equipped him with an army saddle, bridle, holsters, saddle-bags, saddle blanket, picket rope and picket pin. I rode him daily for a fortnight before starting, and found him docile, spirited and fleet. Under an order from the war department applicable to all bona fide emigrants to California or Oregon, I purchased at cost an army rifle, a brace of holster pistols, 200 rounds of ammunition and the small accessories that go with firearms.[10] I had previously purchased a belt revolver,—an Allen five shooter commonly called a "pepper box."[11]

One of my fellow boarders at Newman's was John A. Brewster, already mentioned as a fellow passenger on the steamer from Pittsburgh to St. Louis. He had visited meantime some other western cities and had returned to St. Louis to seek employment. He was a graduate of a Philadelphia medical college, and besides being well educated he possessed pleasing manners and a good address. I had obtained for him temporary employ-

---

[8] If the days are counted from May 15, the actual date of departure, the Pioneer Line reached Sacramento in 151 days, and Reid arrived in San Francisco in 160 days.

[9] Reid complains that the passengers were sold, that is, in the sense of being duped or cheated.

[10] U.S. *Congressional Globe*, 30th Cong., 2d sess., Sen. 580, Feb. 22, 1849. The order was well publicized; see, e.g., *Missouri Republican*, March 25, 1849.

[11] The Ethan Allen self-cocking revolver was popular during the Mexican War and the gold rush. Because of widespread fear of Indians, emigrants were heavily armed; one company even carried swivel guns in its wagons. See Bruff, I, p. 544, n.1; Stewart, *California Trail*, p. 221.

ment in the surveyor general's office, and when I decided to go
to California he proposed to accompany me and we agreed to
travel together and join our fortunes in California. In purchas-
ing our outfit every article of personal wear was got in duplicate,
which gave us at first the appearance of twin brothers. The pony
was to be used in common on the "ride and tie" or rather day-
about plan.[12] We had a small medicine chest suitably filled under
his directions for emergencies. He too procured an army rifle
and ammunition. Each of us had a pair of heavy Mackinaw blankets, a broad rimmed soft fur hat and an india rubber cloak and
india rubber leggins. We took with us many other articles that we
supposed would be necessary or useful on such a trip, including
an assortment of reading matter.

   An enterprising St. Louis man named Tooke advertised that
he would give lessons in the art of smelting gold and silver to
prospective emigrants, representing that a knowledge of the
process would be of great value in the mines. I became one of his
many pupils, paid my fee, heard his lectures, got a booklet with
his formulas and purchased of him a copper basin for washing
gold dust and a cast-iron mould weighing about four pounds for
casting gold ingots of the size and value of $1000 each. I cannot
help laughing still at this bit of preliminary experience. So unnecessary to a gold miner was the process that no part of it was
ever put in use by any of his pupils. My ingot mould was thrown
away in Sweetwater valley, and the poor indian that happened to
find it must have been sorely puzzled to divine its purpose. It
would be a capital weapon for two persons to kill a bear with,—
one to hold the bear, the other to knock him on the head. The
copper basin was much too small for gold washing, and with
some other *relicta* [relics] of the journey was sold at auction for a
song after my arrival at San Francisco.

   On the 28th of April we embarked on a steamer for Independence, reaching it on the fourth day.[13] I rode Don to the wharf

   [12] Reid means that he and Brewster will take turns riding the pony; one will
ride one day, the other the next.
   [13] Reid identifies the steamboat as the *Sacramento* in a phrase crossed out in his
journal (p. 7) and in the diary entry for June 21, above. The boat arrived in
St. Joseph, Missouri, sometime between May 5 and May 9. See Barry, *Beginning
of the West*, p. 847. Reid probably arrived in Independence on May 4, since the
receipt for his passage money (preserved in the Reid Papers) is dated there on
May 5.

where, dismounting, I gave the bridle rein to a deck-hand and went up the passengers' gangway to the main deck, from which I watched the process of loading up. I then noticed that the deck-hands had trouble with Don. He objected to being led or driven over the planks leading to the lower deck. When they began to use blows to make him move I called out to stop, and that I would take charge of him. Going ashore, I threw the rein over his neck, sprang into the saddle and spoke to him, when he walked the plank at once as if he had been used to it all his life.

On the steamer I made the acquaintance of Dr. Sylvanus M. E. Goheen, a prominent physician of Belleville, Illinois, and his brother, Rev. Davis Goheen, of the same place, who were going in our train to California,—the latter on account of ill health. I found them to be men of superior minds and agreeable manners and I counted much on the pleasure of their companionship on our long journey. We put up at the same hotel in Independence, preparatory to our going into camp about eight miles out on the prairie, near the line of Kansas territory.

Just before our departure from St. Louis the newspapers contained accounts of the outbreak of Asiatic cholera at New Orleans, but it had not reached our city.[14] On the first evening at the hotel in Independence, as Brewster and I were in the parlor, a local physican came in and asked if we belonged to the Pioneer Train. On learning that we did he said he had just come from the room of a Mr. Beadles, a newspaper man from Iowa, who was one of our passengers and who had an acute attack of cholera, with no one to attend him. He asked whether we would go to his room and take care of him in his (the doctor's) absence. I had a vivid recollection as a boy of the ravages of the cholera when it visited this country in 1832, and had shared in the dread it then inspired even at a distance.[15] But now when brought face

[14]Reid is mistaken. There were 38 deaths from cholera in St. Louis as early as January 1849, and the Catholic archbishop allowed his flock to eat meat on Friday because physicians recommended abstinence from fish and vegetables. Deaths slowly increased, and cholera became an epidemic in the city by June, when one-tenth of the population died. The cause of Asiatic cholera, from bacteria, was unknown until 1883. Death frequently occurred only hours after an attack. See *Missouri Republican*, Jan. 1, 3, 1849; S. P. Lalumière to Bernard Reid, June 28, 1849; Rosenberg, *Cholera Years*, pp. 115, 135. Holliday, in *The World Rushed In* (p. 476, n. 114), estimates that 1,500 died from cholera in frontier camps and on the trail to Fort Laramie in 1849.

[15]For the epidemic of 1832, when Reid was nine years old, see Rosenberg,

to face with it, I felt no fear of it, and we went together to the sick man's room and nursed him till about midnight, when he died. We were then about retiring to get some sleep when Dr. Goheen came to ask us to assist him in caring for his brother, the minister, who had the cholera. We went at once to his room and remained, rendering such help as we could, till day break, when the patient died. After assisting the Doctor in laying out the remains we got breakfast and went to our room to get some needed rest. We slept till noon, and at dinner were told that Black Harris, a noted Rocky Mountain hunter and trapper, who had been engaged as guide for our train, was lying sick with cholera, in a room near the hotel. Our dinner over, we went to his room and remained with him about two hours, when he died.[16] Thus in the short space of 18 hours, we had waited at the death beds of three members of our train, victims of the epidemic that had broken out so suddenly among the emigrants and the people of Independence. Dr. Goheen gave up his trip and took his brother's remains back to Belleville. He went to California in 1850 and died at Placerville in January 1851 of symptoms resembling cholera. His widow survives and resides in Minneapolis.[17] In the death of Black Harris our train suffered an irreparable loss, as his intimate knowledge of the regions we

---

Cholera Years, chap. 1. Reid's recollection that Robert Beadles was a passenger is puzzling, since a man by that name was listed as a member of the crew from Orange County, Virginia, in the *Missouri Republican*, May 17, 1849. According to that newspaper (Dec. 24, 1849) a Robert "Reedles" died on May 9. Reid lists Beadles's death in the margin of his passenger list, in the Reid Papers, and Searls notes that Beadles, a teamster known as "California Bob," died on May 15; see Searls, May 15, and the list of men who died in Searls's published diary, p. 64.

[16] Reid's recollection of the sequence of deaths is faulty; "Black" Harris was the first of the three to die. See Reid's letter (signed "Gerald") in the Independence *Daily Union*, May 14, 1849, reprinted in Hafen, ed., *The Mountain Men and the Fur Trade*, IV, 117. Cf. Searls, May 24: "This trail was first laid out by 'Black' Harris our intended guide who unfortunately for us died in Independence of Cholera, just before our departure." Harris's death was indeed a great loss to the Pioneer Line. He had been a monumental figure in the fur trade and had served as a guide for a number of earlier trains on their way to Oregon.

[17] In preparation for expanding his diary into a narrative journal, Reid wrote to the editor of the Belleville *Advocate*, requesting information on the Goheens; he remembered their last name and their home town in Illinois. He received many replies, including one from Dr. Goheen's widow. The Goheen correspondence is in Folder 79, Reid Papers. Reid's letter was first published in the *Advocate* on January 20, 1904.

This famous watercolor was painted by Alfred Jacob Miller in 1837. "Black" Harris, the noted mountain man hired as the Pioneer Line's overland guide, is seated in the foreground. *Courtesy: Walters Art Gallery.*

were to traverse and his experience in surmounting such difficulties as we were sure to encounter, would have been of incalculable value to us.

At our camp we found a scene of bustle and activity in the preparations for weighing anchor and setting sail with our "prairie schooners" and other craft on the wide prairie ocean we were about to cross. Several days elapsed before the train was fully organized and equipped, but on the 8th of May orders were given to strike tents and begin to move.[18]

Our wagons were new and well-built, and were brought from St. Louis by steamer, hauled out to camp and arranged as a "corral" or oval enclosure, with a roped gap or gate at one end, into which the mules could be driven for protection in case of an attack by Indians, and for "catching up" and harnessing at every start of the train. There were twenty good spring wagons with square tops, some covered with white canvas, others with black or green oil cloth, and each seated for six passengers. The "lazybacks" were hinged and could be let down flat, making, with the seats, a bed on which three could sleep in the shelter. Tents were provided for the other passengers and train men, but on account of their great weight and trouble they were discarded before reaching the mountains, and then those who could not find shelter in the wagons had to sleep under them or under the sky as a canopy. There were 22 freight and baggage wagons with the usual hooped covers, all loaded to their full capacity and drawn by six mules, and some of the heavier ones by eight. The passenger wagons were to be drawn by four mules each. One of the spring wagons was for the proprietors and their staff. The others were numbered and a mess assigned to each. There were eleven messes of six each, three of five, three of seven and two of nine, according to a list that I made soon after we started, a copy of which is appended in a note.[19] Some of the names were given me at second hand, some of them not complete and others probably mis-spelled. There was at least one passenger at the start— Tiffany, of New York, whose name was omitted from my list. As far as practicable the passengers were permitted to group them-

[18]The date was actually May 9. Searls wrote in his diary on May 9 that it was "the day appointed for our final departure," but harnessing proved difficult, the train traveled only two miles, and several additional baggage wagons had not arrived. Thomas Turner was in Lexington, Missouri, on May 8 buying extra wagons, according to the *Missouri Republican*, May 13, 14, 1849. Searls's entry on May 15 makes it clear that the train started in earnest on that day. The Pioneer Line originally projected April 26 as the departure date; see *Missouri Republican*, April 16, 1849.

[19]The typed copy appended to the 1904 journal is missing, but Reid's original passenger list, in his hand, is in the Reid Papers. Passengers are listed under their carriage numbers, the dead men's names are boxed, and additional names of the dead are written in the margin. See p. 186.

selves into messes based on acquaintanceship, or suppc
geniality. The nine in [carriage] Number 8 were all ;
men from the coast of Maine. Each freight wagon, oi
schooner," had blazoned on its white cover a name presumably
suggested by the fancy of its driver. I remember only these four:
Prairie Bird, Tempest, Albatross and "*Have You Saw the Elephant?*"[20] As matters turned out this last legend, notwithstanding
its bad grammar, was the most appropriate and prophetic of all.

There were in the corral about 300 mules, which, after hitching up the requisite number for the wagons, left a herd of about
sixty to be driven loose as a reserve to draw from as occasion
might arise, to relieve any that might become galled or jaded
at their work. But the proprietors, unfortunately for us, instead
of buying mules "best adapted for the trip" as their prospectus promised, had purchased at a cheaper rate young and soft
mules that had never been broken to harness. The result was
that, owing to the heavy loads and frequent spring rains, the
wagons often sank to the hubs in the soft prairie, and the un-
seasoned mules soon began to show shoulder galls and exhaustion. Then to intensify the wrong done us, before we got a hundred miles on our way the proprietors, through greed to double
their gains, decided to start a second train, and as a nucleus of it
they detached three or four of our wagons and most of our loose
mules; and Allen, who was with us to that point, left us there under Turner's control, and went back with the confiscated mules
and wagons to organize the new train.[21]

Todd and Cunningham were the principal lieutenants to Captain Turner, and he had besides a commissary, two principal
wagon masters, (Moses Mallerson and Robert Green), a wagon
maker, a harness maker, a farrier, and the requisite number of
teamsters and herders, some of these last being Mexican vaqueros skilled in throwing the riata or lasso, but this accomplish-

[20] In general "to see the elephant" meant to face a severe hazard or to gain
experience through ordeals. The expression was used as early as 1834, but it became popular during the gold rush.

[21] The Pioneer Line had decided to organize a new train weeks before leaving
Independence. Neither Reid's nor Searls's diary mentions Allen's presence at the
start of the trip or the loss of some wagons and mules. The company's second
train apparently left late in June. See *Missouri Republican*, March 21, April 5,
June 1, 21, 1849; Barry, *Beginning of the West*, pp. 875–76.

Bernard Reid's receipt for his passage money is signed by S. Todd, one of the Pioneer Line's "principal lieutenants." Note that the destination on the "ticket" is San Francisco. *Courtesy: Archives, Univ. of Santa Clara.*

ment was by no means confined to the Mexicans. Each passenger mess was to drive its own team. Passengers and crew all told made a total of 161 souls in the train at the start.[22]

No pen can adequately describe our start. Half-a-dozen circuses combined in one would have been tame in comparison. Not one of our 300 mules (except an old bell mule, the leader of the herd), had ever had a bit in its mouth or a collar on its neck. To initiate them, one by one, into their new degree, by the ceremonial of being bridled and harnessed, proved to be a "riding of the goat" of the roughest kind. The mules had not been consulted about it when brought from their native heath, Kentucky, and they soon made it manifest that they had not given their consent to the ceremony.[23] I do not mean to imply that when the time came they were "kickers" in the literal sense. They had so many other ways of objecting to the process that they seemed to have reserved that particular mule trait for later stages of their

---

[22] Lell H. Woolley recalled (at the age of eighty-eight) that 150 passengers were on the train; a passing emigrant, James Lyne, estimated the total number of men at over 200; and the published list named 125 passengers, and some of the crew. Reid's total count is certainly conservative, since he listed only 120 passengers. After cross-checking lists and entries in Reid's and Searls's diaries, my count is approximately 131 passengers. Since the crew numbered at least 40, the total number of men with the train was at least 170. See passenger lists in the *Missouri Republican*, May 17, 1849, and in the Reid Papers; Lyne to Henry Lyne, May 22; Woolley, p. 3.

[23] Searls and Woolley also mention trouble with the mules; see Searls, May 9, 11, 15, and Woolley, p. 3. For a discussion of emigrants' problems with mules, see Potter's introduction to Geiger and Bryarly, pp. 35–36; and Mattes, *Great Platte River Road*, pp. 38–39. Cf. Webster, May 26, 27; Wistar, pp. 44, 51.

experience. In a strategical point of view they made the mistake of permitting themselves to be inveigled into following the old bell mule into the corral. Had they clung to the native liberty of the open prairie they might never have come under the yoke that proved in the sequel to be so galling. The corral formed an amphitheatre of about two-thirds of an acre. All hands were piped to their respective posts, the gap through which the herd entered was strongly roped behind them, and the fun began. A vaquero would single out a victim and throw his lasso. If it missed, it sent the whole herd galloping around the arena. If it caught, the galloping went on the same, or faster if possible, with the vaquero and his assistants, on the shorter "interior lines," tugging at the lasso with all their might, to make their "catch" heave-to, or, failing in that, to lasso his feet and throw him broadside, when half-a-dozen of them would pounce on to him to stop his struggling and force a bit into his mouth and a collar over his head. That accomplished, he would be taken to the nearest wagon wheel, firmly haltered there, and then harnessed ready for hitching to a wagon. Meantime other train men were catching, as catch could, other candidates for the degree, and going through a similar process with them. Many of them were very hard to catch, and when caught, to handle. It was a sight to see their wild leaps and contortions to baffle their captors. And who could blame their natural brute instinct to preserve their liberty? From the carriage tops and other points of vantage the passengers looked down for hours upon the exciting contest, and from time to time cheers rent the welkin—sometimes for the man and sometimes for the mule—whenever some feat of special agility or daring on either side was recognized. Towards the last, when the arena was well nigh cleared, Mose Mallerson, the wagon master, a young man of great nerve and splendid physique, was giving chase to a particular mule that had been very hard to conquer. Time after time he had shaken loose from his tormentors and set them at defiance. Then all at once Mose sprang at him like a tiger, clasped his arms around his neck, seized his ear with his teeth, and letting go his arms, held on to his ear with his teeth alone. The startled animal ran like lightning with Mose's body streaming through the air like a ship's pennant in a high wind,—and so they went, mule and man,

round and round the ring—the spectators cheering wildly—till
at last, completely conquered, the mule stopped in its mad career, and submitted to be bridled and harnessed without further
protest.

At last mules enough to man all the wagons were harnessed.
Tents had been struck and loaded up, and all was ready for the
move. One by one the wagons started, but not without dissent on
the part of many mules whose in-born talent for kicking developed suddenly when the whips cracked. These little episodes
caused many interruptions in the order of march, but no serious
damage was done unless it was to the tender heels of the kickers. So much time was consumed in the circus performances that
the sun was setting in the west before the last wagon had left
camp; and at the same time the leading wagon in the procession
wheeled into its place in a new corral to form our camp for the
night—only one mile from our starting point.

Next morning the performance of yesterday was repeated on
a milder scale, and so on from day to day until a better understanding between man and mule came to exist, and "catching
up" became a tame and commonplace affair.

Our larder was supplied at first with a good variety of provisions for the journey, such as sea biscuit, flour, pinole (a sweetened meal made of parched corn), bacon in the shape of hams,
shoulders and "side-meat," salt fish, cheese, beans, coffee, sugar,
tea, salt, molasses, dried apples and dried peaches. Each carriage
had a cooking and table service on a plain scale, stored in the box
attached to the rear of the wagon bed. Every fifth day, army
fashion, the commissary dealt out to each mess its allotment of
rations according to the number of mouths to be fed, and the
passengers took turns in cooking or arranged for that among
themselves. While our first bill of fare lasted we lived on the fat
of the land, but this liberal menu did not last very long.

By our trail it was about a hundred miles to the Kansas river at
a ferry kept by civilized indians, not far from where the city of
Topeka now stands.[24] After passing, not far from our starting

[24] This lower ferry, operated by the Papin brothers, was about 13 miles east
of a second (upper) ferry near present-day Rossville, Kansas. Allowing for the
first campground's location 8 miles from Independence on the Santa Fe Trail,
Searls's figure for the distance from Independence to the Kansas ferry adds up
to some 96 miles; guidebooks gave the distance as 100 miles.

point, the boundary between Missouri and the territory of Kansas, the country was uninhabited except by a few indians and half-breeds occupying huts and tilling small farms here and there at long intervals between the Missouri line and the Kansas river. The whole distance was over a prairie, mostly a dead level, but in some places undulating, with an occasional small water course skirted by a border of timber. Waukarusa creek was the largest stream we had to ford before reaching the river.[25] A tree or a grove of trees where there was no water was a rare sight. On one of the vast plateaus we crossed was the "Lone Elm," a prominent landmark standing like a solitary sentinel in the great treeless waste. How it came to sprout and grow by itself, or to survive the destruction of storm or fire that overwhelmed its companions, if it ever had any, leaving no trace of them whatever, is a question which history or science can probably never solve.[26]

I kept no diary until May 24th, but a week earlier I made the following brief notes of that day's events on a slip of paper, evidently intending to enter them more at length in my diary when opened:

"Thursday May 17th. Leave two carriages with two men to die of cholera. I remain awhile. Lone Elm. Kentuckian. News from back. Snipe. Snakes. Flowers. Peas. Santa Fe trail. Indian homes and spring. Camp at five o'clock two miles off on the Oregon trail. At dark the two carriages came up. The two men were buried together at the last camp."[27]

Excerpts from the day's entry in the diary of Reid's fellow passenger Niles Searls augment Reid's notes: "Two miles from our encampment was passed the 'Lone Elm.'. . . At one o'clock we reached the point

[25] According to Searls, the train started in earnest on May 15, as noted above, and crossed the Wakarusa (not Waukarusa), near present-day Lawrence, Kansas, on May 19, in pouring rain. Because of the river's steep banks, the crossing was difficult. The train traveled only four miles on that day.

[26] The Lone Elm was on Cedar Creek, about 40 miles along the trail. The Pioneer Line reached the spot on May 17. Most diarists on this route noted the tree, near present-day Olathe, Kansas, but it disappeared during the gold rush. See Mattes, *Great Platte River Road*, p. 137.

[27] Reid inserted the notes he made on May 17 in the first page of the copy he made of his 1849 diary. The wording is slightly different from the above quotation, but the meaning is unchanged. The two men who died were passengers Oliver Trowbridge (Canada) and William Millen; the latter's residence was listed as Indiana in the *Missouri Republican*, May 17, 1849, but Searls (p. 64) believed he was from Connecticut.

where the Oregon trail diverges from the Santa Fe road. Following the
latter a short distance, we reached Cow Creek, upon which is the residence of a Mr. Rogers, . . . whose wife . . . was a half-breed.[28] Near the
house was an excellent spring. . . . Those who had been left in the
morning with the sick came in at a late hour, after having performed
the last duty towards them required here on earth. They died a little
before five this evening and both within a period of five minutes, and
were buried in one grave on the ground where we had encamped the
preceding night."

For some reason, Reid did not include another brief entry written on
a slip of paper on May 18, which he inserted in the first page of the
copy he made of the original overland diary. The entry is as follows:
"Start at 8. I rode around by the Indian Spring. Scoured the timber of
Santa Fe creek for game. Saw none. Shot at mark. Initials. Santa Fe
creek fork at 1. Overtake train a mile further and exchange places with
Brewster."

It is to be regretted that I did not then note the names of the
two sick passengers. At least two other passengers had previously died of cholera since leaving our first camp. Whenever a
passenger died on the way I kept a record of it crudely by drawing an ink line around his name on my list; and even after I began my diary I did not always make any other record of his
death. Hence, while my list shows all who died on the way (while
I was with the train), it does not give dates or causes of death,
and my diary does so in a few instances only. Nearly one-half of
those who died were victims of cholera, and most of the others
of scurvy on the last half of the journey. I *italicise* on the printed
list the names of those who died on the way while I was with the
train.[29]

[28] The Mr. Rogers who cultivated a farm was a Shawnee. According to The-
odore Talbot, a diarist of 1843, all his sons were named after U.S. presidents. See
Mattes, *Great Platte River Road*, p. 138. The Oregon Trail followed the Santa Fe
Trail for 45 miles before diverging to the north.

[29] Reid did note the deaths of Trowbridge and Millen in the margin of his passenger list, as well as that of Captain Gillespie of St. Louis, one of Turner's staff,
who died at the first campground. Passengers McDonald and Swift, both physicians, cared for Trowbridge and Millen. No record can be found of the other two
passengers' deaths. On his passenger list Reid noted that 24 men died (not 18, as
he recalled in his "California Gold Rush Letter," p. 225), including the three who
died in Independence. Niles Searls listed 17 dead, and the *Missouri Republican*,
15. David McCollum estimated the number as one-sixth of the "total," Dr. Robert McDonald recalled that 42 died, and an emigrant from Mississippi reported
that deaths were "numerous," falsely stating that the dead were thrown out on
the prairie without burial. From cross-checking lists in the sources below and en-

Captain Turner and his staff had saddle horses and so had several passengers, among them Tiffany, Winslow, Mulford, Dr. Steele and two or three others. An Italian from St. Louis, named Lamalfa, had a wagon with four horses, with an outfit for business in California. He was not of our train, but travelled with us for company and protection.

At one of our earlier camps where there was some timber I went apart some distance to shoot at mark with my pepper-box revolver. Pinning a paper target to a tree I stepped off twenty paces towards the camp, turned and fired. While examining the score after firing, I held the revolver muzzle downwards. This, without my knowing it, caused one of the bullets to roll down the unevenly bored barrel and lodge in the muzzle, thus leaving an air-space between powder and ball. Going back to my base I fired again at the same target. Almost instantly Mr. Tiffany came galloping up from directly behind me, nearly running me down with his horse, and angrily demanding *why I shot at him.* I assured him I had not, and pointed to the tree I had fired at in the opposite direction. Still fuming with anger he said he knew better, and that the bullet had almost grazed his face. I wondered if he was crazy, but a look at my smoking revolver solved the mystery. The explosion of the powder in the air-space between powder and ball had burst off a longitudinal strip of the cylinder in such manner as to hurl it directly backwards, nearly killing or wounding Mr. Tiffany, who was now profuse in his apologies for having charged me with felonious shooting.[30] I soon after threw away the worthless cylinder, but kept the butt, which I afterwards wore for awhile in the mines, projecting

tries in the Reid and Searls diaries, my count is 22, excluding the three who died in Independence. See lists of the dead in the *Missouri Republican,* Aug. 12, Dec. 24, 1849, and in the Reid Papers; Barry, *Beginning of the West,* p. 862; *Missouri Republican,* July 4, 1849, letter from "Rambler" (Dr. Augustus Heslep of St. Louis); Searls, May 15, 17, and p. 64; Bidlack, ed., *Letters Home,* p. 35; McDonald, *McDonald Overland Narrative,* p. 63; and Unruh, *The Plains Across,* p. 436, n. 60.

[30] Such accidents, often fatal, were fairly common on the trail. In practicing shooting at a mark Reid followed other greenhorn emigrants unused to firearms. Cf. Johnson, April 29; Long, May 9; and Sedgley, July 2. Searls, on June 4, wrote that he practiced with other passengers and only one was a good shot. Reid noted that Tiffany came from New York, but Pardon Dexter Tiffany, born in Maine, was a lawyer from St. Louis.

from my belt as a make-believe piece of armor to conform to the prevailing custom of going armed.

The Kansas River bottom was handsomely timbered, and the ferrying process was slow on account of the number of our vehicles and the width of the stream—about 250 yards. We crossed on May 23d [May 22] and camped about a mile beyond on the prairie.

Searls, May 22: "Reached the ferry of the Kansas this morning and were fortunate in finding an opportunity to commence crossing our wagons immediately. The Ferry is owned by two half-breed Indians. . . . Collected around the bank were quite a number of Indians of the Pottawatomie tribe, dressed in their usual grotesque costume and painted or daubed with vermillion. The rear of the train reached the northern bank about sunset and proceeding two miles we encamped on a beautiful plain."

Searls, May 23: "The baggage needing to be overhauled and re-packed, we shall remain in our present position till tomorrow."

The indians of the vicinity are the civilized remnants of the Pottawatomies, Delawares and some other tribes transplanted here when the white man crowded them out of their hunting grounds in the middle states. Near the ferry was a Methodist mission and school.[31]

[31] The Indians were removed west of the Mississippi (from the Old Northwest) by the Chicago Treaty of 1833; cf. Searls, May 22. For the Methodist Episcopal mission, which had closed in 1846, see Bryant, May 19, 1846; Paden, *Wake of the Prairie Schooner*, p. 39; and Barry, *Beginning of the West*, p. 800.

The Kansas River to Fort Kearney

May 24–June 8

As we have seen in the Prologue, the Pioneer Line began hitching up at a campground near Independence on May 9, but it was May 15 before the wagon train finally set out along the trail. After following the Santa Fe Trail for about 45 miles, the train turned on to the Oregon Trail in present-day Kansas. On May 22 it crossed the Kansas River by ferry and camped on the prairie beyond.

Bernard Reid's diary begins on May 24, the day the Pioneer Line resumes the trail. Entries in his diary during this "shaking-down" period are in the form of notes, often cryptic, unlike the flowing descriptions Reid sometimes wrote during later stages of the journey. Yet the meaning is clear, and the varied rhythms of the passages intensify the energy of Reid's prose.

The train now moves northwest, fording tributaries of the Kansas River. It then follows the Little Blue River into what is now Nebraska, and descends into the valley of the Platte River before arriving at Fort Kearney, a military post located about one mile from the river. Eight men have died of cholera by the time the Pioneer Line reaches the fort.

Thursday, May 24. Early start. Finished letters to John and Socrates Newman. Inclosed the former in an envelop to the girls.[1] As the train was leaving I started back on the pony to the post office at the Ferry. Wrote letters on a log to Hughes and Fortier.[2] Paid 10¢ per letter. Started again. Buzzards. Wrong road. Long

[1] "John" is Reid's brother in Clarion; "the girls" are their sisters. Socrates Newman is the son of Capt. Jonas Newman, who owned the St. Louis boarding house where Reid had lived for nearly two years. None of the letters Reid wrote along the trail is preserved in the Reid Papers. See Socrates Newman to Bernard Reid, Dec. 15, 1848.

[2] Hughes and Fortier are Reid's friends in St. Louis.

bottom. Indians. Swamp. Bluff. Storm. Camp on bank of Cross Creek.[3] Mud and water. Wigwams. Wet sleeping. 12 miles.

In the journal based on the diary Reid recalled that on this day, "The train camped for the night near some indian wigwams at Cross Creek, in the midst of mud and water, a sorry sleeping place for those who had to bivouac on the wet ground. My cloak was fortunately large enough to envelop me like the under-crust and upper crust of a 'turn-over.' . . . Distance made today is 12 miles, as indicated by what was called a 'roadometer' attached to one of the wagon axles."[4]

Searls writes on this day: "We are now in camp, waiting for the workmen to construct a road down a steep bank. Near our camp are several Indian camps or wigwams."[5]

Friday, May 25. Wet clothes. Clears up. Rusty arms. Indians and ponies. Six-shooter. Pottawatomies. New road cut to ford. Start at noon. Cross in 1½ hours. Ride the pony. Mounds and monument. Rattlesnake and moccasin. Splendid views. Ride off for wood. Pony scares and runs off. Grab the rope. Sore fingers. Lose glasses. Brewster comes for me with the pony. Return and hunt and find glasses. Beautiful camping ground. 10 miles. Heavy rain at night. All wet.

Reid, journal: "Some Pottawatomies mounted on ponies visited us, inspecting curiously our whole outfit, but wondering most at the rapid discharge of a six-shooter fired for their amusement. Some indian mounds in the vicinity. . . . I tried my "pepper-box" with effect on a rattlesnake and a moccasin."

Searls: "It rained nearly the whole night and to me it was the most dreary night that I have passed since we left the States. . . . It appears as if everything, even the very elements, warred against us. . . . Several Indians have been in camp and some suspicions are entertained; a strict guard will be kept."

Saturday, May 26. Rode the pony. At 9:30 came to a creek beautifully set off with fine oak trees. Kentucky company passed

[3] Almost certainly this is Soldier Creek. See Bryant, May 19, 1846; Farnham, p. 302; Searls, May 24; Sedgley, May 29; and Staples, May 28; all identify the stream as Soldier Creek.

[4] The "roadometer" (frequently called an odometer by emigrants) was commonly used on the trail and considered fairly reliable.

[5] Henceforth, each excerpt from other diaries or from Reid's journal (1904) that appears after an entry in Reid's diary is for the same day, unless otherwise noted, and all excerpts from Reid's writings are in material preserved in the Reid Papers.

before us. Repaired the road. Cut down trees. Threw in bushes. Crossed in 2 or 3 hours. Mounds. Monumental pile. Deep ravines. Camp on the sloping bank of Little Vermillion, swift, deep, muddy. Timber bottom on west side half a mile wide. Deserted cabin. Graves,—indian and white: Capt. Ashley, Chariton County, Mo. Hagin. Some nameless.[6] Pontoon wagons. Hard work unloading. Carrying baggage. Pulling empty wagons over. Two float off and overturn. The first with Tom Turner inside with a quart of whiskey,—both safe.[7] The next was carried off by the current. Lamalfa in boat after it. Two men swam to the wagon—in the drift [pile of tangled tree tops]. Danger of their drowning. Jumped in. Gained the boat. The men got out on the drift. Lamalfa frightened. Wagon lost. At last, just at dark I find it. They throw me a rope and I secure it to a tree till morning. Clothes all wet. Dry clothes sent over. Pass over. Borrow dry clothes. Change. Stand guard over the baggage on the west side of the creek. Encampment remains on the east side. Lamalfa and two others relieve us at half past one. Lie down on my arms in my cloak by the fire. Another sleeping beside me. The guard takes us to be Pawnees; call to us, and receiving no answer aim their rifles at us! and call again, threatening to fire if not answered. At last I awoke in time, probably to avoid being shot! Fine business![8] Now in Pawnee limits. Guard duty in such a scene. Reflections.

Sunday, May 27. Took all day to cross the balance over. Hands too sore to help. Three or four companies encamped here awaiting the fall of the water. Kent County Md. Chariton, Mo. Kentucky. Tennessee. N. Carolina. St. Louis County. We encamped in woods on west side. Slept out at fire.

[6] Like many other diarists, most notably Goldsborough Bruff and James Hutchings, Reid begins to record graves seen along the trail. The burial sites were emblems that intensified the emigrants' fear of death. Many of the graves recorded by Reid were also noted by Bruff and Hutchings, thus aiding in verification of the Pioneer Line's progress along parts of the trail. For a complete list of the graves recorded by Bernard Reid, see Appendix B, p. 208.

[7] In his journal (p. 114) Reid recalled that Captain Turner was a heavy drinker, and many of his future problems were caused by the increasing use of alcohol.

[8] Woolley (p. 14) recalled a garbled version of this incident. Wagon trains became more vigilant in Pawnee country because the tribe was thought to be hostile and dangerous; the Pawnees, however, had been decimated by disease and warfare with the Sioux. Cf. Delano, May 27; Dewolf, June 13; Long, May 11; Searls, May 29; Wistar, pp. 69–70; and Wood, May 23.

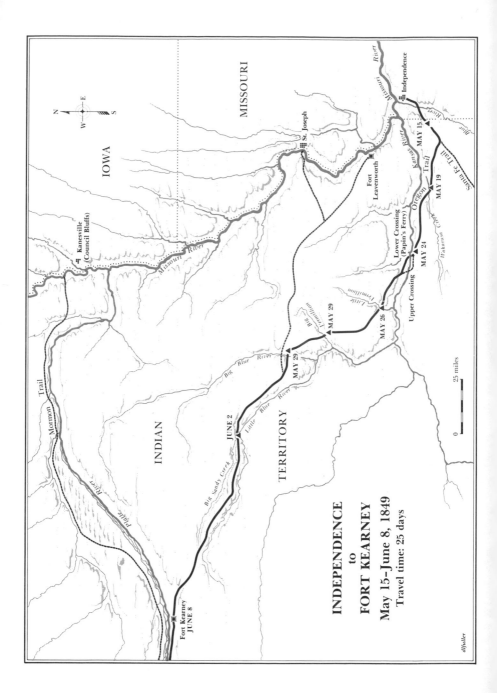

INDEPENDENCE
to
FORT KEARNEY

May 15–June 8, 1849
Travel time: 25 days

Searls, whose messmate, Charles Sinclair, has been sick with cholera since May 21, writes: "Far from home, and the friends he loves, . . . his case seems truly distressing. Charlie [Mulford] has been all attention to him since his first attack and . . . has done everything in his power to smooth our new companion's pathway to the grave. I shall take his [Mulford's] place tonight in watching over his, apparently dying, pillow."

Monday, May 28. Started early. Rode the pony. Kentucky train got the start. I passed all and advanced alone, passing grave of Roush, of Illinois.[9] 15 miles to a clear, rapid creek. Fished, read, bathed and slept till 5 o'clock. Train had camped at noon, and were delayed. They came at last late in the evening, and crossing the creek without difficulty, camped on the west bank. Grave of Woodson, Ky.

Tuesday, May 29. Had a pleasant day's drive of 15 miles to the Big Vermillion. Passed grave of Ingraham, Tenn. Vermillion very steep on the east side but otherwise not difficult to ford. Encamped on prairie on west bank. Grave of James H. Marshall, of St. Louis, with cross,—died in 1844,—surmounting a beautiful and commanding eminence,—at sunset against the sky. Passed three spring branches with running water. Brewster and I stood guard the third watch—from 1 to 3 Considerable disaffection brewing.[10] My watch stopped.

Wednesday, May 30. Left [carriages] Nos. 17 and 19 with Sinclair expected to die. Rode the pony. Heavy rain. Overtook the train which had got ahead of me, at a little winding stream skirted with timber. Difficult crossing after the shower. Rode on over high prairie ridges to the Big Blue. While the train was crossing Brewster and I went in search of Alcove Spring.[11] Fine

[9] The gravestone of Henry Roush, in Union Township, Pottawattomie County, Kansas, is in one piece today. See Barry, *Beginning of the West*, p. 845.

[10] Cf. an undated letter from a Mormon, Almon W. Babbitt, printed in the St. Joseph *Gazette*, Oct. 19, 1849: "I met the Pioneer company . . . this side of Independence. They were getting along very slow, and the passengers generally dissatisfied with their fare." On July 20, 1849, the *Gazette* had printed an undated letter from "Dr. Price," who wrote that the passengers were "much dissatisfied." As early as May 17 Dr. Augustus Heslep, who spent the day with the Pioneer Line near the Lone Elm, wrote that he feared the train would pursue "a troublesome voyage"; *Missouri Republican*, June 6, 1849.

[11] Alcove Spring had been named in 1846 by the overlander Edwin Bryant, who thought it "one of the most romantic spots" he ever saw. Reid is using Bryant's diary of his 1846 trip as a guidebook. See Bryant, May 27, 1846; and Reid, journal, p. 24.

picturesque glen. Names on trees and rocks. Honeysuckles, cedar, currants, gooseberries, strawberries. Island. Not hard to ford. Got over after the train, both on the pony. Went fishing. Indian skeleton lodges. Large timber. Camp on the west bank. Mrs. Keyes' grave on east bank. New grave on other side of tree.[12] [Mileage left blank.]

Searls: "Our company left camp this morning at an early hour, but in accordance with our preconceived intention, our mess, together with No. 11, remained . . . with our esteemed and dying messmate. . . . [Sinclair] quietly breathed his last at four o'clock p.m., May 30th, aged 23 years. . . . His grave was prepared. . . . Unable to procure other conveniences we wrapped him in his blankets and with sorrowful hearts consigned him to the 'cold earth.'"

Thursday, May 31. Left the Blue. Traveled pretty well till noon. Camped for dinner and grazing at a small run. 14 miles. Started again at 4. Went about 6 miles further, passing the grave of B. F. Adams, of Ohio,[13] and another without a name. Difficulty of getting wood and water at camp on open prairie. Alarm of Indians about.

Searls: "Mr. Dodson of Chicago was taken sick yesterday morning with Cholera. . . . As usual we have been favored with a copious downpour of rain. Scarcely a day passes in which it does not storm more or less, in consequence of which we are continually exposed by sleeping on the wet ground."

Friday, June 1. Cloudy. Rode on in advance to a hollow of pools, passing a party with ox teams from St. Joseph and another from Weston, Mo.[14] Two new cases of cholera in our camp;

[12] Mrs. Sarah Keyes, mother-in-law of James Reed of the Donner party and traveling with the Bryant party in 1846, died at the age of seventy; her grave was near present-day Manhattan, Kansas. Bryant (May 29, 1846) wrote about her death and burial, and a number of diarists using his guidebook, like Reid, mentioned the grave. The unnamed new grave noted by Reid was identified by Long, May 9, and Johnson, May 16, as that of John Fuller, a teamster, who had shot himself accidentally.

[13] When passing this grave Charles Long (May 10) noted that Adams, aged twenty-one, was "from my native state about my own age."

[14] The trails from St. Joseph and Independence converged about eight miles beyond the Big Blue, near present-day Marysville, Kansas. It was from this spot that another forty-niner, William G. Johnston, had described the scene looking back along the trail on May 9: "There seemed to be an unending stream of emigrant trains. . . . It was a sight which, once seen, can never be forgotten; it seemed as if the whole family of man had set its face westward."

Richard Smith of No. 5, and Foncannon, a driver,—the latter was somewhat sick before. Passed a grave with a cross—John Degnier, aged 39, of St. Genevieve, Mo., and grave of H. L. Dunlap, of Indianapolis. At 10 miles nooned at a hollow of scattering timber and sloughs of water. At encampment grave of J. Landon, of Oxford, Ohio. After dinner passed grave of John Eathy. In the evening crossed a small timbered stream with steep banks, and camped on the hill beyond in the prairie. Fine prospect all around. Distance 16 miles. Mules so hard worked they gave out some this afternoon.

Searls: "A more disagreeable day I have not seen since we started. We have two more cases of Cholera this morning."

Saturday, June 2. Drove today. Passed two graves together. John Abbott, aged 78, New Albany, Ind., and Sloan McMillen, Louisville, Ky. Crossed two branches of the Little Blue and camped after passing the last one.[15] Distance [mileage left blank.] The driver, Reuben Foncannon, was buried this morning.

Sunday, June 3. Rode the pony. Loitered behind the train. Gathered flowers. Roses in abundance. High prairie table land. Unequalled view. Grows tiresome at last. No breakfast. At 18 miles came to the Little Blue, or Pawnee River, at noon.[16] Pony in the creek. Trouble with him. Swim for him. Afternoon travel 6 miles. Camp on Little Blue again. Pretty stream. Met return party from Kentucky. Sent one letter.

Reid, journal: "When Don was turned loose at noon he made straight for the river and . . . got into a bank of quicksand. . . . I swam across to his rescue and with a good deal of difficulty got him out on terra firma."
Searls: "This day has been the best day's travel made since we started. Distance twenty-five miles."

Monday, June 4. Keep up the Blue. Carriage No. 17 upset and broke. Grave of Daniel Collins of Mo. Fine vistas in river bottom. Cottonwood. Burr oak. Grave of Joseph Lewis Wells, of Lincoln County, Mo., made today. Camp on bluff of second bottom. Jacob Keller, of Indiana, a driver and companion of Foncannon,

[15] The two branches are Little and Big Sandy creeks.
[16] The river rises in Nebraska and joins the Big Blue in Kansas. Pawnee Creek is not another name for the river; the creek flows into the Little Blue. The valley was much admired by emigrants, even in bad weather; cf. Decker, May 10; Perkins, June 12; and Pritchard, May 13.

Monday, June 4. Keep up the Blue. Carriage No. 17 upset and broke. Grave of Daniel Watkins of Mo. Fine vistas in river bottom. Cottonwood. Burr oak. Grave of Joseph Lewis Wells, of Lincoln Co. Mo. made today. Camp on bluff of second bottom. Jacob Keller of Indiana, a driver and companion of Foncannon, was buried after dark. Children on the prairie. Watered pony out of my hat. Distance 26 miles.

Tuesday, June 5. Rode pony. Passed three ox trains. Overtook Tipton. Camped for noon on the Little Blue. Large baking. Hot work. Afternoon went hunting on pony with Burns, up the valley of the river after leaving the trail which now strikes up towards the Platte. Rode considerable distance. Saw five antelopes coming towards us. Got in a ravine. Another hunter of our party scared them. Running shot.

Killed a rattler. Shot at maid at a buffalo scull. Saw no more game. Galloped a race with Burns. Camped on the high bank of a chasm or slough in the table land. Brought our wood and water with us from the Blue. Muddy water here and a few elms. 10 miles from the Blue. Total distance to day 25 miles.

Wednesday, June 6. Appearance of rain. Rode pony. Last 3 days started at 4:30 a.m. Crossed the slough, which in high water is the bed of a stream, flowing into the Blue. 5 or 6 miles further crossed another similar slough with no timber save a single tree in sight within a vast range. On its west bank, a little to the left of the road, is a grave with this inscription: — "Here lie the remains

A page from Bernard Reid's 1849 diary. *Courtesy: Archives, Univ. of Santa Clara.*

was buried after dark. Children on the prairie.[17] Watered pony out of my hat. Distance 26 miles.

Searls: "I got out to walk and was soon in advance of the train. . . . I lay down to await the coming of our carriage and was soon in a sound sleep. When I awoke I found two hours had elapsed and our company had passed me long since. . . . I struck out on foot. After having travelled till the perspiration stood in big drops on my brow and . . . mounting a small eminence . . . I saw our team and mess in the bottom of the valley. . . . The whole top and body of the carriage was literally crushed to atoms. . . . Another of our teamsters was taken with cholera today at noon and is now a corpse."

Tuesday, June 5. Rode pony. Passed three ox trains. Overtook Upton.[18] Camped for noon on the Little Blue. Large baking. Hot work. Afternoon went hunting on pony with Burns[19] up the valley of the river, after leaving the trail which now strikes up towards the Platte. Rode considerable distance. Saw five antelopes coming towards us. Got in a ravine. Another hunter of our party scared them. Running shot. Killed a rattler. Shot at mark at a buffalo scull. Saw no more game. Galloped a race with Burns. Camped on the high bank of a chasm or slough in the table land. Brought our wood and water with us from the Blue. Muddy water here and a few elms. 10 miles from the Blue. Total distance today 25 miles.

Wednesday, June 6. Appearance of rain. Rode pony. Last 3 days started at 4:30 a.m. Crossed the slough, which, in high water, is the bed of a stream, flowing into the Blue. 5 or 6 miles further crossed another similar slough with no timber save a single tree in sight within a vast range. On its west bank, a little to the left of the road, is a grave with this inscription: —"Here lies the remains of Mrs. Alice Hibbard, wife of Lemuel Hibbard of St. Louis, Mo., aged 34 years and 1 month, died 31st of May 1849." Nooned on the open prairie. No wood or water. Large diameter of the country. Platte bluffs and knobs [sand dunes] in

---

[17] Male diarists invariably noted the presence of children and women on the trail, and many commented in particular on the women; the percentage of females in wagon trains in 1849 is estimated at only 5 per cent. When Joseph Hamelin saw a young woman on the trail, he wrote: "My little old heart went pit-a-pat, it did." See Jeffrey, *Frontier Women*, p. 108; and Hamelin, June 19.

[18] S. J. Upton, another passenger.

[19] "Indian Bill" Burns, one of Turner's staff.

view. Start at 3. Storm blows up black and terrible. Grave of Franklin Wilson, aged 17, of Washington County, Arkansas. At noon a one-horse wagon passes us. Left Independence 21st May. Brought us European news. After starting, the storm breaks over us with tempest-like fury. It was with difficulty I could keep my seat in the saddle. Reached the bluffs overlooking the Platte bottom about 4 p.m. Bottom apparently 3 miles wide and very wet since the rain. Camped near the river bank opposite Grand Island and immediately opposite a small island to which we had to wade for wood.[20] Distance 18 miles.

Searls: "We shall remain here till Friday to recruit our animals, and air our baggage and provisions which have been damp for many days."

Thursday, June 7. Fine clear morning. Went over to the small island on the pony to get wood. Beautiful spot. Sweet briar, wild roses, gooseberry, willow, dogwood, cottonwood, etc. Grape vines in abundance. Large river. Water like the Missouri, but shallow. Richard Smith died. Buried at 1 o'clock, with masonic ceremonies. Auction of his effects. Quarrel of Bob and Dillard.[21] Light bread. Camp deliberations. Remained in camp all day.

Friday, June 8. Pleasant but cloudy. Started at 6. Ride pony. Pass returning trains. Camp for dinner within 2 miles of Fort Kearney.[22] Distance 10 miles. Commenced a letter to Mary.[23] Start after noon. Great hail storm. Gathered up the scattered

[20] Grand Island was a well-known landmark. About 52 miles in length, it divided the Platte River, and its cottonwood trees were a contrast to the treeless banks of the river. The Platte was a curiosity because of its great width (nearly 2 miles), shallowness, and "flatness" (hence the name given by French trappers), which made the water appear level with or even higher than the surrounding country. See Mattes, *Great Platte River Road*, pp. 161–64.

[21] "Bob" is a trainman, perhaps the one called "Chihuahua Bob" by Searls on July 5; R. S. Dillard is a passenger.

[22] Formerly Fort Childs, Fort Kearney was renamed in honor of the Mexican war hero, Gen. Stephen Kearny, after his death in 1848. The misspelling "Kearney" was common in 1849 and became so standard as to be perpetuated in the spelling of the modern city of Kearney. Though the official name is "Kearny," Reid's contemporary usage is retained in the text of the diary. The fort was established in 1848 to protect emigrants and to keep peace between the Pawnees and the Sioux. In his journal, June 8, Reid recalled that soldiers at the fort had helped repair wagons with army materials. The fort was some 325 miles from Independence. For an exhaustive description of it, see Mattes, *Great Platte River Road*, chap. 6.

[23] Reid's older sister.

Fort Kearney (officially spelled Kearny) was sketched by overlander James F. Wilkins on June 4, 1849. The drawing conveys his impression, shared by most emigrants, that the fort was "a miserable looking place." *Courtesy: State Historical Society of Wisconsin.*

wreck of the train and moved on to the Fort. Camped nearby, 2 miles from our noon camp. Bought 12 lbs sugar for our mess, at 25¢ per lb. Turf houses, stables and ditches at the Fort. No fortifications. Well of cold water. Supper at the house of a Mormon family [the Knowltons]. At noon camp some emigrants who came up the Platte told us of their skirmishes with indians two or three days before.

Searls: "All the storms which I ever before experienced were as nothing compared with the one we endured this day, just before reaching Fort Kearney. The rain fell in torrents accompanied by a whirlwind and by hail the size of hickory nuts. Two of our carriages were overset by the gale and one of them crushed to atoms. Mules and loose stock were stampeded and ran for hours. Captain Turner, who was on horseback, was struck on the finger by a hailstone which dislocated the joint. In the short space of ten minutes no less than three inches of hail and rain fell. . . . There are no settlers here except a family of Mormons who keep a boarding house and with whom a large number of our men made an excellent supper of bread, milk, fresh butter, doughnuts and all the little et ceteras."

A newspaper correspondent who signed himself "Pawnee" wrote from the fort on June 13: "The Pioneer Line of fast coaches reached here on the 8th. . . . A great error was made in fitting out this line, resulting either from ignorance or lack of means. The baggage wagons are entirely too heavily loaded, . . . and the carriages . . . are drawn by but two mules, and small ones at that. . . . A strong feeling of discontent prevailed throughout the entire company . . . and the chances are strongly in favor of a general exploding. . . . The devil himself would find it impossible to give satisfaction to an incongruous crowd of one hundred and twenty persons . . . thrown together for the first time, as is the case with the Pioneer Line. There are to be found doctors, lawyers, divines, gentlemen of leisure, clerks, speculators, etc. etc., tumbled in together and obliged to stand guard, cook victuals, bring wood and water, wash dishes, and haul wagons out of mudholes. Can anything imaginable be more difficult than the smoothing down of such a heterogeneous mass."[24]

[24] The letter appeared in the *Missouri Republican*, July 6, 1849. Dale Morgan has written that "Pawnee" was Capt. Stewart Van Vliet, then quartermaster at the fort; see Morgan's note in Pritchard, p. 22, n. 13. To my knowledge, no passenger was a clergyman.

Fort Kearney to Fort Laramie

June 9–28

The Pioneer Line now follows the Platte River through present-day Nebraska to the forks of the North and South Platte. About fifty miles beyond the forks, along the South Platte, the trail crosses the river. It descends from high bluffs near the landmark of Ash Hollow to the south bank of the North Platte. The route then moves along the river into what is now Wyoming. Near the confluence of the North Platte and Laramie rivers the trail reaches Fort Laramie, a private trading post bought by the United States government on June 26, one day before the arrival of the Pioneer Line. This is the end of the easiest stage of the journey. The passengers have become increasingly disillusioned about the progress and management of the train by the time the Pioneer Line reaches Fort Laramie. Nine men have died so far, and others are seriously ill.

Saturday, June 9. Got breakfast for the mess and then went with Brewster to Knowltons[1] for our breakfast. Quite a luxury. Finished my letter and sent it by a Mr. Sullivan of St. Louis. Overtook the train at noon camp. 11 miles. Saw mirage, and yellow and indigo wild flowers. After noon passed grave of Joseph Hunter, of Columbus, Ohio, aged 56. He was the captain of his company. Half a mile further came to the grave of John D. Bradshaw, of Johnson County, Mo., aged 40. Soon after came to a well recently dug, of pure cold water two feet below the surface. Cry of "buffalo!"[2] Something seen over the river. Camped

---

[1] The Mormon family who kept the boarding house where Reid, Searls, and other passengers had eaten supper the night before.

[2] The train is now in the heart of buffalo country. Many diarists wrote about the excitement of the chase. See Delano, May 31; Dewolf, June 18; Johnson, May 17; Long, May 8, Perkins, June 16; Searls, June 15; Swain, June 16; and Tiffany, May 25.

on dry bottom near the river bank. Distance since noon 7 miles. *Sunday, June 10.* Start at 6:30 up along the Platte bottom. Bonnell and Stoyell supersede us (Brewster and I) as cooks. Ride pony. Thousand islands—real gems.[3] After noon saw pretty cactus in bloom. Also beds of a handsome fragrant orange colored flower—leaf like a rose geranium. Prairie dog village. Camp after crossing Plum Creek. Distance 19 miles. Slept in tent. Thunderstorm.

Searls: "We passed through a village of Prairie Dogs this afternoon. The first intimation we had of our proximity to these pigmy barkers was the observing of a small animal on the trail, bearing a close resemblance to a rat, though considerably larger in size."

Monday, June 11. Clears up prettily. Learned that carriage No. 4 was sent back to the fort for flour. Wet road. Travel only six miles. Encamp near two new graves at the shore. In the afternoon go about 9 miles. Brewster and I on first watch at night. Mosquitos bad.

Searls: "It was discovered that a mistake had been made in the computation of the amount of flour on hand, and that we are deficient in that article to a large amount. A wagon has therefore been sent back to Fort Kearney for a supply of that article. Nothing of interest has occurred to vary the monotony of the journey."

Tuesday, June 12. Brewster and others went to hunt buffaloes. Start with train at 6:15. Remain behind fixing my rifle. Tried to take the distance across the river. Too windy. Saw two wolves within gunshot at a recent camp ground. Could not discharge my rifle before they trotted out of sight. Saw a party of horsemen at the foot of the bluffs in full chase of something at which they were firing. Walked to them. They had killed an old wolf. Walked to the noon camp. Afternoon struck off to the bluff on foot alone. Ascended some of the highest peaks. Flowery slopes. Green parterres.[4] Romantic serpentine valleys. Abrupt gorges.

---

[3] Other diarists commented on the number and variety of the islands in the Platte. Perkins (June 16) counted "nearly 30" and thought their appearance "very charming." Reid, who had a surveyor's interest in geography, here likens the river to the St. Lawrence, with its thousand islands, though he had never seen the St. Lawrence.

[4] Parterres—ornamental gardens with plants and pathways arranged in patterns. Here Reid's imagination soars.

White sand steeps resembling rock. Storm coming up. Sublimity added to the scene. Te Deum. Fading, still fading, etc. Gathered flowers. Growing dark under the black curtain of the sky. Turned down the valley to seek the camp. Saw a young antelope. Drops rain. Hurried on down the plain. After a long run discovered that I had gone far past the camp. Turned and reached it wet and exhausted after dark. Lay down in the tent. Storm breaks over us. Mules driven into corral. Pony and horses frightened. Found by aid of the lightning and tied them to the wagon wheels. Tent leaked and water came in under and over us. Hard time of it. Distance 18 miles.

Diarist Ansel McCall, ten days' travel time ahead of the Pioneer Line, wrote on this day: "For the last three weeks we have been waiting anxiously for the grand Pioneer Line of fast coaches . . . [to] dash by us. Some grand stage men of St. Louis had organized this line of coaches. . . . Their passengers were all to be of the first-class—grass widowers, *gamboliers*, bankers, brokers and men of fashion. They were to be attended by skilfull *valets*, etc. . . . I presumed, at Independence, to advise two young men . . . who proposed taking the conveyance, to be cautious in making their contract, and . . . keep back the larger portion of their passage money to provide against . . . failure to carry out the agreement, as they could have no legal redress on the plains."

Wednesday, June 13. Cloudy with occasional sunshine this morning. Rations. Auction of cabin stores and Lamalfa's stores.[5] Bought a bottle of lemon syrup, 50¢. High times. Scramble for molasses, tobacco and raisins. General discussions. Turner's speech in the corral. Motion put and carried to put bedding in carriages and walk more. Dissatisfaction. Proposal to split the train. Lie in camp till 2 p.m. Meantime the auctions and waifs lightened up the train somewhat.[6] Some liquor spilled out on the prairie. Traveled 5½ miles in the afternoon. Camped near a clear running stream nearly parallel with the river and near it. I

---

[5] Joseph Lamalfa carried goods in his wagon and intended to trade in California; Woolley (p. 4) recollected that passengers called Lamalfa "Macaroni" because he carried so much of it. The cabin stores came from a wagon or wagons owned by a man named Campbell, ostensibly traveling with the train, like Lamalfa, and selling goods and liquor to the passengers. On July 11 Campbell will be dismissed from the train.

[6] By "waifs" Reid means stray articles. In his journal, June 2, Reid recalled that Turner had also unloaded a ton of cured meat, but there is no record of this in either Reid's or Searls's diary.

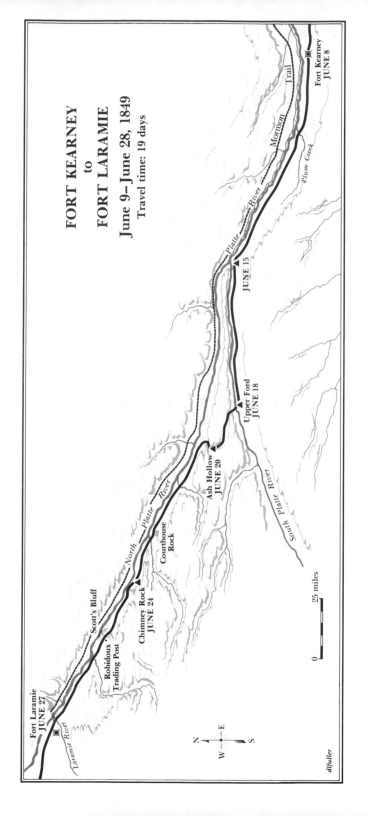

FORT KEARNEY
to
FORT LARAMIE
June 9–June 28, 1849
Travel time: 19 days

Fort Kearney
JUNE 8

Plum Creek

Mormon Trail

Platte River

JUNE 15

Upper Ford
JUNE 18

Ash Hollow
JUNE 20

South Platte River

Courthouse
Rock

North Platte River

Chimney Rock
JUNE 24

Robidoux
Trading Post

Scott's Bluff

Fort Laramie
JUNE 27

Laramie River

N
W — E
S

0   25 miles

dlfuller

went over after train starts to bathe and change clothes. Storm comes up before I reach the train again. Camp near bank of some stream along which is some willow and cottonwood timber. Heard this morning of murder by indians at the Loup Fork, of Harrison Rowe, brother of Cyrus Rowe of No. 8.[7] At night Mr. Peabody comes to camp. He had left the Kentucky train (just in our rear), and joined a pack-mule party of five who left Independence on the 27th of May. Brewster and I walked over with him to their camp nearby. Drs. McDonald and Swift and some others of the party propose joining them. We would too if we had the animals.

Reid, journal: "It was also determined by a decided vote to restrict the right of passengers to ride in the spring wagons. Until now many of them had persisted in riding, though the mules could scarcely drag their loads. Henceforth none but the sick are to ride, and the blankets are to be hauled in the carriages to relieve the heavy wagons."

Searls: "A considerable uneasiness and discontent has prevailed among our passengers for several days, owing in a great measure to our slow progress. All sorts of abuse has been awarded to Captain Turner, some blaming him for not going faster, others for travelling at all during the continuance of the present state of the bad roads. . . . Captain Turner resolved to lighten up by destroying everything not essential to our comfort. Liquors to a large amount were turned out, and extra articles of various kind broken up, after which a meeting was called in the Corrall."

Thursday, June 14. Train starts at 6:30. Clear weather but muddy bottom. Take pony today as Brewster has boils and cannot ride. Remain behind awhile with Peabody. Some others remain also. Introduced to Capt. Long of the pack party. An ox train from Independence comes up soon, and then comes the Kentucky train. The ox train left on the 15th May. Travelled 7½ miles and camped for noon on the bank of the river, where there is a little timber and shrubbery. Large rose trees, wild geraniums and other flowers deck the river bank. Grass very short and thin. Brewster and I make out a list of our expenses and purchases and he gives me his due bill for $100.[8]

[7] The Loup Fork joins the Platte along the Mormon Trail from Kanesville (Council Bluffs), Iowa. Rowe's brother apparently had come from Wisconsin. Foster (p. 25) and Lord (June 17) mentioned this murder; see also the St. Joseph *Gazette*, Aug. 3, 1849.

[8] Evidently Reid paid for the two men's clothing and supplies. On Septem-

After dinner start with train on pony. Buffalo seen on the bluffs. Several gave chase. I followed. Did not get in sight. Hunted through the hills alone all afternoon. Saw no game. Romantic glens. Cedar. Roses. Grass. Sand. Labyrinths. Scenic painting on the stage. Descended upright steeps. Plain opens at a pretty winding timbered stream. Hopes of getting a cooling draught of clear, fresh water. All dry! Beautiful sunset. Found our camp just beyond another timbered branch. Bottom filled with pools of water. Close to the bluffs. Picturesque situation. 15 miles all day. Made our bed out-doors. After midnight threatened rain. Took up our bed and walked into the tent. Almost a stampede among the mules. Kentucky train camped near us fire two shots. Probably indians about.

Searls: "An attempt was made by Indians last night to stampede our animals but without success."

Friday, June 15. Clear morning. Passed the grave of Capt. Pleasant Gray, of Huntsville, Texas.[9] High knob near the road. Forks of the Platte. Met two wagons from Salt Lake and one emigrant wagon, returning from Fort Laramie. Camped off to the right of the trail a little above the forks. Distance to-day 10 miles. Lay up all afternoon waiting for the wagon of flour from Fort Kearney. About 4 o'clock a herd of 8 or 10 buffaloes appear in the river bottom about a mile from our camp. Brewster, Mose [Mallerson], Rogers, Tiffany, Dr. Steele, Todd [and] Cunningham, Patterson and others on horseback, gave chase and ran them towards the bluffs, where three were shot. Two of them were brought to our camp and one to the camp of an ox train nearby. Not being at the corral when the alarm was given I had no chance to get a horse in time, so I shouldered my rifle and struck off alone to the bluff to head the buffaloes should they chance to come that way. I went about three miles without seeing any of them. Saw an antelope but could not approach near enough. At the extreme point of a deep narrow ravine overhung by stunted trees, and cut into caves and alcoves by the rain and

ber 13 Brewster will add to the note for his share of the pony. Only $50 of the debt was ever repaid. See John Brewster to Bernard Reid, July 16, 1852.

[9]According to Bruff (June 25), Gray's grave was beyond, not before, the forks of the Platte; Gray, aged forty-three, died of cholera on June 9.

winds, I saw a horse without saddle or bridle. I could not account for his being there unless the indians had stolen him from
some camp and hid him in the wild, secluded spot, and perhaps
half a score of them were now sleeping or watching behind one
of the intervening crags. I had no ammunition with me but the
charge in my rifle, and had there been "indians about" guarding
their prize I might have been in a bad fix. I found the horse
picketed, and that he had a gunshot wound on the hip. Saw no-
body about and led the horse to the camp. Found he belonged to
Mr. Mulford of No. 17, who had shot him accidentally when
hunting.[10] I met Brewster coming from the chase loaded with
buffalo meat. So we will have quite a feast on a new dish for me.[11]
Brewster, in the chase, lost one of the holster pistols and the
horseblanket. Two teamsters left the train today.

Saturday, June 16. When the train started Brewster and I went
back to the hunting ground to search for the lost pistol and blanket. Hunted for more than 3 hours in vain, then set out to overtake the train. As we passed our camp ground an ox train came
up. We showed them the carcases of the buffalo and they cut off
some slices of pretty good meat that had been left. We walked on
at a rapid rate. The sun was hot, the road dusty and the wind
blew almost a tornado. It was impossible to keep my hat on. I
had to walk bent against the wind to keep from being blown off
the trail. It was hard walking, and as it was over a dreary sand
waste without water, we suffered such thirst that we had to
drink out of a muddy stagnant pool. We overtook the train at
1:15 p.m., encamped on a high table land above the river bottom
over a part of which we had been since morning. The abrupt
bluffs had gradually sunk into gently rolling elevations, and the
trail, leaving the bottom, had crossed the points of these. Once at
home, as the camp really seemed to be, we prepared a good

[10] The horse belonged to Niles Searls, Mulford's friend and messmate. Searls
wrote on this day that the horse was shot by "a passenger," but recollected years
later in his published diary (p. 67) that Mulford had wounded the horse. The
animal remained so weak that it was abandoned again on June 22.

[11] Reid recalled in his journal that he and one of Turner's staff went buffalo
hunting on June 11, shot one of a herd of four, and carried the meat back to
camp, where it was a "welcome treat" to many of the men. But his comment here
that buffalo meat was "a new dish for me" suggests that his retrospective tale of a
successful hunt on June 11 was a product of wishful thinking.

drink of lemonade to quench our thirst, and regaled ourselves on a dish of piñola mush and molasses, hard bread, cold coffee and buffalo steak. The train had travelled 12 miles. We started again in the afternoon and went 11½ more to a beautiful campground on the river brink, to which we descended through a picturesque defile in the bluffs, now running close to the river and quite high and rugged. Opposite us in the river were several small islands, some of them handsomely timbered. At our noon camp was the grave of W. W. Goodwin of Perkins County, Ala., and in the afternoon we passed the grave of S. W. Moore, of Jackson County, Mo.[12] Today Drs. McDonald, Swift and Hoy, Lewis [Louis] Sloss, and the driver "Yankee," of our train, joined Capt. Long's pack party,—and one of that party joined our train in place of Dr. Swift.[13] His name is [space left blank].

Sunday, June 17. The trail follows the river bank. In two or three miles we came to a spring oozing out of the river. A little further on the wind was blowing clouds of sand across about 200 yards of the trail from an abraded bluff on our left. The sand was driven like a snow drift covering up the grass and scanty vegetation in its path. I was some distance behind the train on foot and did not venture to pass through this sanddrift on the road. Making a detour to the left, I waded throu the [word illegible] sand where it was only knee high. I never saw anything so dreary. It was a Sahara on a small scale. The bluff seemed about half swept away in this manner, and probably it all came from a slight breach in the sod a few weeks ago. The vegetation generally along the trail this morning is scanty but flowers are numerous. I counted seven or eight kinds in bloom, besides cacti of different kind and other plants not yet in bloom. In the afternoon I met with several conical cacti in bloom. They were very pretty. I pressed one.[14] Just as we came into camp four buffaloes were seen a little ahead of us. Two gave chase on horse-

[12] When Bruff passed this spot on June 26, Goodwin's initials were obliterated; he was twenty-four and died on June 9. Moore died on June 11, and by June 26 his address was obliterated.

[13] Dr. Hoy did not leave with the others; see Reid's diary entries on June 29 and especially July 22, when Hoy finally left the train. According to Dr. R. H. McDonald's recollection, two men from the pack train joined the Pioneer Line; see McDonald, *McDonald Overland Narrative*, p. 65 and appendix. Searls mentions the teamster "Yankee" on June 4; he is the third crew member to leave the train.

[14] This is probably the cactus flower that Reid will send to his sisters from San Francisco; see p. 151.

back and two on foot. The chase was kept up sometime, but the game got away. One of the horsemen lost Brewster's rifle. Todd was thrown from his horse and badly bruised. As it was some distance from the camp a carriage was sent to bring him in. Mr. Rowe has serious symptoms of cholera. He drank cold water to excess this morning. Dr. Brewster prescribed for him. Camped on a gentle slope between the bluffs and the river, near a slough of tolerably clear standing water. Distance 20 miles. We have let the pony run loose these two days to recruit him and heal his chafed back. The walking has been hard on me owing to a sore ankle. Hard wind at night blowing towards the river. The wind has been almost incessant in that direction for some days. Wolf of No. 10 shot an antelope today, the first brought to our camp. Duhring and Brewster are cooks today.

Searls: Messmate Charles Cranson "was taken with severe pain in the legs and arms to-day almost depriving him of their use and resembling in some degree a paralytic stroke."

Monday, June 18. Start at 6:30. Clear and windy. Saw some of the broad flowered cactus in bloom. Color pale yellow. Passed through a field of about 100 acres crowded full of the yellow prairie flower. Camped for noon 12 miles from the ford of the South Platte. Distance this morning 11½ miles. Rations served at noon. No ham. Half the dry bread mouldy. Walked some in the afternoon. Feet very sore. Saw more large broad pale yellow cactus in bloom, a little like a peony. Camped at the upper ford.[15] Most of the trains had crossed at the lower ford. Distance 21 miles. Some of our party in advance on foot found a stray steer and drove him into camp. When the train arrived they killed him and distributed the beef. He was in good condition and his meat was quite a luxury. Our mess got a good share. The camp is on the river brink. Pretty good grass. No wood, and buffalo chips[16] very scarce. Indian wigwam in the distance a couple of miles up the river. Very windy. Slept out doors under the lee of a tent.

[15] The upper ford, near present-day Brule, Nebraska, was 53 miles from the lower ford; these fords were the most popular crossings along the South Platte. The upper ford was considered dangerous, but the river was shallow at this time. The "shifting" bottom Reid notes the next day was quicksand.

[16] Dried buffalo dung used for fuel. Some diarists used the French trapper's term, *bois de vache*, though it was spelled in picturesque ways.

Searls: "Saw the dead body of an Indian deposited in a tree near the river. Reached the ford a little before sunset and encamped for the night. Some of the passengers ran down and shot a fine fat ox near camp, which they found several miles off. The beef is delicious."

Tuesday, June 19. "Catched up" early to ford the river. Started staff carriage first. It stuck in the sand several times. Next big bacon wagon with 12 mules. Got over pretty well. Passengers generally wade over. Put Brewster's clothes and mine on pony and wade across. Half a mile slantwise. Water not up to wagon beds. Bottom always shifting. Noticed something like gold tinsel among the sand in the river bed. Got a basin full of sand and pebbles to wash out. Back and shoulders badly, badly scalded in the hot sun. Before crossing I went up to the wigwam. It proved to be a mausoleum resembling an indian lodge, and in it were two indian corpses buried in state,—one on the ground in robe or blanket, the other immediately above him on a raised platform or scaffolding. The wigwam was of elk or buffalo skins dressed and sewed together, 20 steps in circumference, 21 feet high. The poles meet and cross at the top,—surrounded by the stars and stripes. Great seam ornaments with tassels like military buttonholes, and some buffalo tails swinging outside.[17] After getting dinner on the north bank we started over the bluffs towards the North Fork. Rolling prairie flattens as we go. Few flowers, but both species of cactus in bloom. Grass scant. Storm blew up black and threatening. Drew up in line to meet it. A great deal of wind with some rain and a sprinkle of hail. Went on after the storm, and camped near the head of a hollow leading down towards the North Fork. No wood or water near. Some time after the rain, I felt chilly and had an attack of nausea. Rode on, hoping soon to reach camp and wrap myself in blankets,—but soon became too faint and dizzy to remain in the saddle. Got into the carriage and Brewster gave me a warming pepper draught, and I soon felt better. Took a cup of hot tea and slept in the wagon. We have come about 13 miles from the river. Charles C. Cranston [Cranson] of Ann Arbor, Mich., died this evening in carriage 17. He had been sick for some time and somewhat deliri-

[17] Few diarists described this scaffold, and none so vividly as Reid; cf. Hutchings, July 9; Lord, June 15; McCall, June 7; Searls, June 19. This is Sioux country, and the tribe placed their dead above ground, probably to protect the bodies from wolves, the scavengers of the prairie.

ous. This morning he attempted to cut his throat. His disease was not certainly known.

Searls writes on June 20 of Cranson's death "last night at 8 o'clock. His death was probably occasioned by congestion of the brain. This is the second member of our mess who has been called away by the hand of death. . . . May he rest in peace in this, his solitary place of interment."

Wednesday, June 20. Started early after burying Cranston. Our mess and some others had no breakfast. Crossed some steep broken ridges and began to descend the winding hollow [Ash Hollow] in which there is a small stream. Felt much better this morning. After going 3 or 4 miles we camp on the bank of the stream, where there is some stunted cedar and plenty of grass. The water of the creek has sunk in a couple of hours quite under the sandy bed, and has to be got at by digging. Flowers are numerous. Some new kinds. Wild sunflowers, and a crest-like white cluster of blossoms. Rained a little at intervals while in camp here. Washed out the sand brought from the Platte. Found scales of mica resembling gold and silver in brightness, and came to a sediment of fine black sand which I wrap up and put away to test sometime. The hollow widens. Stunted cedars shooting out of crevices of calcareous rock gradually give place to small groves of ash on sloping hill sides and bushy bottoms. Find a large plant like a turnip or thistle with a large white flower. The stalk containing a yellow sap. Just before leaving the hollow and entering the valley of the North Fork, I was behind the train reading some names on trees, when a very fine looking indian came across the hollow towards me on a dun pony. He was naked down to the waist and his long black hair was plaited in a queue behind. He was armed with bow and arrows and spear. Could talk no English. We shook hands and made signs, but to little purpose. He rode and moved with dignity and agility. Soon Francisco came up and tried to talk to him but could not except by signs. Soon leaving us he started up the precipitous bluffs, which his pony climbed like a mountain goat.[18] In a moment the

[18] The Indian is a Sioux brave. The Sioux, much admired by emigrants for their physical beauty, were generally friendly to whites in 1849; cf. Delano, June 4; Farnham, June 5; Johnston, May 21; and Pritchard, May 26. Francisco is a Mexican teamster. This is one of a number of occasions when Reid roams alone in the surrounding countryside, perhaps lulled by the friendliness of the Indians en route.

Rachel E. Pattison's grave, noted by Bernard Reid on June 20, can be seen today near Lewellen, Nebraska. From Webb, *Gold Rush Trail*, p. 81. *Courtesy: Todd Webb.*

bottom of the North Platte opened to view. The river and opposite bluffs presented an appearance similar to what we had seen before below the fork, but the bluffs on the south side showed a marked difference of character. They are high, rocky and precipitous. In some places overhanging—frequently resembling turrets, castles and embattled fortresses, crowned by a few stunted cedars.[19]

These cliffs are sand and crumbling and whitish sandstone. They are cut into at irregular intervals by deep ravines through

[19] Few emigrants mentioned these formations, which were called Castle Bluffs. Cf. Kirkpatrick, June 7; Holliday, *World Rushed In*, p. 161.

which, after heavy rains, run clear streams that dry up or sink under the sands very soon after the rain ceases. At the mouth of Ash Hollow was the grave of Rachel E. Patterson, aged 18.[20] We camped about 5 miles up from Ash Hollow in tolerably good short grass on a pretty level lawn running into an angle in the bluffs. Distance today 11½ miles. D & B [Duhring and Brewster], our cooks for the week, served up this evening a nice rich soup, the first we have tasted on the trip. It was really excellent, and with boiled and fried beef, good biscuit, piñola mush and molasses and tea made a very good supper for hungry men. A large train of 40 ox teams is on the opposite side of the river, and an ox train from Independence that we passed at Ash Hollow is camped near us. Slept in tent. Mosquitoes were so bad that we had to keep a smudge fire at the tent door to smother them. Had a miserable night, owing to my scalded back, waist, shoulders and arms. Passed a grave today decked with twigs of cedar.

Thursday, June 21. Made an early start. Road at first wet and miry; soon became sandy and broken by ravines. Wagons and carriages sink deep in the sand, and some stalled. Walked and drove alternately with Mr. Duhring. Commenced reading Father De Smet's letter.[21] Saw a new flower. Leaf like rosemary. Purple petals, long and narrow around a yellow center. Mr. Bonnell today saw some artemisia (wild sage). 10½ miles to noon camp. Very hot sun. Baxter of Michigan came to camp. He was a fellow passenger on the Sacramento. Belongs to the train of 40 wagons on the other side. Hunting 46 lost oxen. Went 8½ miles in the afternoon and camped close to the river. Sand and some grass. Passed this morning two new graves, and this afternoon the grave of John Hoover, aged 12.[22]

[20] The grave of Rachel E. Pattison (not Patterson) can still be seen near Lewellen, Nebraska, and is now covered with glass to protect it from the weather. The young woman, a bride of three months, died of cholera on June 19, 1849, the day before Reid passed by. See Mattes, *Great Platte River Road*, p. 301.

[21] Reid may have met Pierre De Smet, the Belgian Jesuit missionary and explorer, in St. Louis, where De Smet had his headquarters. But it is more likely that Reid meant to write "letters," referring to De Smet's *Letters and Sketches, 1841–42* (Philadelphia, 1843), which could have been one of the books he took along in his baggage.

[22] The boy died of cholera on June 18; the headboard of his grave read, "Rest in peace, sweet boy, for thy travels are over." See Bruff, July 2. In his diary on June 18 Vincent Hoover wrote a detailed and moving account of his younger brother's death.

Passed another sleepless night like the last. In addition to my scalded back myriads of mosquitoes were trying to devour us.

Searls writes on June 22: "We have been annoyed several days with mosquitoes, but until last night were enabled to battle them with some success. They came, however, with the twilight of last evening in myriads, falling like famished tigers upon their prey."

Friday, June 22. Up at 3:30 and off at 5. Close to camp crossed a small run on the bank of which stood a lone tree! The bluffs near the trail this morning have sunk into gently rolling hills. Wild sage bushes plentier, and sunflower, blue lupin, the white-crested flower, bronze flower, yellow flower and cacti (not in bloom) are plentier. Some banks on the river side are covered with volcanic and other pebbles of every kind, color and shape. Sun hot. Some clouds. 9 miles to noon camp. Begin a letter to Kate.[23] Passed grave of William L. Stevens, of Boone County, Mo. Then a row of bare sand mounds. About 9 miles from noon camp crossed a handsome creek of clear water 20 feet wide, winding down a ravine studded with cedars. Near east bank of creek grave of E. Morse, of Poland, Ohio, aged 66. An Indiana camp at the creek. Shrill voices of children playing on its banks. Clouding up as for rain. Saw a new clustered purple flower with long pistils supporting globules. Camped near a fine clear, cold spring to right of trail. Total distance 20 miles. Stood guard second watch. Slept tolerably well.

Saturday, June 23. On the first mile passed graves of three of one company from Bristol, Indiana. All died of cholera. Ellis Russel, aged 53, June 14; Samuel P. Judsen, aged 49, June 15, and N. T. Phillips, aged 32, June 17. Soon came in sight of Court House and Chimney Rocks. Rode over towards the former. Found it farther than supposed.[24] Crossed a sandy stream; ascended ridge. Found it too far to go on. Turn towards camp. In the afternoon, riding along, a gust springs up. Sand clouds.

[23] Reid's younger sister. He mailed the letter at Fort Laramie on June 29.
[24] These striking formations were mentioned by all overlanders. A number of other diarists commented on the deceptive distance of the landmarks because of the clear air; see Delano, June 7; Swain, June 29; and Wistar, June 12. Reid does not express the excitement and wonder of diarists like Pritchard (June 1), Johnson (June 5), and Lord (June 22). See Mattes, *Great Platte River Road*, chaps. 11 and 12, for exhaustive descriptions of the landmarks. Cf. Cross, June 17, and Hutchings, p. 189, for identification of the three men from an Indiana county.

Put on goggles. Lose spectacles. Go back 4 miles. Cannot find them. Trot along to overtake the train. Magnificent sunset. Chimney Rock and architectural ruins in the distance. Pass 5 encampments—11 graves all day. Reached camp at 9 o'clock. No wood or water. Cold supper. Distance today 26 miles.

Sunday, June 24. Lay in camp till 4 p.m. Busy cooking. Walked up to grotto spring and chimney rock. Fine water, wild spot. Names. Grave of J. Griffith. Walked around the base half way— 400 paces. Climbed to base of column.[25] Thousands of names. Flowers—grass—fragrant shrub. Hard lumps of rock—soft rock—culled flowers. Mounds and castles in the vicinity. Singular scenery—train far ahead. Brewster and Perce [Pierce, a passenger] on horseback. Take a near cut over the bottom. Alkali fields. Ride and tie. Overtake the train sometime after dark. Passed grave of Joseph Geser of St. Louis, aged 36, a native of Switzerland. Died June 21 of consumption. Camped after 9 o'clock near the river. Cold supper again. Distance 16 miles.

Searls: "Descending from the [Chimney] rock we struck off in an easterly direction to an encampment situated about ¾ of a mile, near which was a spring bubbling forth from the bottom of a ravine. . . . Its temperature was almost that of the freezing point."

Monday, June 25. Started early—travelled fast. Left the river bottom about 6 miles from camp. Left Scotts Bluffs on our right. Grave of M. Roby of Ohio, aged 20, of Company I, Mounted Rifles, died June 19th of cholera.[26] Ascended a beautiful valley shaped like a horseshoe. Magnificent scenery on both sides. Valley terminates at dividing ridge. Several pure cold springs.

[25] Chimney Rock is shaped like a funnel, and to emigrants it was the most fascinating of the landmarks. The fine spring water in the nearby grotto had made the site a favorite campground for trappers. See Decker, May 28; Perkins, June 28; and Sedgley, June 29. The grave of J. Griffith, noted by Reid, is mentioned by Bruff, July 5, as being on the northwest side of the rock; Griffith came from Buffalo, New York. Hutchings, p. 189, noted that by July 16 his body had been disinterred by wolves.

[26] Scott's Bluff was named after a sick trapper, Hiram Scott, who died at the spot in 1827 or 1828. According to legend, Scott died after being deserted by his companions. Of two roads that wagons could take from this point, the Pioneer Line chooses Robidoux Pass; cf. Searls, June 25. The soldier who died, identified as James Roby by Bruff and Cross, was one of the Mounted Riflemen, who were marching from Fort Leavenworth to Oregon in 1849 to establish forts for the protection of emigrants. See Bruff, July 6; Cross, p. 116; and Howell, pp. 13–14.

James F. Wilkins made this sketch of Fort Laramie on June 24, 1849. The fort was dubbed "Camp Sacrifice" by one forty-niner because of the massive unloading there by many wagon trains. *Courtesy: State Historical Society of Wisconsin.*

Graves of F. Dunn and Joseph Blakely, R.I.P. Roubidoux store.[27] Accident to No. 1. Distance this morning 16 miles. Camp for noon near summit. Start at 5:30 p.m. Went on half way to Horse Creek, 6 miles. Slough water. On reaching the summit of dividing ridge get first glimpse of Rocky Mountains—one large peak and several smaller ones to the left of it—the Laramie Peaks. Saw also the Black Hills [of eastern Wyoming]. Passed grave of Rufus Adams, aged 59.

[27] This trading post, described by many emigrants, was operated, in all likelihood, by Antoine Robidoux, a member of a well-known family; few diarists spelled the Robidoux name correctly. See esp. Perkins, June 28: "Below the spring in the ravine a Frenchman has established himself in a little cabin as a jack of all trades, Blacksmith, Shoemaker, Tailor &c, & keeps a little stock of groceries, hardware, &c. Some of his prices were amusing enough to us though not to the unfortunate traveler whose misfortunes compel him to refit here." The grave of F. Dunn of Illinois is well recorded; he died of cholera on June 13, at the age of twenty-six. See Banks, June 14; Parke, June 14; Mattes, *Great Platte River Road*, pp. 438–53; and Bruff, July 7, and Hutchings, p. 190, who recorded the other grave as that of Joseph Blake, not Blakely.

Tuesday, June 26. Started early. Walked all forenoon—pony running loose. Crossed a slough,—then Horse Creek. Good water. No good grass near. Passed level bottom and ascended long rolling, sandy hills. Camped at edge of the hills on a gravelly point. Distance 14 miles. Took a bath in the Platte. Some rain. Walked in the afternoon. Train went very fast. Narrows.[28] Threatened storm. Camped after dark. 12 miles since noon. Turner had gone ahead in the morning to Fort Laramie to make new arrangements.

On this day, at Fort Laramie, diarist James Wilkins wrote: "A gentleman from Turner and Allen's pioneer line encamped with us last night. he gives a very unfavorable account of the 'pioneers' they being still a week or more behind.[29] He himself bought a horse and left them in disgust leaving his trunk and everythink behind but a couple of blankets. His object is to catch up with an ox train in which he has a relation and who he believes to be 100 miles still in advance. *so much for mules.*"

Wednesday, June 27. About 12 miles to the Fort.[30] Go on within 3 miles and camp. Get dinner, and start again to another campground half a mile west of the Fort. In the morning met an express with pack mules bearing letters to the States from the fort. No letters ready. Met two men who informed us of the purchase of the fort by the U.S. troops the previous day. On coming to the Laramie river, which was rapid and breast deep, many of us had to wade or swim across. Bonfire of wagons etc. east of the river. The Fort about as Bryant describes it. An old fort nearer the junction of the rivers abandoned.[31] Quadrangle—towers, adobe walls—swivels[32]—inner court, shops, etc. Cards, letters and

[28] Reid is probably referring to a narrowing of the Platte; cf. Geiger and Bryarly, June 13, who noted that the river at this spot became "much narrower."

[29] Here Wilkins is mistaken, of course, the Pioneers being only a day away

[30] Fort Laramie, owned by the American Fur Company since 1835, was near the junction of the North Platte and Laramie rivers, opposite present-day Fort Laramie, Wyoming. It was originally called Fort John on the Laramie. The United States government bought Fort Laramie on June 26, for the protection of emigrants. Searls, June 27, mistakenly wrote that the cost was 1,000 dollars; the actual cost was 4,000 dollars. See Mattes, *Great Platte River Road*, p. 494.

[31] For accounts of the massive unloading and breakup of wagon companies that commonly took place at Fort Laramie, see John P. Reid, *Law for the Elephant*, pp. 48–50; Batchelder, June 8; Castleman, June 27; Johnson, June 10; Kirkpatrick, June 10; and Love, June 11. Edwin Bryant arrived at Fort Laramie on June 22, 1846. The deserted fort noted by Reid was Fort Platte, a post of the fur trading firm Sybille, Adams and Company, until 1845.

[32] Guns defending the gate.

names on posts and walls inside and outside. Crowds of emigrants. Met Augustine Pasquier, going to Fort Bois on Little Missouri, where his Uncle Primo and Major Harvey have a trading post.[33] Went on to camp. Distance today 12 miles. Turner has bought light wagons instead of five of the heavy ones, and tomorrow something will be done to lighten up.

Searls: "This is the point at which many of the emigrants change other modes of conveyance for pack animals. Wagons are being burnt or sold at prices varying from twenty-five cents to thirty dollars. . . . Captain Turner has purchased several light wagons and the heavy ones composing our baggage train will be abandoned. Provisions for sixty days are to be taken and we are promised that within that time we shall reach Sutter's Fort."

On this day David McCollum, one of the three passengers in No. 17 from Ann Arbor, Michigan, at the start of the trip, writes to a friend in Ann Arbor of his dead messmates and home town friends Charles Sinclair and Charles Cranson: "The journey is long and fatiguing and the Lord knows when we shall get through. . . . The property of Sinclair and Cranson must be sold, and will bring but a trifle. I have all they left in my possession and shall do the best I can with it and pay it over to their friends if I live to return. . . . I have written to their families. . . . Dr. Ormsby sold his waggon for $35 to the Pioneer Line and they leave a heavy one and cannot sell it at any price. . . . This is a miserable country since the time we struck the Platte River."[34]

Thursday, June 28. Busy all day cooking and overhauling our baggage. Threw away some lead shot, and other heavy articles. Many other passengers did the same. Turner lightened up the provisions and his own baggage, and all seems to bid fair to go better. Bought 15 lbs. sugar of [passenger] Jones at 15¢, for

[33] Pasquier was probably an acquaintance from St. Louis. Harvey most likely is Major Alexander Harvey (notorious for his violence), who with the Frenchman Charles Primeau founded the St. Louis Fur Company in 1846. "Uncle Primo" could be Primeau. No information has been found about Fort Bois, but many "forts" on the Little Missouri (in present-day South Dakota) were no more than settlements with a few log houses.

[34] David McCollum to J. H. Lund, June 27, 1849, and Dr. Caleb Ormsby to wife, June 30, 1849, in Bidlack, ed., *Letters Home*, pp. 19, 20, 34. Ormsby, also from Ann Arbor, was at the fort with another wagon train. A teamster named Gilman died at the fort, bringing the total number of dead to ten. Despite the failure to carry out its unrealistic promise of a speedy trip, the Pioneer Line had made fair time to the fort, and was only a few weeks behind the first wave of emigrant wagons. Fort Laramie was approximately 336 miles from Fort Kearney. See *Missouri Republican*, Dec. 24, 1849; passenger list, Reid Papers; and Morgan's chart of travel for many wagon trains in Pritchard, appendix.

Brewster and me. Went over at dark to see Pasquier. On returning he gave me some dried buffalo meat.

Searls: "Baggage of various kinds has been destroyed and additional
mules will be hitched to some of the carriages, so that we live in hope of
making better progress for the future. The country around us presents
a dreary desolate appearance."

In a letter dated August 1, a newspaper correspondent from Fort
Laramie who signed himself "Joaquin" reported that the Pioneer Line
had passed the fort; its journey, he wrote, had been "unfortunate all the
way."[35]

[35] The letter, which was published in the *Missouri Republican* on August 29,
1849, wrongly stated that the Pioneers had passed the fort on July 2.

Fort Laramie to South Pass

June 29–July 19

The trail now moves west beyond Fort Laramie, entering the Black Hills (Laramie Mountains) of present-day Wyoming. The terrain is the roughest yet encountered, and the landscape becomes arid and desolate. The trail crosses the North Platte River approximately 110 miles from the fort. After fording the river, the Pioneer Line leaves its banks at a great bend in the course and faces a short but difficult stretch of alkali flats, with water holes poisonous to oxen. Beyond the flats, however, lies the welcoming valley of the Sweetwater River, a mountain stream with clear, sparkling water. On the banks of the river the Pioneer Line's mules break down and the passengers, gathering as if in a town meeting, force the captain to unload. Having discarded 11 tons of goods and some of the wagons, the Pioneer Line advances up the valley, moving along an easy grade to reach South Pass, at the summit of the Rocky Mountains. Here overlanders cross from the Atlantic to the Pacific watershed. Their arrival at the Continental Divide is an emotional and symbolic experience.

Friday, June 29. After breakfast and fixing up to start I finished my letter to Kate. The train moved on while I rode down back to the fort to mail the letter. Wrote also to Father Damen. Crowds of emigrants about the fort. Saw some Sacramento passengers. Bade goodbye to Pasquier. Started on and met Dr. Hoy near fort. Waited until he returned and went with him to Captain Hooker's camp about a mile, and got a good milk and bread dinner. Accident to the turtle soup. Went on after dinner 10 miles to Piney hills. Broken knobs and ravines—stunted pines and cedars. 4 miles further the warm spring. Passed grave of W. More, of Pike County, Ill., J. M. Hay, aged 14, Dr. McDermet, of Fairfield, Iowa, A. Hammond of Winchester, Ill., and

W. Brimer of Cherokee train. Dr. McDermet's grave had a gold-leaf inscription on the head-board. Took the right-hand road on the level above the hills.[1] Saw our train in the distance. Overtook it near a small stream of excellent clear water. Camped half a mile west of it. Cold supper. Total today 20 miles.

Reid, journal: At "the camp of Captain Hooker's company of dragoons en route for the Pacific Coast . . . I got an excellent dinner. I would have had the luxury of turtle soup, but as there is many a slip between the soup and the lip, an accident unfortunately upset it just before serving. I little thought then that just thirteen years later I would be fighting beside my host, General Joseph Hooker, in the same army corps in the civil war."

Searls: "We frequently meet with emigrants returning home, even after having reached nearly to the South Pass. Some are deterred by sickness or accident from proceeding farther, others by the reports of the poor feed for stock in the mountains."

Saturday, June 30. Started early. Went on foot up and down hills and ravines. Laramie's peak to left about 15 miles. Crossed a small swampy stream half sunk in sand and mud. Not good water. Good spring a little distance up to the left. Previously crossed a small, clear stream. Both streams timbered. Afterwards passed down along the dry bed of a stream. Thence ascended the ridge and bluffs. Sometimes in view of the Platte and at last descended a long slope of three miles to Horseshoe Creek near its mouth. Crossed over to a bottom of elms, box elder and high grass, where we camped. The carriages scattered here and there, each beneath the shade of a spreading elm or cluster of elder.[2] It was a delightful place for a noon camp on a hot day. Distance 16 miles. The stream is 6 or 8 paces wide, quite shallow, and has a clear gravelly bottom. Bathed in its limpid water. 5 or 6 other camps in the vicinity. Thunder cloud threatens to break on us before starting. Rained some after a while. Cross two or three gullies running full from the rain on the hill.

[1] The trail forked west of Fort Laramie. The right-hand road wound through the Black Hills, and the left-hand road moved along nearer the Platte River. The Pioneer Line takes the right or hill road; on July 2 Reid writes that the trails converge. Dr. McDermet's headboard, noted by Reid at this spot, was his medical sign; see Lord (also a physician), June 27.

[2] Cf. Cross, June 26: "This spot surpassed any encamping ground we had met with since starting on the march [of the Mounted Riflemen]." Yet when Bruff camped there on July 14, the grass was poor.

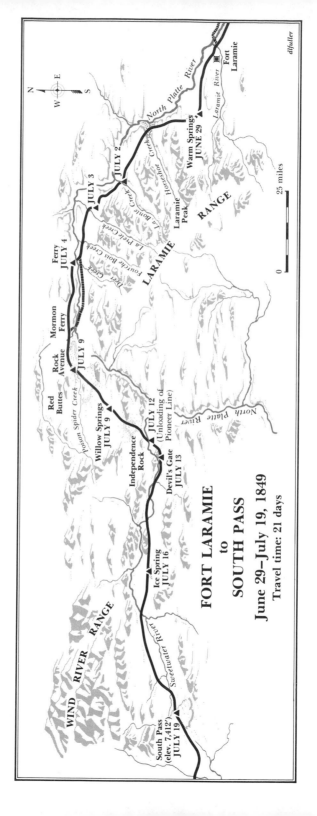

FORT LARAMIE
to
SOUTH PASS
June 29–July 19, 1849
Travel time: 21 days

Camped at dark near the river bank. Distance this afternoon 6 miles. Rain some at night, our tent was left at the fort. So four of us have to sleep out-doors.

Sunday, July 1. A clear morning. Followed the river about a mile. Came to a remarkable cañon[3] or pass between perpendicular rocks from 500 to 1000 feet high. Issuing from the cañon the river suddenly sweeps around an abrupt but graceful bend. Geo. W. Kelsey and I took our rifles and climbed the highest cliffs, and followed the edge of the overhanging brink around the semicircle.[4] The grand views afforded us of the boiling river far below us and the precipitous cliffs, fully repaid me for the toil of the difficult ascent. The top of the cliff was strewn with fragments of almost every species of rock, many of them bearing marks of volcanic action. I gathered specimens of several kinds of rocky pebbles and crystals. Numerous wildflowers were growing on the top and in the crevices of the rock. On the very edge of the precipice were two circular cups in the rock filled with clear water from last night's rain. Being thirsty we leaned over and drank a better draught than the muddy Platte a thousand feet below us could have afforded. Could have remained all day on such a spot, without tiring, gathering gems and flowers and musing on the grandeur of the scene, but the train was already miles in advance and necessity dragged us away. Descending a ravine a rabbit started up before us. I shot it but unfortunately the shot mangled it too much to carry it to camp. Passed along the river bottom and through ravines. Climbed spirally the great dividing ridge, and about noon caught sight of the train corralling. Just then a deer approached us within shooting distance. I shot and missed. We took different directions to follow it. I started three antelopes but could not get a shot at any. Ranged the hills and hollows for some hours till completely tired, and came to camp in dividing ridge about 3 o'clock. Found nearly everyone in camp asleep in the shade. Remained in camp till 6, till a broken wagon could be mended. Travelled six miles on the ridge. Total distance today 18 miles. Laramie Peak in our front the last 10 miles. Road very circular.

[3] Reid uses the Spanish word for canyon throughout the diary.
[4] Kelsey is another passenger, one of two men named Kelsey who were from Louisiana.

On this day diarist Ansel McCall, in camp just beyond South Pass, wrote: "We get no tidings of the Great Pioneer Line or its gay and festive passengers."

Monday, July 2. Called up by the bugle before dawn. Started at sun up. Kept along the same ridge. Laramie Peak to our left. About 3 miles left hand road comes in. Began to descend the ridge. Long, steep and difficult in places. Mack's [passenger John McKaraher's?] wagon upset with him inside. Not much hurt. Passed grave of Thos. M. Rankin of Lewis County, Mo., aged 28.[5] From summit of this ridge great view in all directions. Range of rugged peaks bounding half the horizon. The foreground a great basin of smaller hills, broken, barren and desolate. About 7 miles came to La Bonte river, small and clear. Timbered. New flowers like lilies and tulips. Camped about a mile from crossing and near the stream. Bathed and washed clothes. Started at 2:30. Two miles brought us to an oval valley about 4 miles long, which evidently had been long ago the crater of a volcano. Lava. Upheaved rock. Burnt clay and sandstone. Red dust and gypsum. Small stream and spring. Line of timber. Rocky cone near gateway of valley—a kind of sentinel rock. Pass through another somewhat similar valley, with a small stream and spring. Ascended the ridge and camped half a mile below the summit on west side. Water half a mile to the right. Discovered that I had lost my revolver out of my belt. Went back on foot across the ridge to the spring where I had filled the canteen. Found the revolver just where I mounted Don. Total distance today 18 miles. Slept outdoors. Cold air. Almost frost. Castellated rocks near.

Searls: "Our evening's march has been the most toilsome to our mules of any for several days. Our course has been through the very heart of the Black Hills. . . . Game appears abundant. . . . Game, however, has not sufficient attractions to allure us out very often, being too much fatigued with traveling to devote any great portion of time to the pleasures of the chase."

Tuesday, July 3. Started at sun-up. Right cold. 5 miles came to a small creek. Descended its bed 200 yards. Another mile La Prele creek smaller than La Bonte. Some timber, poor grass. 3½

[5] Bruff (July 14) noted that Rankin's grave was on the side of a hill and that he died on June 25; cf. Hutchings, p. 191.

Goldsborough Bruff sketched this ferry made of dug-outs at the Deer Creek crossing of the North Platte River on July 20, 1849. It seems more elaborate than the two "rude machines" used by the Pioneer Line on July 4, and described by Niles Searls. *Courtesy: Henry E. Huntington Library.*

miles Fourche Bois, 30 feet wide.[6] Poor grass. 4 miles to Platte. 5 up Platte to Deer Creek. Reports of 1000 to 2000 teams between us and the ford, and no grass. U.S. train[7] grazing up the creek. Had 3 or 4 days start of us. Bad prospect. Grave of C. B. Pratt of Canton, Ohio, aged 52.

Searls: "Emigrants are crossing from a short distance below us to a point thirty miles above, at every place practicable. The usual method is to prepare some two or three 'Dug Outs,' pin them together by means of cross timbers, thus forming a kind of scow capable of carrying a wagon. . . . Our company has purchased two of these rude machines, one near us and one two miles below."

Wednesday, July 4. A sorry way to celebrate the Glorious Fourth. Turner decided on ferrying the Platte at this place,—the bag-

[6] Since Edwin Bryant packed from Fort Laramie in 1846, his guide was no longer so useful; Reid's mention of Fourche Bois Creek suggests that he is now using Clayton's or Ware's guide, which both mention this creek. William Clayton's *Latter-Day Saints' Emigrants' Guide* was published in St. Louis in 1848, and Joseph E. Ware's *Emigrants' Guide to California, 1849,* in 1849. For this succession of creeks, all tributaries of the Platte, see Paden, *Wake of the Prairie Schooner,* p. 186.

[7] The Mounted Riflemen, on their way from Fort Leavenworth to Oregon.

gage train at Deer Creek mouth,—the carriages one mile below, on raft made of dug-outs. Carriages sent down to the ferry, and mules and horses sent out to graze for the day. Another train ahead of us at ferry.[8] We have to wait. Dull business. Shoot at mark. Mend up things. About 4 p.m. commenced ferrying our carriages. Got the last over at 10 p.m. In the afternoon Davidson and I went in to swim over the Platte. Water very cold and current too strong. Nearly exhausted when third way over. Began to feel uneasy as the current swept us down. Davidson seized with cramp. I was powerless to help him, and called for help from shore. None offered to come as none could probably have reached us in time. Providentially we were carried by the current to the point of a bar, where I got on my feet and caught Davidson as he was being swept past senseless. I could not have struggled much longer. We waded to the boat on the north side and were safe.[9] After all were ferried over Mr. Rogers and some 20 others got up a jollification in honor of the night of the 4th. The welkin rang till midnight with their volleys, cheers, songs, toasts and carousals.[10] Band of little children today.

Searls: Messmate Charles Mulford prepared a July 4 dinner of "fresh fish, peach pies, etc. . . . At one o'clock the cloth was laid—yes, a *Cloth*, for this time we spread a large piece of canvas upon the ground upon which we placed our dinner."

Thursday, July 5. Lay in camp till 4 p.m. Mules then brought down and we travel on. Road very sandy and hilly, about 6 miles.

[8] The ferry was one of a chain that emerged as wagon trains arrived in such numbers in 1849. Augustus Burbank, June 27, wrote that "a general crossing was going on with canoes, wagon beds, and rafts for a distance of twenty-five miles or more up the river." John Evans Brown on this day noted that his train was assisted in crossing the river by "Mr. Turner of the Pioneer Line."

[9] John M. Davidson is a passenger. The two men were lucky to escape drowning in this dangerous river, where a number of deaths were reported. Stansbury, July 25, estimated that 28 men in all had drowned; cf. Chamberlain, June 20; Farnham, June 24; and Tinker, July 11. Reid states in his journal entry for July 4 that he was a good swimmer.

[10] William Rogers, known as "Uncle Billy," is another passenger. Cf. Badman, July 4: "The government troops and Pioneer Line was firing salutes all the while till 12 o'clock at night." It was a day of celebration on the trail. Diarist P. C. Tiffany, for example, produced a cake especially baked by his wife, William Swain's train had a lavish feast compared with everyday fare, and Charles Parke made ice cream at South Pass with cream from two cows, hailstones, salt, and two buckets; James Wilkins, however, ate a dinner of "hard sea bread and a tin cup of indifferent water."

Dust flying in thick clouds. Camped on the river bank sometime after dark.

Searls: "Gaming has prevailed to a large extent among our passengers for the last few days. . . . Large sums of money are staked and lost."
Another diarist, Dr. Israel Lord, is camped close by with his train. He writes of a Pioneer Line passenger who is recovering from cholera: "Dodson is in camp. He looks like anybody but himself. It would be a refinement of flattery to say he looked human." C. B. Dodson, from Illinois, left the Pioneer Line on July 11 to travel with Lord's train.

Friday, July 6. Up at dawn. In about 5 miles we came to the ferry and camp of the 3d Division U. S. troops for Oregon.[11] Camped for noon about a mile farther on. Some of the train have found what seems to be gold among the sands of the Platte. Take a swim. Arrange baggage, books, etc. Almost a stampede among Uncle Sam's horses. They ran past us and frighten[ed] an ox train passing. Came 8 miles farther in the afternoon. Dustier than ever. The whole train often hid from view. The wind in our face. Pretty camp on river bank. Total today 14 miles.

Searls: "The heat being intense, our company lay by till near night. . . . We did not encamp till 9 or 10 o'clock, but toiled on through a cloud of dust. The full moon made it sufficiently light."

Saturday, July 7. Rode the pony. Took rifle and half a dozen cartridges and struck off to the right of the trail. Saw some antelopes. Followed them up to get a shot. Was led into a wide valley or plain some miles off the road, spreading for miles in every side, but without water. Places that had been shallow lakes or ponds were now covered with some salt or alkali substance, white as snow and half an inch thick. Away up the valley rose a line of curious looking rocks, resembling the ruins of some old Roman wall. They stood in detached masses like towers or fortresses, some round, some square, and shooting up in a thou sand different shapes.[12] The surrounding plain was covered

[11] At Fort Kearney Col. W. W. Loring had divided the Oregon battalion of Mounted Riflemen into three divisions; the first and second divisions crossed at the Mormon ferry, about 20 miles upstream from the Deer Creek crossing, and near present-day Casper, Wyoming. The Pioneer Line travels near part of the battalion most of the way from here to Soda Springs. See Loring, pp. 332, 334.
[12] The "rocks" Reid describes here were curiosities known as the Red Buttes. Frémont (*Report of the Exploring Expedition*, p. 54) remarked that they were "lofty escarpments" of red sandstone.

with herds of antelope, but they could not be approached or
taken in ambush. Shot 3 or 4 times at 400 yards. Picketed pony
in grassy bottom, and started on foot with my rifle to range the
ravines. Started a gang of five buffaloes. Shot one in the flank
but did not stop his speed. Went back some two or three miles
for the pony. Too late to chase them. Started back towards the
river. No water or food all day. Great thirst. Soon grows dark.
Shot a hare. Went on and on towards the river. Saw the bluffs, but
they seemed to keep receding. Tantalized often by bushy valleys
that I supposed contained running water. Found only beds of
dry sand. Aimed to strike the trail 6 or 7 miles west of where I
left it. A fire off to the right. Heard a shot. A hunter's bivouac
probably, not near the trail. On, on, on, still farther, passing
plains and ridges and ravines in almost endless succession. At
last struck the trail but found no camp near. It was in the desert
crossed by the road after it left the river. About 2 miles to the
bluffs. Found them precipitous, rocky, and full of chasms and
defiles, altogether impassable by man or horse. Headed several of
the ravines, making repeated trials to pass the bluffs. At length
found a place to crawl safely down. It was midnight when I led
the poor pony to the water's edge and into the river. He swal-
lowed the grateful draught with great avidity, and stooping
down I followed his example. I now felt but little hunger. It had
been merged in the more imperious thirst. Picketed the pony.
My bed on the beach, with the saddle for a pillow.

Searls: "Another day of wind and dust has succeeded. Owing to the
sandy roads, we rolled only a few hours before encamping. Corralled in
the river bottom opposite a small island. Upon examination the grass
was found good upon this island and the mules were swum over and it
was further resolved to remain here till tomorrow in order to recruit
them after their fast. . . . Distance eight miles."

Sunday, July 8. Slept soundly. Rattlesnake in a clump of grass
at my feet when I awoke. Killed him with my steel ramrod. Saddled up, and back to the road again.[13] Found a train and learned
that our train was yet behind, not having marched in the after-

[13] Reid describes this adventure in great detail in a letter to his brother James,
Nov. 27, 1849. On this day Joseph Sedgley met up with the Pioneer Line and
wrote that the train had lost 30 men from sickness. This claim was an exaggera-
tion (10 had died), but it reflected the view among some emigrants that the
famed Pioneer Line was an ill-fated wagon train.

noon yesterday. Returned to meet them. Every cloud of dust mistaken for the train. Went back 5 or 6 miles to the river. Found some of the advance guard, and waited an hour till the train came up. At 10 o'clock got some cold scouse [mush] and bacon. Camped for noon before leaving the river. Distance yesterday 10 miles, this morning 6. Started about 6 in the evening. Filled the casks with water. Took pony to go up along the river to search for my ramrod which I left this morning where I killed the rattlesnake. Road diverges to the right. I kept up the river bank. Some bluffs and difficult ravines to climb. Grows dark. Rocky barrier again. Give it up. Two emigrants herding cattle. Strike off northward to road. Clear moonlight presently. On the trail found Francisco lying at the roadside. Had been kicked by a mule. Helped him up and into his saddle and went on with him. Get into a broken region of ups and downs. Camp in a kind of long oval valley. Poor grass. No water. Distance since noon 10 miles.

Searls: "Clouds of dust enveloped the train almost suffocating both man and beast. A strong southwest wind blew the hot sand into our faces until to bear up under its scorching influence was almost impossible. . . . Near sunset . . . we rolled out of camp . . . and we continued our march over an excellent hard road till 11 p.m."

Monday, July 9. Keep up the valley. Sometimes broken and irregular. Dead oxen strewn along every half mile. Sloughs of bad water. Rock Avenue.[14] Mules greatly exhausted. Ours gave out with others. Camped for noon at a little swampy run of sulphurous water, all tramped up by oxen and mules. Poor grass. Went three miles further and camped for the night at willow spring at head of valley. Another camp at the same place. Good water, but grass grazed down, short. Total today 12 miles.

Reid, journal: "The poor half-starved and overworked animals have indeed a hard time of it. Many of them are turned loose till their shoulder galls have time to heal. These galls become no doubt very painful and itchy. On one occasion I saw a mule, just unharnessed, practicing quite a feat of contortion by standing on three legs, curving itself into a circle, and scratching the galled wound on its shoulder with the toe of its hind foot."

Searls: "A number of companies are encamped in our vicinity, in one

[14] Now known as Poison Spider Creek Pass in present-day Natrona County, Wyoming. Cf. Bruff, July 23; Gray, June 22.

of which are several Ladies. We were treated this evening to a vocal concert from them which was really entertaining."

Tuesday, July 10. Climbed prospect hill, one mile. View of Sweetwater Mountains—Intervening plain—8 miles. Camped for noon on a small run, not very good water. Afternoon came to a larger, swifter stream—Greasewood Creek. Good water. Left the usual route to Independence Rock and kept down to the left along the creek and camped in pretty good grass. Total today 14 miles. Mose and Green talked of leaving.[15] Fudge!

Searls: "Great anxiety prevails among the passengers on account of our slow progress. The mules are evidently too heavily laden still, and are failing under their hard fare. It is now becoming a serious question how we shall get through. All are of opinion that under our present organization and with our present loads we cannot accomplish the journey. Something must be done to relieve us from our present uncomfortable position or we shall soon be compelled to disband and proceed as best we can. The only feasible plan appears to be, to destroy baggage. Our wagon masters say that unless this or some other plan is devised they shall leave the train and push on. A number of passengers are preparing to do the same."

Wednesday, July 11. Kept down the valley of the creek 5 miles to the Sweetwater. Picturesque plain through which we passed, encircled by mountainous peaks. Climbed a pile of bare rocks thrown up in vertical strata. Gained the summit. Sense of awe and grandeur. Camped close to a clear cold spring gushing from the foot of the granite pile. Commenced a great work today. Pioneer train on its last legs, and needs reform. Meeting called in the corral at 1 o'clock to adopt measures for lightening the train. Col. Rumsey Pres't. I am Vice President,—Dr. Brewster Secretary. Funny scene. Dr. Pitts, Kinsey, Peters, Turney, O'Brien and Pres't. figure more or less,—each in his way. Committee appointed to draft resolutions. Rogers, Flinn, Peters, Alden, Heath, Treadwell, Perce, Waters, Merrie, Mallerson, Rumsey.[16]

[15] The train has halted frequently on this stretch and moved slowly compared with others that reached the Sweetwater only one or two days after crossing the Platte; see Decker, July 9–11; Delano, June 20–22; Geiger and Bryarly, June 22, 23; and Pritchard, June 13–15. Mose and Green are the wagon masters, Moses Mallerson and Robert Green. On this day James Hutchings claimed that he met the passenger train beyond Devil's Gate. Hutchings, whose diary was rewritten, is mistaken. The Pioneer Line reached that spot on July 13. Hutchings noted that the passengers were very unhappy about their experiences.

[16] All the men are passengers except Moses Mallerson, the wagon master. He

Meeting reassembled at 4 to hear Committee's report. Report adopted with great unanimity, viz: cut down each man's baggage to 75 pounds all told. Dismiss Campbell's wagon with 4 mules.[17] Appoint a committee of five of general superintendence—another committee of one from each mess to weigh and load the baggage. To allow all physicians together 75 lbs. extra. To have a hospital tent. To reduce the passenger carriages to 12 etc. Standing committee,—Waters, Capt. Reed, Peters, Todd, Ware.[18] Measures to be carried into effect tomorrow.

Searls: "By the reduction of baggage and wagons . . . , it is computed our baggage train will be relieved of twenty-three thousand pounds weight."

Thursday, July 12. A scene of destruction began. Trunks, bags, boxes were brought out, opened and ransacked. Cut down to 75 lbs. a man. The scene can be easily imagined. In the evening the plain was scattered with waifs [stray articles] and fragments, looking as though a whirlwind had scattered about the contents of several dry goods, hardware and variety shops. Men and boys from three or four other trains camped nearby were loitering around like vultures waiting for their prey,—and not even did they wait, but handled and snatched and begged and eyed curiously the various objects of their desire before they were cast from their baggage. Some 30 lbs. we concluded to pack on the pony—162 going into the wagons. Gave away several books. Davidson agrees to take my Blackstone's Commentaries for me.[19] Most of the train appeared dressed out in their newest and best, having discarded their old suits. On the whole it was a busy and important day. Moved 5 miles up the river after dark.

---

may have been included because the passengers needed expert advice, but Reid's mention of Todd (staff) as a member of the standing committee at the end of this entry suggests that at least two of Turner's assistants favored the passengers' more stringent decisions on unloading.

[17] Campbell is the sutler traveling with the train and selling goods to the passengers; Reid has already mentioned an auction of Campbell's "cabin stores" on June 13.

[18] All these men are passengers except Todd, a staff member.

[19] Reid had read Blackstone's *Commentaries* "half through" in Clarion when he was reading law; he bought the text in St. Louis and included it in his baggage. See Reid, journal, July 12; and Reid to Thomas Sutton, Nov. 27, 1847. Reid's total of 162 lbs. for himself and Brewster is higher than the allowance and does not agree with the amount given in the letter to his brother excerpted below un-

Independence Rock was sketched by James F. Wilkins on July 10, 1849. In the shadow of this landmark, on July 12, the Pioneer Line unloaded 23,000 pounds of baggage. *Courtesy: State Historical Society of Wisconsin.*

Searls: "The sacking of baggage commenced this morning. . . . Gold was here, merchandise: law and medical libraries, articles of clothing of every description. Ammunition, etc., were abandoned by their possessors. Our teamsters and Mexican herdsmen were soon arrayed in the cast off finery of their unfortunate fellow travelers. . . . To look upon the profuse destruction of property was enough to cause a sigh. . . . By the arrangements of the Committee, our carriage was one of those destined to be left, but other means for our conveyance not being in readiness, it was decided for us to take it along till tomorrow. We left the scene of destruction a little after sunset and rolled till within two miles of 'Independence Rock,' when we encamped. Distance six miles."

Dr. Israel Lord, a real curmudgeon, camped near the Pioneer Line and wrote: "Our train took as many as twenty trunks and discharged as many . . . of less value and more weight. [The Pioneer Line has] overloaded, and overdriven and badly selected mules. The passengers pay $200, and cook their own food, watch the camp, harness and drive their own teams, and generally go on foot. This is paying pretty dear. . . . They are a hard set, are the Pioneers, for sure. Half of all, I should

---

der this entry. Lord, July 11, estimated that the discarded property was worth 5,000 dollars.

think, perhaps more are gamblers and hard drinkers, men without character, and perfectly reckless."

In a letter to his brother James, written from San Francisco on November 27, 1849, Reid recalled this reorganization of the Pioneer Line in some detail: "We advanced up the North Fork of the Platte with a great deal of difficulty, and arrived at the mouth of the Sweetwater completely broken down—unable to budge another inch. Here Turner had not the manliness to come forward, acknowledge frankly that they had failed to fulfil their contract, and request us to lighten up our baggage. No, he merely dodged the responsibility and at the same time sought to accomplish the same end by a shallow trick. In order to *frighten* us into the measure of lightening up, he induced his master teamster and wagonmaster in whose efficiency was our whole dependence, to threaten to leave the train next day and go ahead on their own hook with pack mules. The passengers understood the trick; but at the same time they saw the necessity of sacrificing their property for the sake of getting along. A meeting was called, and a committee appointed to frame resolutions to be reported to an adjourned meeting. Their report was unanimously adopted. Every man's baggage, including everything, was to be cut down to 75 pounds. The account before was 100 lbs. *exclusive* of bedding, arms, and ammunition, which averaged about 45 lbs. Several had extra baggage for which they were to pay T. A. [Turner and Allen] and Company 70¢ a pound for transportation.[20] I had 34 lbs. extra, making my total about 184 pounds. So I had to throw away 110 pounds. A singular scene was presented that day in camp. All trunks and sacks were out and open, and trumpery of every description was strewn about the plain. Each man appeared dressed out in a new suit, having doffed all his old clothes in preference. And then what a weighing by balances, and a weighing in the mind a question—'shall *this* or *that* go?' 'Shall I most need this book or that coat?' And people from other trains camped near gathered around, and hovered around like vultures, awaiting our departure to pounce upon their prey. Many of them were even too impatient for that, and would dab into trunks and piles of plunder, handing out some attractive article with a 'do you want this here?' 'Are you goin' to leave that thar?' At last the separation was completed—each man's 75 lbs. was weighed by a committee, and the rest fell into the hands of the *Philistines*. So much did the passengers sacrifice,—but they demanded of John [Thomas] Turner that he also should make some sacrifices. Deaths and desertions had rendered four or five of the carriages unnecessary. That day's work, and the consumption of provisions had made four or five of the wagons unnecessary. These we resolved we would take no further—for we the passengers had actually been carrying the wagons and carriages along from Independence, walking instead of riding, and almost daily hitching to with ropes and pulling the teams one by one out of mud-holes, across creeks,

[20] Reid is mistaken here; Turner and Allen charged 20 cents per pound for extra baggage.

and up steeps. Turner had a scape-goat, or stool-pigeon who pretended to own two wagons in the train, with their contents.—They were bro't along to speculate off the passengers. One was loaded with *liquors*! the other with delicacies in the way of eatables.[21] Large sums were demanded of any who hungered or thirsted for any of these things. On close inquiry and cross-examination it turned out that 'the firm,' and not their scape-goat, owned these commodities. It was accordingly resolved that they should go no further, and that the mules that hauled them should henceforth be for the benefit of the passengers. Thus 'retrenched and reformed,' in two or three days we made a new start and got along tolerably well for a while."

Friday, July 13. Roused up early and off before breakfast. Took charge of the pony with his pack. About two miles to Independence Rock, remarkable only for its isolated position and for the thousands of names carved and painted on its surface.[22] The southerly end of it pretty close to the river where the trail crosses it. Saw a very few names that I knew. Among them those of Fathers De Smet, Point and Mengarini put there under the monogram "IHS" 8 years ago.[23] 3 or 4 miles farther Devil's Gate, a perpendicular cleft in the granite rocks, through which the Sweetwater flows. The road is through a very pretty but not so steep gap. Tolerably good grass. Both committees proceeding with their business agreeably to the action of the meeting. Decided to leave Cunningham's load of liquors.[24] Turner had it knocked in the head, 4 or 5 gallon kegs. Another meeting called

[21] The "scape-goat, or stool-pigeon" is Campbell. Reid's entry for July 11 indicates that Campbell had one wagon, and Searls wrote on July 11 that one of the committee's resolutions decreed that "Mr. Campbell be allowed four mules of his present team and withdraw from the train." It seems, therefore, that Campbell had one wagon. Reid remained a strict temperance man. He wrote home that he "took no kind of spirits (considered indispensable by many)" throughout the trip. See Reid, "California Gold Rush Letter," p. 229.

[22] Three famous landmarks along the Sweetwater River were Independence Rock, Devil's Gate, and the Ice Spring, mentioned by all diarists. Independence Rock supposedly received its name when a party of fur trappers celebrated July 4 at the site in 1829. For Devil's Gate, noted by Reid on this day, see Stansbury's fine description, pp. 65–66. Reid writes of the Ice Spring in his entry for July 16, below.

[23] "IHS" is a symbol for Jesus, appropriated by the Jesuit order. Reid may have met the three Jesuits in St. Louis, which was their headquarters. From his diary entry dated June 21 we know that he knew, or knew of, De Smet. The other Jesuits were De Smet's fellow explorers.

[24] This is the second time a load of liquor had been spilled out on the ground (the first was on June 13). Since it was a large amount and in the possession of Cunningham, one of Turner's "principal lieutenants," it may have been intended to stock the company's proposed trading post in California. Wilkins, on Septem-

but not organized. Went on at 3 o'clock. Took a swim in the Sweetwater. Camped in a bend of a small run or slough, the bank of which formed a circular wall around us. Distance today 14½ miles. Dead oxen by the roadside at almost every half mile have annoyed us ever since leaving the Platte ferry.[25]

Saturday, July 14. Started on foot. Mr. Bonnell has occupied the wagon for 3 or 4 days with a sore foot. Road very sandy. 4 miles another gorge in the rock through which the river rushes over and around fallen rocks. Sides craggy but not vertical. Bright scales in the sand under water and in the rocks along shone very much like gold.[26] Leave the road and walk through the pass. Stop an hour viewing the massive piles of rock and listening to the roaring of the waters. Found the camp two miles beyond the pass. Tired and footsore. Weather very hot. Hard walking in the sand. Todd bro't up today Mr. Elder of No. 9 to replace Mr. Wattles, who goes to No. 18. Walked on in the afternoon and camped in the river bottom to right of the trail near Pomeroy's and the Buffalo train. Total 15½ miles.

Searls: "Our wagon was abandoned yesterday and the larger one, formerly appropriated to baggage, given to ten of us in its stead. . . . We have united of our own free will and hope to have a pleasant time together. . . . Near us is a train from Buffalo, N.Y., who are engaged in preparing pack saddles for packing."

Sunday, July 15. Brewster and I are cooks this week. Start early and take a new cut-off recommended by Pomeroy.[27] Cross river at his camp. Re-cross three miles below. Difficult crossing. Camp near a point of rock jutting into the river. Excellent wood, water and grass. Do a large baking. Went on foot over sandy road and hilly points through a picturesque gap in the rocks, in which we had to cross the river twice,—having crossed it to

---

ber 19, wrote of the incident: "That was the time an Irishman observed when the old Cogniac 'watered the plain.'"

[25] The alkali water on this route poisoned cattle; many diarists wrote about the sight and stench of dead cattle on this stretch, though few indicated any sympathy for them. See Foster, June 24, 26, 30; Hale, June 25; Searls, July 10, Sedgley, July 9; and Swain, July 18.

[26] Gold existed in this region, but there was no rush of miners until 1869.

[27] Trains took a cutoff here to avoid a long bend in the serpentine Sweetwater. Pomeroy is Theodore S. Pomeroy, of Lexington, Missouri, captain of a "mercantile train" selling liquor and groceries to emigrants. The diarist Joseph Hamelin traveled with this train, which proceeded to Salt Lake City.

north side a mile below. Camped at dark in river bottom. Total 16 miles.

Monday, July 16. Wakened up at 3 by the warning bugle. Got breakfast in a hurry and hastened off at daylight. Between one and two miles crossed the Sweetwater and struck off to the left,—leaving the river it is said for 16 miles. Seven miles brought us to the ice pond, where we camped for noon. Ice is found in the marsh on the right of the trail by digging 6 or 8 inches, through the outer turf. Blocks of it were obtained 6 inches thick and clear as crystal. The water in the marsh tastes strongly of alkali. Started at 12 and had a hard drive of 10 miles to the river. Corralled on the north side. Timber sage and a few willow bushes. On the way got a view of the snow peaks of the Wind river mountains ahead of us. Bold scenery about our camp. Chilly air and cloudy sky all day. A few drops of rain in the afternoon. Total today 17½ miles.

Searls: "We resumed the march long before sunrise, owing to having a march upwards of twenty miles without grass or water and in order to get in advance of some two hundred wagons encamped in our vicinity. . . . By eight o'clock we reached one of the greatest curiosities witnessed during our journey. . . . The Mormons have named this place 'Ice Spring.'"

Tuesday, July 17. Struck the river again in 4 or 5 miles, and crossed it twice at points near together. Camped 7 miles from start. Baked pies at noon. Morrison and Kilburn of Fort Madison, Iowa, now packing, came to our camp to see Brewster. They are in a party of six who left St. Joseph on June 7. Afternoon passed a spring on our right. A little farther at a cañon of the river, struck over high hills to the right. Dykes of rock across the road. Granite spring and some ponds on the left. Whitish looking muddy water. Camped after dark in a small dry ravine. Spring over a ridge to the northeast. Brewster and I stood guard 2d watch. Total today 15 miles.

Wednesday, July 18. —In a mile crossed Strawberry creek and soon after Omaco creek, clear cold water one rod wide. ¼ mile below road found a snow bank. 3 miles farther crossed Willow creek nearly as wide.[28] Nooned here. Got view of the snowy peaks to the north west. Afternoon went on 5 miles to the Sweet-

[28] These streams are all tributaries of the Sweetwater River. Bruff on July 31 noted that Omaco and Strawberry creeks were almost dry.

water, where we crossed it for the last time, camping on the south side. Snow on its banks near us. Distance today 16 miles.

Searls: "In the Valley of Wind River we found a vast bank of snow some eight feet deep, and here we indulged in a game of snow balling."

Thursday, July 19. Ascended the ridge, leaving the river finally to the right. Table mountain to our left. Gradually ascended towards the summit of South Pass, which is 9 miles from our start.[29] At 7 miles I went over this to the Sweetwater, ¾ of a mile to the right of our trail. Took a bath. Reflections on bidding adieu to Atlantic waters. Cast flowers upon the bosom of the swirling stream, to be wafted homeward. Adieu sweet water! Speed thee toward my home, while I wander on to the shores of the Pacific. Returned to the trail a little before reaching the pass. Alone I stood upon the summit 2000 miles from home, with another 1000 miles of a dreary way before me! As I looked down on the Pacific slope, the long vista widening in the distance, it seemed like entering upon a new world. Found the camp a mile beyond the Pacific spring. Distance this forenoon 13½ miles. At the spring I mingled and drank a draught of the Atlantic and Pacific waters.[30] West in the afternoon to the dry Sandy, 10 miles. Water saltish and found in holes.[31] Picturesque appearance of table rocks seen on our afternoon march. Several singular Buttes scattered over the plain.[32]

Searls: "In leaving this point and descending to the west, it seemed like abandoning the world and all of interest it contained with prospects exceedingly dubious."

[29] This smooth gap in the Rocky Mountains is 7,412 feet above sea level. Diarists wrote emotionally about the Continental Divide. See, for example, Delano, who on July 29 took a "parting look at the Atlantic waters which flow towards all I hold dear to earth," and stood beside the trail to watch "long trains of wagons with their way-worn occupants bidding a long, perhaps a last adieu to eastern associations, to mingle in new scenes on the Pacific coast."

[30] Pacific Spring is about 3 miles from South Pass, and its waters run west into the Colorado River. Reid recalled in his journal entry for July 19 that he carried a cup of water from the Sweetwater to mingle with the water in the Spring, cf. Wood, July 3.

[31] Because 1849 was a wet year, there were pools of stagnant water in the usually dry river bed.

[32] These are the Oregon Buttes, near present-day Farson, Wyoming. The Oregon Territory extended to the summit of the Rockies at this time. The distance traveled from Fort Laramie was approximately 280 miles.

South Pass to the City of Rocks

July 20–August 11

Beyond South Pass many wagon trains, including the Pioneer Line, diverge from the Oregon Trail and take Sublette's or Greenwood's Cutoff, bypassing Fort Bridger. On this route the wagon train fords the Little and Big Sandy rivers and crosses a desert before reaching the Green River, a tributary of the Colorado. Beyond the river, the trail moves along the lovely Bear River Valley and then swings north to the celebrated Soda Springs, in what is now Idaho. The Oregon Trail continues north to Fort Hall, but the Pioneer Line chooses to follow Hudspeth's Cutoff, opened on July 19 by forty-niners. Hudspeth's Cutoff moves west across mountain ranges for some 130 miles of unmapped territory. Emigrants taking this route believe that it leads to the Humboldt River, but it meets the California Trail from Fort Hall at Cassia Creek, saving only about 25 miles. Just beyond the creek the road from Salt Lake City joins the trail near a landmark soon to become known as the City of Rocks, close to the present-day Nevada border. On this stage of the journey the Pioneer Line's mules falter badly, and provisions are almost exhausted.

Friday, July 20. Went on to Little Sandy in the forenoon, 10 miles. Passed the old road leading off from the left. Post office—letter in split stick.[1] At Little Sandy grave of Rev. Robert and Mary Gilmore, both died of cholera on the 18th.[2] Distressing history of the Gilmore family. Creek bottom full of the stench of

---

[1] The "split stick" held messages from emigrants to friends in other wagon trains; when Bruff passed the site on August 3, a board nailed to the stick was "plastered with notices." The old road noted by Reid led to Fort Bridger.

[2] Bruff noted the Gilmores' common grave on August 3 as that of "Robert Gilmore and wife." The Gilmores may have died on July 18 from mountain fever (now called Colorado tick fever or Rocky Mountain spotted fever), which could have caused symptoms resembling cholera.

dead oxen. Camped on the opposite hill. Late in the afternoon went on 9 miles to the Big Sandy. Crossed it and went nearly two miles up along the hill. Camped in the sand and sage. A long way to water.

In 1903, apparently after copying his original 1849 diary, Bernard Reid placed advertisements in Missouri and Sacramento newspapers, inquiring about the fate of the two Gilmore children, abandoned by their wagon train after the parents died on the same day. An excerpt from the July 20 entry in his journal tells us about "the distressing history" of the Gilmore family:

"Rode Don today and was some distance in advance of the train when I reached the bluffs overlooking the green valley of the Sandy, which wound its way like a silver thread through the center of the valley. From my perch on the bluffs no sign of life was visible, but on the bank of the creek I could discern an emigrant wagon apparently abandoned by its owners, as no men or animals were in sight. In the valley, near the foot of the bluff, I observed a rude head-board indicating a new grave, and on going to it and dismounting I read this double inscription.

'Died of cholera, July 18, 1849,
Rev. Robt. Gilmore, of Saline County, Mo.
Died of cholera, July 18, 1849,
Mary, wife of Rev. Robert Gilmore.'

I remounted and rode slowly towards the abandoned wagon, my mind filled with the sad reflections inspired by so pitiful a story. On approaching nearer I was surprised to see a neatly dressed girl of about 17, sitting on the wagon tongue, her feet resting on the grass, and her eyes apparently directed at vacancy. She seemed like one dazed or in a dream and did not seem to notice me till I spoke to her. I then learned from her in reply to my questions that she was Miss Gilmore, whose parents had died two days before; that her brother, younger than herself, was sick in the wagon, probably with cholera; that their oxen were lost or stolen by the indians; and that the train they had been traveling with, after waiting for three days on account of the sickness and death of her parents, had gone on that morning, fearful, if they delayed longer, of being caught by winter in the Sierra Nevada mountains, where the Donner party of Missouri[3] had been caught three years before and many of them perished of cold and starvation. The people of her train had told her that probably her oxen would yet be found, or at any rate some other train coming along with oxen to spare would take her and her brother and their wagon along. Her story, as she told it with simplicity and modesty, but with deep feeling, was inexpressibly sad and touching. Who could tell the deep sense of bereavement, distress and desolation that weighed on that poor girl's heart, there in the wilderness

[3] Actually of Illinois.

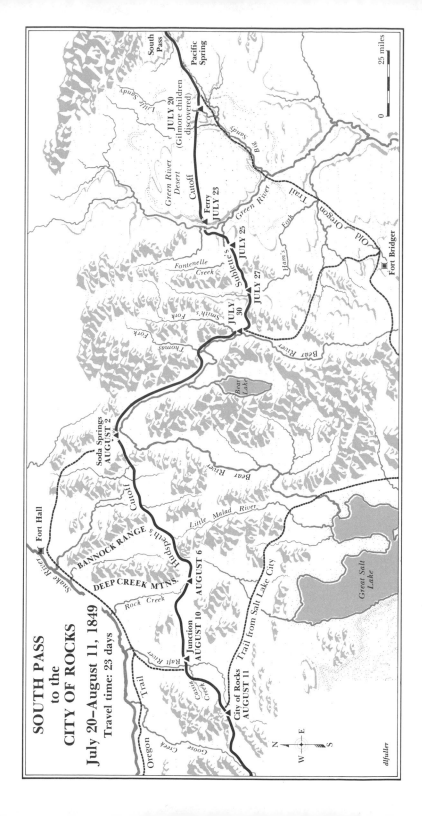

**SOUTH PASS
to the
CITY OF ROCKS**
July 20–August 11, 1849
Travel time: 23 days

South Pass

Pacific Spring

JULY 20
(Gilmore children discovered)

Little Sandy

Green River Desert

Cutoff

Big Sandy

Ferry
JULY 23

Green River

Sublette's
JULY 25

Fontenelle Creek

JULY 27

Ham's Fork

Old Oregon Trail

Smith's Fork

JULY 30

Thomas Fork

Bear River

Fort Bridger

Bear Lake

Soda Springs
AUGUST 2

Bear River

Fort Hall

Snake River

BANNOCK RANGE

DEEP CREEK MTNS.

Hudspeth's Cutoff

Little Malad River

Rock Creek

AUGUST 6

Junction
AUGUST 10

Raft River

Cassia Creek

City of Rocks
AUGUST 11

Trail from Salt Lake City

Great Salt Lake

Oregon Trail

Goose Creek

N
W E
S

25 miles

0

dljfuller

with no telling what fate was in store for her and her sick brother?
While we were conversing some other passengers on horseback came
up, two of whom were doctors, who immediately examined and prescribed for the sick boy, and soon others came up on foot, and when the
sad story was passed from mouth to mouth a handsome purse was soon
raised to purchase other oxen, if the chance should offer, and to supply
any other needs of the orphans. Our train, when it arrived, camped in
the vicinity, and before we moved on we had the satisfaction of knowing
that another ox-train from Missouri, arriving soon after ours, were able
and willing to take the deserted children and their wagon with them
and care for them.

In the ups and downs of my subsequent experiences in California I
failed to trace out the future history of the Gilmore children, though
the subject was often on my mind, and it was not until December, 1903,
that I learned what had become of them. In answer then to a communi-
cation in a Missouri paper I learned from a Mr. Burgess, of Washington, Kansas, that his uncle, Henry F. Parsons, of the train that took
charge of the waifs at Little Sandy, married the girl, Nellie Gilmore,
soon after their arrival in California. After living for some time there
they returned East and resided first in Wisconsin, then awhile in New
York City, and afterwards in Michigan, and [she] died at Howard,
Wisconsin, in the beginning of December, 1903, at the age of 71, after
the date of my inquiry about her in the Missouri paper. Her husband
died in 1885. Her nephew informed me that she often wondered what
had become of the young man that had found and befriended them
when they were deserted on the prairie and that she invoked many
blessings on my head. Her brother Charles recovered from his sickness
and died in Michigan in 1878. What a satisfaction it would have been
had I not delayed in tracing them until it was too late!"[4]

Saturday, July 21. Lay by all day.[5] Began to sprinkle rain about
10 a.m. Rained for a couple of hours. Quite cool, with raw wind
from the N.W.

[4]Reid wrote a letter of inquiry about the fate of the Gilmore children to the
editor of the *Republican* (Marshall, Mo.), published Nov. 13, 1904 (clipping, Reid
Papers). He received three letters from Nellie Gilmore Parsons's nephew by marriage, B. B. Burgess of Washington, Kansas; he also received a postcard from a
Mrs. Edwards of Sacramento, whose father had seen Reid's letter of inquiry in
the Sacramento *Union*, Feb. 5, 1904. Mrs. Edwards knew the Gilmore story and
believed that the brother had died. The Edwards and Burgess correspondence is
in the Reid Papers. Cf. Luella Dickensen (p. 89), who also wrote affectingly
about two orphaned children cared for by her wagon train in 1846. The Gilmore
story was reported by the Pittsburgh *Gazette*, December 7 and 16, 1903, from
information provided by Reid.

[5]Searls noted that the train traveled 20 miles on this day, but Reid's entry must
be correct. The day before (July 20), Searls had written that the train planned to
remain the following day at the Big Sandy, a popular campsite, in order to prepare for the desert crossing, and his entry of July 22 makes it clear that the train
was in camp the preceding day.

Sunday, July 22. Bugle and gun waked us up between 12 and 1 for a long drive of 35 miles across the desert to Green River by Sublettes Cut-off.[6] Hoy and McKaraher leave for Salt Lake, packing.[7] Send a short letter to Mary with McK. Fussy time getting all things ready in the dark. Roll out before day. Level plain—day break—mountain scenery on the right—gorgeous sunrise. Sleep walking—dead oxen—dry ravines. Halt at 22 miles for noon. Walked all the way. Sage hen, for dinner. Water scant. Went on after dinner on foot ahead of train. Passed horsemen and footmen. Walked nearly 4 miles an hour. Sprinkle of rain. Tried to catch some to slake thirst. Came in view of Green River Hills. As I advanced they seemed to recede. Ravine after ravine—ridge after ridge. Overtook and passed Sackett and Andrews, both nearly done for. Guessed it was still 2 miles to the river. Continued to guess so for two or 3 weary hours. Sundown. At last a glimpse of the river down a long gap in the hills. High bluff point. Steep winding road. Rocky by-path. Stop to rest. Long walk down the bottom. Dry bed of a stream. Follow its windings. In a mile or two came to a small spring of alkaline water. Followed a mile or two farther—saw a light—Heard voices. Hailed. Recognized Dunning's voice. Found him, Chas. Kelsey, Candee, Brewer and Davidson around a blazing sage fire. Sea biscuit and raw bacon. They share their store with me. Several re-inforcements of weary pioneers come in from time to time. Lie around with feet to fire, indian style. Extremes of heat and cold. No blankets. Miserable, tedious, sleepless night. Walked today 51 miles. Train stopped 6 miles back on the hills.

In a letter to his brother James on November 27, 1849, Reid recalled this long trudge across the desert: "I am compelled to say, in the face of Fremont and others, that after passing the great prairies between the confines of Missouri and the Platte river, the main characteristics of all scenery whether mountain or plain are barrenness, solitude, and desolation. A stretch of country that we crossed, 1500 miles wide, seems to

[6] William Sublette reputedly opened the cutoff in 1830. It moved due west across a desert in order to avoid the detour to Fort Bridger, and is sometimes called Greenwood's Cutoff after another mountaineer believed to be the real pathfinder; see Bruff, Aug. 2. Those following Ware's *Emigrants' Guide* (ed. Caughey, p. 25) believed the distance across the desert was 35 miles. Diarists reported differing mileages to the Green River, but all were higher than Ware's.

[7] Hoy, McKaraher, and the other men mentioned in this entry are all Pioneer Line passengers.

me totally worthless and irreclaimable for a series of ages. True here and there, on the margins of rivers, a strip of ½ a mile to 2 miles wide, may produce rich grass, but the frosts that come *every week in the year*, as I am authentically informed, would put cultivation out of the question. Besides even these green spots are but oases in a great desert,—they are too much isolated,—cut off from the rest of the world by deserts too vast, dreary and inhospitable, ever for centuries to be made the permanent and flourishing settlements that some men imagine. Let Whitney build the railroad and I won't begrudge him the adjoining land![8] There are millions and millions of acres there, for the fee simple of which I would not give a dime. One desert we crossed extended from Big Sandy to Green river (the *upper* Colorado of California) a distance of 53 miles without a drop of water. It took the train two days to cross it.—I walked it in a day. It was reported in our guide books to be only 35 miles, and under that impression I set out to reach water the same evening. After travelling 8 hours at a rapid pace, I began to look out for the river. Every mile I had a deep ravine to pass, and as I rose to the summit again I felt always sure of beholding the river but was still doomed to disappointment. Oh, how anxiously I still pushed, weary, thirsty, but with unslacked pace. I had overtaken and left far behind many a footman of our train and several horsemen too—for the poor animals were fagged. After twilight [an] hour or two I began to think it was a dream—that I might not be really awake and walking—but that I might before long awake and find my toiling across the desert a mere illusion of the brain. Supposing the guide book to be nearly correct, and conscious that I must have walked far beyond the given distance, I could not otherwise account for the non appearance of the river. I certainly had not turned back on my track—I knew my course by the sky, and the beaten road was before me. It began to grow serious. My thirst was intense—and I was very weary,—but I kept on. At last I came suddenly upon the point of a high promontory overlooking the plain far below. In this plain close by I thought I could distinguish the silver line of a stream. It was a glad sight, but it increased my thirst. The road wound circuitously down the side of the promontory,—I thought I would take a direct path towards the stream. I soon found myself among ledges of craggy perpendicular rock, and could advance no farther that way. I soon found my way down at last with difficulty through clefts and gorges, and stood

[8] Asa Whitney was a merchant and railroad promoter who unsuccessfully petitioned Congress for a transcontinental railroad via South Pass, to be paid for by land sales. Cf. Dr. Caleb Ormsby to wife, July 24, 1849, in Bidlack, ed., *Letters Home*, p. 29, written near Fort Bridger: "The whole western world thus far, is good for nothing except to serve as a bridge to California . . . not worth a dime." See also William Wilson, August 6, 1850, near Hudspeth's Cutoff: "Senator Benton [of Missouri] and other big men may talk and humbug the country and you greenhorns about a railroad to the Pacific, but if you and I live a thousand years, we will never see the resemblance of such a thing." Reid and these other emigrants, of course, did not anticipate irrigation.

on the plain below. The stream I thought could not be half a mile off. Turning into the sandy bed of a dried-up brook, I hurried on towards the river. I walked a mile without a sign of water—and climbed up the bank of the brook to satisfy myself I was not winding through some tortuous labyrinth,—but all was clear and tolerably straight. I wondered if I were Tantalus or not.[9] Turning into the ravine again, I followed it more than two miles farther, and saw light on the bank and soon heard the sound of voices. The party proved to be three [10] of our train who had started very early. They had been down at the river bank, still some distance further, and purchased a piece of bacon and some biscuit from a small train they found there: and they had returned to this spot on account of the wild sage, with which to keep a fire through the night. There was also near, a small spring of water in a bed of the stream I had followed down. Oh, how sweet to my parched palate was the taste of that cold water! I drank as though I had thirsted for a week. Returning to the fire, I was kindly furnished with a share of the biscuit and bacon. The latter we stuck on a stick and broiled in the flame. That repast seemed as delicious to me as any gala-day-feast could be. After some time small additional parties from our train began to arrive, and to enter our circle. At midnight the ring numbered a dozen,—at daylight 27. The night was too cold to sleep, without blankets as we all were, and our only resource was to keep up a blazing fire,—and for that purpose no fuel in the world can beat the wild sage, which grew all around high enough to shelter us while [sleeping?] from the wind. The train did not arrive till next day."

Searls, still on the desert with the Pioneer Line, writes: "The wind commenced blowing a gale about noon, rendering our rolling quite difficult, from the clouds of dust which enveloped us. . . . We toiled on till the glorious sun sank behind the western horizon. The mules began to exhibit signs of exhaustion and some were taken from the harness unable to go farther and pull their loads. . . . At 10 p.m. . . . the mules . . . were corralled and there kept close till morning. For my part, completely exhausted by the fatigue, I rolled up in my blankets and was soon dreaming of home and absent friends. Distance forty-five miles."

Monday, July 23. Welcome dawn of day at last. Went down to the trains on the river bank. Hard coaxing to get anything to eat. At last a young lady—of an emigrant family—just up and kindling her fire, agrees to give me a breakfast. The rest of our crowd scatter around and seek a bite somewhere. Some of them

[9] In Greek mythology Tantalus (the son of Zeus) stole the food of the gods and gave it to mortals. His punishment was to stand in water under trees laden with fruit. When he tried to drink, the water disappeared; when he tried to eat, the wind blew away the fruit. His name is the provenance of the word "tantalize."
[10] Actually five, as Reid's diary, July 22, indicates.

brought provisions and cooked for themselves. I had a first rate breakfast of excellent coffee, pancakes, rolls, ham, etc. and had a chair to sit on and ate off a table under an awning. Something new on the trip. They were a nice friendly family from Galena, Ill.,—did not learn their name. They did not want to take any pay, but I made them accept half a dollar. Told me to call upon them again anytime it suited. In an hour or two the train came in sight. Turned to the left to the lower ferry—two miles below this one. Got Brewster to go to the camps and get some breakfast. I drove the carriage down to the river through a steep gap between pillared rocks like an embattled gateway. Began ferrying over—one wagon at a time. Tried to take a nap under the shadow of the carriage. Mosquitoes too bad. Took a swim and washed some clothes in the Green River. Cold and swift. Got all across about 4 p.m. and camped on the west bank. Distance for the train today 8 miles. Three graves reported near. Did not see them. Mountaineer's lodge near. Monte bank.[11] Dirty looking squaws and fine fat ponies. Ferry owned by a mormon. Good flat boat. Charged $2.50 per wagon.[12]

Searls: "A more woebegone looking set of fellows than emerged from our camp this morning could not easily be found. . . . We descended several dangerous hills, one of them one-half a mile in length, and finally, after dragging rather than travelling nine miles, reached the river, making in all fifty-two miles from the Big Sandy."

Tuesday, July 24. In camp all day. Trains crossing over and camping about us in great numbers. Growing city of wagons, tents, men, women and children, whites, indians, negros, horses, oxen and mules. Motley crowd. After breakfast, rigged my lines and went fishing. Out till 3. Lazy work. No luck. Then went into

[11] The "monte" observed by Reid was a game of chance; the monte "bank" may be a reference to the banker in the game, or it may be Reid's shorthand for a monte game played on the bank of the river.

[12] The Green River was a favorite resort for trappers and mountaineers. Ferrying was difficult, though the river became fordable by August. Prices for ferrying varied widely in response to demand and competition. The Pioneer Line used the Mormon ferry at Names Hill, so called because of the many names carved on the rocks. Searls, July 23, gives a different charge (two dollars) from Reid; Staples, July 29, also wrote that the charge was two dollars. It is not clear whether the passengers or the Pioneer Line paid these charges, but they were certainly unexpected. For the ferries at this spot, see Unruh, *The Plains Across*, p. 259.

a job of mending coat and trousers. Numerous rents in both. Projected exploration of Colorado [Green] River.

Wednesday, July 25. Very cold morning. Start at 8. Down the river bottom two or three miles, then up the steep bluffs. Beautiful view back. Then down towards the river again. Cross a small branch. Then over another series of hills and hollows, and halted for noon on the banks of a swift, clear stream emptying into Green River, some 3 or 4 miles below. Stream said to be Bear Creek. Afternoon moved up the creek valley about 5 miles and camped where the trail leaves the creek bottom. Pretty scenery. Passed grave of J. Merrill, aged 23, of Lexington, Mo., died July 6, 1849.[13] Distance today 15 miles.

Searls: "Every few days we come across a canvas lodge occupied by some Canadian Frenchman who dignifies his establishment by the name of a trading post, though the title of 'Gambling Hell' would convey a more correct idea of its uses. . . ."

On August 3 Joseph Middleton arrived at this site and wrote, "One of the French Canadian trappers told me . . . that the Pioneer Line passed here about 8 or 10 days ago with very poor mules."

Thursday, July 26. Rolled out at sun up. Bitter cold morning. Struck over the hill to the left of the creek, and kept on S.W. by W. up and down, up and down until about 9 we began to ascend a wide ravine leading up the side of the dividing ridge or wall of the Great Basin.[14] Fine rills course down the ravine fed by springs and the mountain snows. The rills are bordered by thickets of quaking asp [aspen], and underbrush and groves of tall, tapering graceful firs. Altogether a grateful sight after the expanse of desert traversed. Hard pulling up the mountain side. Another spring and rill near the top. Halt for noon. Hear of trouble in California. Blockade. Express for the Oregon and Fort Hall

[13] The stream is not Bear Creek but Fontenelle Creek, a popular campsite; Searls also identified it incorrectly as Bear Creek. Most trains were uncertain about the route because guidebooks gave sketchy directions for the cutoff. See Bruff, Aug. 7; Goldsmith, pp. 51–52; and Tiffany, June 7, for descriptions of the beautiful campsite. Bruff also identified J. Merrill's grave, noted by Reid, but gave the date of death as July 9, 1849.

[14] The name given by Frémont, in 1844, to the region between the Rocky Mountains and the Sierra Nevada; none of its rivers drain into the sea. The Bear River Valley is part of the Great Basin. The Pioneer Line, as Reid surmises by the end of day, does not reach the edge of the Great Basin until July 28. See Cline, *Exploring the Great Basin*, esp. p. 3.

troops now on the way.[15] Family jar [tiff] in our mess. Afternoon
kept up to summit of ridge. Another higher and more rugged
mountain ridge still beyond. Descend into the picturesque dell
between them and bear away south west. Meet here my hospitable friends of Green River breakfast memory. Passed an ice cold
spring close on our right. Sharp crested ridges of bare rock
in parallel lines. A pretty gap in one of them. Camp in a small
stream one step wide coming down a ravine in the mountains on
the N.W. Distance today 18 miles. The high ridge crossed today
cannot be the wall of the Great Basin as was supposed.

In his journal Reid recalled the petty irritations of the trail: "A regretta-
ble family jar comes to a head in our mess. . . . Perhaps there is no situation so trying upon the infirmities of human temper as a long trip
like this under circumstances not favorable for promoting cheerfulness
and good humor. Grown men are apt to become children again and
make mouths at one another on very slight provocation. And here I will
mention a trifling incident, which though not the cause of present un-
pleasantness, illustrates what I have been just saying. For a good while
back our rations of sugar had been growing small, and at our frugal
board some were given to complain that others were taking more than
their share. This led to unpleasant bickering, and to avoid its continuance I proposed to make a little muslin purse or sugar bag for each of
the mess, into which the sugar ration was to be equally distributed when
served by the commissary every fifth day. Then each man could help
himself at meal time out of his own stock, and no one could complain.
This was assented to, and I was appointed to spoon out to each man his
equal modicum of sugar. It worked like a charm, and there was no more
bickering from that cause."
   On this day diarist Alonzo Delano recorded a highly colored version
of the Pioneer Line's reorganization on the banks of the Sweetwater,
told to him by a man purporting to be a former passenger. Far ahead

[15] Reid refers here to a supply train of about four hundred wagons sent from
Oregon under the command of Lt. George Hawkins with provisions for the
Mounted Riflemen at Fort Hall; see Bruff, Sept. 8, and p. 556, n. 21. An entry in
Perkins (July 27) sheds light on Reid's reference to trouble in California. Traveling near the Pioneer Line, Perkins met a mountaineer who reported the stale
news that "England had objected to Gov. Smith's proclamation excluding foreigners from the gold region and would try to force her subjects in." Gen. Per-
sifor Smith, en route to California via Panama in January 1849, had issued no
proclamation but had written to the Secretary of War and consuls on the South
American coast that he would treat foreigners in the gold region as trespassers;
Smith was military governor of California from February to April, 1849, and repeated his pronouncement against foreigners in March. See Bancroft, *Works*, VI,
272–73; and Bean, *California: An Interpretive History*, pp. 115, 127, 166. Reid
may have met the same mountaineer.

along the trail, in the Thousand Spring Valley in present-day Nevada, Delano wrote: "At night a man came to our camp who had taken passage at St. Louis in the Pioneer Line of spring wagons, which were advertised to go through in sixty days. He was on foot, armed with a knife and pistol, and carried in a small knapsack all his worldly goods, except a pair of blankets, which were rolled up on his shoulders. He told us that at Willow Springs their mules gave out, and there was a general distribution of property, a small proportion of the passengers only obtaining mules, the rest being obliged to go a thousand miles without supplies, in the best manner they could, trusting to luck and the emigrants for provisions. The passengers had each paid two hundred dollars for their passage, but now, like the Irishman on the towpath, were obliged to work it out."

Friday, July 27. Rolled out early. Cold as usual. Kept down the dell. Road rather undulating. Seven miles halted by a small run. Our team of two mules nearly used up. After dinner started with 3 mules and a horse. Wound round a pass to the right and enter the valley of Ham's Fork of Green river. Nearly as large as the Sweetwater. Runs south. Kept up the creek bottom 2 or 3 miles to where the road crosses it and winds up the mountains to the west. Halted here three hours and got supper. Total so far 12 miles. Started again before sundown and wound our way up on the very edge or crest of a high angular promontory to the very peak. It grew dark long before we could reach the summit to enjoy the fine prospect it would afford. Then struck off due west by moonlight, along a level ridge of table land,[16] broken by two eminences, till after winding over another higher mountain summit crowned by firs and poplars, we camped about 10:30 without water. Total today 22 miles. Got no sleep on account of myriads of mammoth mosquitoes.

Saturday, July 28. Started off at dawn without breakfast. Found ourselves surrounded by wilder mountain scenery than we supposed last night. Kept along the sloping sides and undulating summits of ridges and down deep glens—a very crooked labyrinth-kind of road, passing at one place through a thick grove of white poplar and mountain firs,—mingled with roses, shrubbery and a variety of bright flowers. Saw more flowers this morning than at any time since leaving the Platte valley. At length descended a very long, steep, crooked hill to a small cold

[16] This is Ham's Fork Plateau.

On July 28 Bernard Reid describes this "very steep and dusty" trail that descended from the Bear River Mountains to the lovely valley at the base. The descent is depicted here in a detail from a drawing by James F. Wilkins, dated August 1, 1849. *Courtesy: State Historical Society of Wisconsin.*

brook,[17] where we halted and breakfasted. Had the luxury of a thorough bath in the mountain brook before breakfast. Distance this morning about 7 miles. Took a good nap under the wagon. Waked up for dinner and another start. Struck N.W. over a long high hill 2½ miles to summit. Very steep and dusty descending. Difficult job. 3 miles more to the bottom of steep. 4 miles more gently descending to camp and Bear River after passing small brook within 2 miles of the river. Beautiful valley of Bear River. Luxuriant grass and some small growth of [three words illegible]. Imposing mountain scenery especially to the north. Doubt as to whether we have come by Sublettes cut-off or not. Mouth of Smith's Fork 4 miles to the north. Gigantic gateway for its passage. Stood guard on first watch. Lovely moonlight night, but cold. Total today 17 miles. Mr. Stowe came into our mess today.[18]

Searls: "Owing to the difficulty in obtaining opportunities to write, I have resolved to write only weekly for the future."

Sunday, July 29. Got up late. In camp all day. Examined maps and compared notes. Lovely and majestic scene spread out before us in the calm soft sunset. Oh, for the artist's pencil! Had a bath in Bear River. Shallow muddy banks. Sandy bottom. Water not clear. Current dull. 100 feet wide.

Monday, July 30. Received by Capt. Turner a note from Col. E. J. Kewen this morning. Surprised that he is with Dr. White's party, traveling with the 2nd Division Oregon troops 6 or 8 miles behind us.[19] They fell behind by taking the Fort Bridger road. We start early. On crossing Smiths Fork 4 miles from our camp, left a note for Kewen. Clear, pretty trout stream. 14 miles halted for noon on river bank. While at dinner Kewen drove up in a buggy with Miss F. White. Glad to see him. Was introduced to his friend. A Shoshonee indian, with a boy, three squaws and a papoose on a board and half a dozen fat ponies came into camp, and excited some curiosity for a while,—especially the papoose done up so

[17] Rock Creek.
[18] J. B. Stowe is a passenger from Carriage No. 6.
[19] Col. E. J. C. Kewen and Dr. Thomas J. White are with the company of Mounted Riflemen, White having become a civilian doctor with the troops after the two army surgeons became sick with cholera. Kewen, Reid's former fellow boarder at Newman's in St. Louis, and a suitor of White's daughter, will become attorney general of California later in the year. See Cross, June 22.

curiously fastened on the board and hung to the saddle-bow. The indian and boy tried their skill in archery. The target a dime set up on the end of a split stick. The boy won 3. Afternoon proceeded towards Thomas Fork. Made a great circuit to avoid swampy bottom. Crossed the Fork. Passed the encampment of the troops [Mounted Riflemen] on its bank, continued the circuit and camped on the bank of the Fork within two miles of our noon camp. Distance today 21 miles. Captain Porter's tent.[20] [He] treat[s] and relates the Wilcox tragedy.

Searls, on July 27, wrote about "the Wilcox tragedy." Some men of the Oregon regiment told him that their guide, "a Mr. Wilcox of New York, was shot the other day by an Indian who had brought an express through to the forces from Fort Hall. . . . Wilcox had resided for some time in Oregon and was acquainted with the Indian. Some suppose that it was in revenge for some former deed that he was murdered."

Tuesday, July 31. Early start over the mountain ridges in the bend of river westward. High hills—deep hollows—narrow rocky passes. Another Thermopylae.[21] Went ahead of train. Took cut-offs. Gained the river. Trader's lodge. Borrowed a fishing line and tried to fish. Talk with trader.[22] Train camped near. Kewen and Dr. White's family come along again, at noon. Introduced to the Doctor and Mrs. White. Gave the Doctor Mr. Chenie's letter.[23] Invitation to call. Afternoon went ahead to fish. No luck. Train came up and passed. In 6 miles crossed a stream 10 ft. wide. Government troops camped on it. 7 miles farther

[20] Porter is Andrew Porter, who was a lieutenant colonel, not a captain, with the Mounted Rifles. In his journal (1904) for this date Reid identified Porter as FitzJohn Porter, a future general with whom he served in the Civil War. But Reid's memory failed him here, for FitzJohn Porter was an instructor at West Point from 1849 to 1855 (*Dictionary of American Biography*, XV, 90–91).
[21] Reid is reminded of the mountain pass famous in Greek history. The wagon train here is still following the course of the Bear River.
[22] Thomas "Pegleg" Smith (1801–66), whose wife was a young Indian; a number of emigrants met the celebrated mountain man at this spot, near present-day Dingle, Idaho. See Bruff, Aug. 15; Cross, June 26; Decker, June 24; Pritchard, June 27; and Chamberlain, July 8, who wrote that Smith "appears happy as a lord."
[23] Chenie was a fellow surveyor in the surveyor general's office in St. Louis; his first name remains unknown. The letter may be a letter of introduction Chenie gave Reid to Dr. Victor Fourgeaud, a former St. Louis physician who had migrated to California in 1847, and who was probably known to Dr. White, a former St. Louis physician himself. See Reid to James V. Reid, Nov. 27, 1849.

crossed a mountain rill,—turned up same half a mile and camped at sundown at foot of a gigantic mountain pile crested with green. Total today 24 miles. Poor Eastman of No. 16, who had been wasting away from debility and inaction, during the whole trip, was found in a baggage wagon dead, as the train came into camp.

In his weekly entry of August 5, Searls wrote: "Death has taken another victim from among our number in the person of Mr. J. Eastman who died of consumption of the lungs, July 31st. He was a native of N. Hampshire and until our arrival at Fort Laramie, a member of the mess to which Charles [Mulford] and I belonged. Thus have three out of six composing our mess at starting from Independence been called away by the hand of death."

Wednesday, August 1. Kept up along the bottom some distance, crossing several rills from the mountain slope on our right. Struck up a ravine leaving river to our left and corralled for noon at 2 fine springs on left side of trail. Saddled the pony again this morning and rode on with Kewen ahead of the general party who remained to bury Eastman. After dinner kept up the ravine and over several ridges, re-entering the river valley and camping near foot of hills some distance from river, at which is the government train. Spring ¼ mile from our camp. Gave $2.50 this morning to Day family, from St. Louis, in distress. At noon camp grave of John Clawson.[24] Total today 23 miles.

James Wilkins noted that the Pioneer Line was "about one day before us with they say about half the number of passengers they started with and they have thrown away about half the baggage."[25]

Thursday, August 2. Traversed today the most remarkable country I ever saw. Nature some day long ago was in agony here and the traces of her convulsive writhings are left forever. We are approaching the great northern bend of Bear river, where it turns suddenly from north to south, sweeping around the point

---

[24] Bruff, August 16, wrote that Clawson, aged fifty, of Savannah, Missouri, died on July 11.

[25] Wilkins received correct information that the Pioneer Line was one day ahead. It is doubtful, though, that half the passengers had left the wagon train at that time.

James F. Wilkins, the artist, reached this curiosity of the trail, the Steamboat Spring, on August 3, one day after the Pioneer Line. *Courtesy: State Historical Society of Wisconsin.*

of a high, rugged, pine clad promontory, the terminus of a long unbroken chain of mountains. The surface of the plain and the hill sides are strewn with volcanic rock,—black, heavy and porous, like cinder. Mineral or gaseous springs spout up in hundreds of places, gathering about them mounds of conical form and considerable height. Visited several of them. The soda well on the bank of a little stream to the right of trail sparkles with a bead as pure and strong as that of any soda fountain. I drank nearly three pints of it. Near it are several large mounds, formed by boiling springs bubbling up in different places on their surface. Some of the water is warm. The Steamboat Spring, north of the creek, and on the river's edge, boils up furiously with a fitful pulse through an aperture a foot in diameter in the solid rock. Its water is warm, and it takes its name from the noise it makes.[26] A little farther on near the trail, a square hole opens in

[26] These springs were noted landmarks at the place where the Wasatch Range terminates in present-day Idaho; cf. Cross, Aug. 1; Geiger and Bryarly, July 11; Long, July 7; Perkins, Aug. 8; and Pritchard, June 29. Bryarly thought it "the most interesting spot on earth I ever beheld." Most of the springs are now submerged under Soda Point Reservoir.

the level grassy plain,—at the bottom of which effervesces a strong soda and iron spring. I drank a cup of it, sweetened. Tasted like the mineral water of the confectioners, lacking only the flavor of syrup. We camped beyond this spring, opposite the bend of the river. Near the first soda spring saw lots of Snake Indians, old and young. They wanted powder, shot and money in exchange for their commodities.[27] Several of them came into camp. Distance this morning 10 miles. Drew rations to-day. Only sugar enough for 5 days. Coffee issued for 25 days and exhausted. No more rice, salt, dried fruit or beans. When I remarked to Charley, the Commissary, that we were running rather short, he answered, "You have flour, side-meat and coffee,— what more do you want?" High times indeed![28] Soon will follow half rations, if even that much. Three or four miles in the afternoon brings us to the cut off or forks of the Fort Hall and new road.[29] Fort Hall road turns up a valley to the right. Cut-off keeps due west across a wide volcanic plain. We had heard of this cut-off on the way, but it was not determined till it could be seen whether to take it or not. It is as well beaten as the other, and is said to save 140 miles. Its place of rejunction with the old trail is yet uncertain.[30] Curious appearance of this wide plain. Ledges of basaltic scoria running for miles like a ruined wall of mason-

[27] Shoshoni were also called Snake Indians; cf. Wood, July 19, and Bruff, August 17, who wrote: "Camps and moving bodies of Snakes (Shoshoni) in all directions. . . . Great trade going on." Searls, on August 5, remarked that the Shoshoni had a fine appearance, "many of them possessing an intellectual expression unlooked for by me."

[28] The Pioneer Line supposedly had kept provisions for 60 days when it unloaded at Fort Laramie; see Searls, June 27, quoted above. The commissary, Charles Falkner, was one of the few who had recovered from cholera; see Searls, May 12.

[29] This is Hudspeth's Cutoff, opened on July 19 by the captain of a Missouri wagon train, Benoni Hudspeth, whose guide was John J. Myers (it is sometimes called Myers' Cutoff). See Parke, July 19; Pritchard, pp. 159–60; Wood, July 25; and Paden, *Wake of the Prairie Schooner*, p. 308. Wilkins, traveling the trail on August 8, was informed mistakenly that the Pioneer Line had left via the Cutoff on August 7, and correctly that its mules were in poor condition; see his diary entry for August 8.

[30] The Pioneers are entering unmapped territory. Cf. Searls, Aug. 5: "All is now uncertainty with regard to the route. The road having been opened this season, no written work describes it, and none have returned to tell of its peculiarities." (This passage is transcribed incorrectly in Searls's published diary.) See also Perkins, Aug. 8; and Sedgley, p. 39.

work caved in and blackened by fire. Here and there were chasms, fissures and sinkholes dark deep and yawning like the portals of hell. A large part of the plain, at some former period, has fallen in like the roof of a vast oven. Bear River, after sweeping suddenly around the promontory[31] through a deep chasm of basaltic rock, flows away southward along the eastern edge of a wide valley extending as far as vision extends. About two miles from the bend and near our trail are several conical elevations of considerable height. I walked to all of them while the train went on. The first one,—a solitary conical mound to the left of the trail, rises up regularly, its sides covered with rich verdure to the very summit. Here a different spectacle presented itself. A steep black crater 200 feet in diameter and 50 or 60 feet deep, with bowl-shaped bottom yawned before me. Its whole inner surface was composed of crumbling masses of black scoria. I had no cicerone by my side as if at Aetna or Vesuvius, to tell me of its last eruption and how many cities, hamlets, villas and palaces were overwhelmed in its torrents of lava. Half a mile south-west is another very similar but larger opening on the plain, with no mound around its sides. To the north-east and close to the trail are two parallel elongated mounds with rocky crests, and near them on the north a larger mound with plain traces of two craters on its top,—but their inner sides and bottom are overgrown with herbage and, are not so well defined as the first described crater. All alone. Reflections and aspirations.

From top of last mound saw our train winding into a ravine leading up into the mountains. Seemed 4 to 5 miles away. Started off at a brisk walk to catch up. Sun went down behind the selvedged [bordering] rim of the mountains, and still I seemed to draw no nearer to them. Deceiving distance. For an hour after sunset the foothills seemed only half a mile away. Another hour passed and I had not yet reached them. It must have been 10 miles across the plain from the craters. On entering the hills the road turns southwest. Ravine level at first, then winds with a gradual rise a long, long distance to the top. It was moon light, but the road seemed lonely. Grisly bears are said to roam in

[31] The promontory was called Sheep Rock (now Soda Point). It is near present-day Alexander, Idaho.

these mountains. I had no weapon with me,—so if one should cross my path I would have to be very polite with him. At length on the mountain side near the trail, among the high sage bushes, I noticed a large, dark slow-moving object. I was studying how to make my best bow to bruin as I approached him,—when lo! he turned out to be an inoffensive horse, fagged out and left behind the train. I tried to lead him along but could not, then tried to drive him but it was no go. With his nose to the grass he had taken his stand and I could not move him. So I left him and trudged on, reaching the top at last, and was cheered by the melodious braying of our mules about a mile ahead. A little further I saw our camp fires blazing and heard our herding bell. I was well nigh exhausted when I reached the camp about 10:30 p.m., having walked 5½ hours at nearly 4 miles an hour. Total distance today 31 miles. The train had made this long march to reach water. Camp on a pretty, bright cold stream rushing down from the snowy peaks of the neighboring mountains. Roses and willows. Went to bed with a cold supper.

Friday, August 3. Lay by in the forenoon. I do not feel very well. Find this creek to be Reid's River, a tributary of Bear River.[32] Bathed and washed clothes. Start at 3 p.m. Strike westward across a high mountain. Ascent long, but easy. Descent on the other side steep, sideling and terribly rugged,—the worst hill of all yet. Upset a baggage wagon and broke a wheel of carriage No. 6. 5 miles to another branch of Reid River at the foot of the mountain. Camp on the west bank. From the summit of today's ridge we had a view of more stately, rugged and picturesque mountains than anywhere else on the trip thus far. On all sides of us they reared their lofty peaks without running in ranges or assuming any regular order of place. They seemed like a group of giants clustered confusedly together, and each trying to overtop the other. Stood guard tonight from 1 to 3. Hardly well enough to be out of bed.

Saturday, August 4. Starting delayed on account of breakage yesterday. Turned in again at dawn and tried to sleep, but did

---

[32] This is probably Fish Creek. Diarists traveling this new route—Farnham, Perkins, Sedgley, Swain, and Wilkins, for example—had no maps or landmarks to guide them. Reid's description of the trail is the most explicit, even though he cannot identify points of interest.

not succeed well. Took no breakfast. Drank a cup of flour and water. Started about 10 a.m. I rode in the carriage. Over 2 or 3 points of ridges and through a gap 4 miles to Reid [Portneuf] River at a bend we just touch and leave it again bearing S.W. about 8 miles further to a small stream fringed with very tall rushes,—some 8 feet high. Some of the train shot some duck, among the rushes, and Brewster and Stowe had caught some trout in Reid River this morning, on which we regaled ourselves. Felt some better and could eat a little. Distance today 12 miles.

Sunday, August 5. Started on foot today. Went a mile south up the creek, then crossed and bore S.W. towards a range of mountains. At 3 miles further began to ascend. Ascended gradually 3 m. to foot of steep range, then wound up in defile nearly two miles to summit. Descended westerly 2½ miles to a small brook running south. Halted for noon. Nearly done out with fatigue and weakness. Afternoon turned up a ravine through another range, two miles to summit of ravine or entrance into a singular elevated valley one or two miles wide extending N & S. Went south down the valley 8 miles to a small brook which we crossed and followed down one mile and camped opposite a lofty steep abutment or promontory like the gable end of a gigantic house. Rode pony in the afternoon. Got a bottle of sweet milk from a train camped near, and had a hot supper of bread & milk. Total today 22 miles.

Monday, August 6. After another hot breakfast of bread and milk took pony and returned the milk bottle. After going about 8 miles south-westerly, crossing a small creek, turned westerly into a long, winding narrow defile up a high mountain, nearly 5 miles to the top, at noon. Verily "Alps on Alps" arise. Many of the mules gave out. Grand mountain view. I climbed an adjacent peak. Descended extremely steep grade for one mile, then more gentle descent 4 miles to edge of wide bottom where we expected water, but to our sore disappointment none could be found, in all that valley, and a placard by the roadside informed us it was still 13 miles to water. It seemed hard for us, but harder still for the poor mules. A shower seemed gathering in the heavens and how fondly we hoped it might bless us with rain, but it went by. There were two 10 gallon casks of water in the train which was doled out to each mess merely for drinking. We got a dry dinner, and about 5:30 p.m. moved down the valley south 5 miles, then turned west toward the range skirting the valley,— two miles over rising benches to the mountain—then a mile to summit through a defile, then by gradual descents over benches of table land 7 miles to a hollow in which was a good good spring [Rock Spring]. It was a severe forced march for everything living in the train. Those on foot suffered the worse, unless perhaps the teamsters, many of whom had sunk under the trial. The mules stood it better than I had expected. Oh, how glad was everybody when the campfires of the trains ahead gleamed in our sight. It was past midnight when the last of the train arrived. We spread our beds at once and slept till day—though some messes went to cooking supper. Total today 33 miles.

Tuesday, August 7. Train rested till 2 p.m., then rolled out southwestward over rising tables 5 miles to foot of mountain. Then due west through a narrow pass with lofty summits on either side, keeping on with an easy ascent 4 miles to mouth of cross ravine in which are some springs. We pitched our camp here crowded in with several other trains. The sky was clear and starry, but we could only catch a glimpse of its zenith, so closely did the mountain summits hem us in on all sides. Around a blazing camp fire a circle of singers with a violin among them kept up a serenade till near midnight. Total today 9 miles.

Wednesday, August 8. Up at 3, got a hurried breakfast,—filled the water casks and off at sunrise. Follow the defile N.W. 3 miles another spring and camp. Then northerly 2 miles to summit of defile. A good spring across a ridge 300 yards left of trail. Then descend along the same narrow pass 3 miles to a spring and small run on the left, then another small run comes in from the right. Kept on till 10 o'clock, and halted for noon and in a wide space on the bank of the run. Good place for wood, water & grass. Hot work cooking. Stoyell climbed an adjacent peak and had a view of Salt Lake to the S.W., and of a plain immediately west of us some twenty or more miles wide.[33] High mountains beyond and no water except the run we are on which bears off to the N.W. An indian in camp today traces a map of the region west of us, making it five sleeps [nights] to Humboldt River.

[33] R. S. Stoyell is Reid's messmate; he is looking down at the trail from Salt Lake City. The train is encamped at Muddy (now Sublette) Creek.

Started 3 p.m. and follow the run westerly, and at 6 miles we cross its dry bed, just below where its water sinks in the sands, and camp in the edge of the plain. Distance today 18 miles.

Thursday, August 9. —Lay by in the forenoon to rest the mules for a probable long drive without water. Filled all casks and rolled out at 2 p.m. southwesterly towards a gap in the mountains. The road terribly dusty, with a head wind. Level plain. Nothing but gravel, sage and dust. After crossing one or two dry branches we were surprised to find water at 13 miles. At dark we crossed another dry bed of a run. The water in it sinks a little above the trail. A few rods further we come to a smaller run and good spring, and camped for the night. Total to-day 13 miles.

Friday, August 10. —Rolled out towards the mountain to the south west. At 3 miles we meet a creek coming from a gap in the range, and we follow up its banks. Enter the gap at 2 miles. 3 miles further we camped for noon. High peaks all around us. Continued up the creek afternoon, crossing it after awhile and bearing off up along a gently rising ridge from which we looked down southward upon a wide valley seemingly without water.[34] At the end of 17 miles camped near a good spring. High peak near us on the west. Night very cold.

Saturday, August 11. Bitter cold morning. Appearance of an old crater near. Early start down the valley southward. Pony had no water last night. Took him to the spring this morning to water him. Met Dr. White there at an emigrant camp.[35] Rode on with him. 4 miles a little stream with some camps on it. At 7 miles halted for noon at a run of clear cool water on a stony bed. Had a good bath. Saw numerous trains moving along westward on a trail away to the south of us. It must be a road from Mormon City.[36] It enters a gap in the mountains south of the one our trail enters. At 2 miles after noon halt we enter our gap.[37] 2 m. fur-

[34] The Raft River Valley.

[35] The same Dr. Thomas White whom Reid had met on the trail on July 30. Searls wrote on August 5 that the White family had left the Mounted Riflemen (on their way to Fort Hall) at the junction with the cutoff, and that henceforth they would travel with the Pioneer Line; cf. Cross, Aug. 2. White and his family will be with or near the passenger train as far as the Humboldt Sink. The camp is on a branch of the Raft River.

[36] This road from Salt Lake City will soon converge with the trails from Hudspeth's Cutoff and Fort Hall.

[37] Cassia Creek Canyon.

ther to a spring. Another 2 miles enter a rocky dell some 4 miles long by a winding road running among the most grotesque rocks standing out singly in the valley, or grouped fantastically together.[38] There were sphynxes and statues of every size, and haystacks and wigwams and castles, and towers, and pyramids and cones and projecting turrets and canopies, and leaning columns, and so on throughout a thousand varieties of fantastic shapes. The dell is bounded on the south by an immense wall on which rise at intervals tall conical towers of bare rock. Through this wall we passed by a grand gateway guarded on either side by one of those gigantic watch towers. I call them the "Pillars of Hercules."[39] Our road descends gradually about a mile to its junction with the Mormon road. Here we get some information, but very vague. Went on. About 4 miles further we camped on the plain a mile or two off the trail, where we found water near the foot of the range on the west,—in the bed of a stream nearly dry. We had previously crossed the bed of a dry stream in which we learned there was running water 2 days before. Total today 22 miles.

[38] All diarists remark on this astonishing spot, later called the City of Rocks, near the present-day town of Almo, Idaho; but none describes it more graphically than Reid. Cf. Bruff, Aug. 29; Lord, Aug. 17; Perkins, Aug. 15; Swain, Aug. 26; and Wilkins, Aug. 13. The distance traveled from South Pass was approximately 355 miles.

[39] These were called Steeple Rocks or Twin Sisters by some emigrants.

The City of Rocks to the
Humboldt Sink

August 12–September 9

Beyond the City of Rocks, where the trail from Salt Lake City meets the California Trail, the route descends into a broad valley, climbs steeply to the summit of Granite Mountain, and sharply drops to the Goose Creek Valley. The trail then moves southwest along the Hot or Thousand Spring Valley in present-day Nevada until it reaches the headwaters of the Humboldt River. The emigrants now begin an even more uncomfortable and wearying stage of the journey, tormented by suffocating dust, extreme heat during the day, and biting cold at night. The trail follows the Humboldt River approximately 300 miles to its Sink, where the river disappears into the desert sands. The Humboldt is a lifeline to the travelers, but its water becomes progressively filthier and more offensive, and the surrounding landscape is arid, the soil heavily impregnated with alkali. The hardships along the Humboldt reach nightmarish proportions for the unfortunate Pioneer Line. The mules are exhausted, the commissary issues only flour for rations, many passengers exhibit symptoms of scurvy, and "deep gloom" prevails.

Sunday, August 12. Our cooking week over, this is my day to drive. Back to main road and then through a windy ravine of gradual ascent. At 4 miles camped for noon at a spring and small rill. Some ox trains here. 2 miles more to summit. Here we saw an exceedingly rough, steep and broken mountainous valley before us. Singular bluffs or buttes—some white—some red—some standing—detached like islands—some in connected chains,—all crowned with flat dome and cornice, tufted over on top with small cedars. From summit 4 miles to creek—called by some Goose Creek, running north,—crossed a branch of it one mile back.—This whole descent is the most rugged and difficult for wagons I ever saw. We would be dropped down steep hills and immediately wind up others to have the pleasure of getting down again at the risk of our necks. At one place an axle of a baggage wagon was broken. At another the road pitched down for 100 yards at an angle of 45 degrees. The teams were all driven down with both hind wheels locked and men holding on to a rope behind. It looked dangerous to sit in a carriage and manage 4 mules on such a steep. However I got down without accident,—though, being the last of the train, the train-men, who were tired out, had left their post at the top of the incline, and I had to plunge down with wheels unlocked and without the two lead mules being unhitched as had been done with the other teams.[1]

Some messes caught plenty of trout in the creek where we made noon halt. Rations issued at this camp. For the last 24 hours we had to live on boiled bacon and piñola mush, hot for supper and cold for breakfast. Looks like hard times a-coming. After a rest of 3 hours we proceeded at sundown up the creek, southerly 3 miles, and camped in a rough spot among the sage. Stood watch tonight. Poor grass on the hill side. Total today 13 miles.

Searls: "Another week has passed, bringing with it the usual routine of fatigue and exposure.

"How different is the figure now cut by the redoubtable 'Pioneer Line,' from that made at our departure from the abodes of civilized men. Rejoicing at the comforts in store for us while on the 'unknown expanse' and with the prospect of a speedy arrival at the goal of our desires, we set out, elated in spirit, only pitying those less fortunate in their choice of conveyance. How sadly have we been disappointed."

Monday, August 13. Keep up S.W. along the creek. At 7 miles enter a cañon with barely room for the road. Bottom soon widens again. 10 miles noon halt on creek. Kept on up the creek in the afternoon. At 1 mile, several warm springs to right of trail. 8 miles farther camp for night on creek. Total 18 miles.

Tuesday, August 14. Off at 6, at 2 miles creek forks,—keep

---

[1] The descent of Granite Mountain was one of the worst of the trip. Cf. Decker, July 2; and Farnham, July 31, who wrote, "The descents were frightful. . . . To look up at the waggons coming down, it did not seem as if they could be held back to come down steady."

up the left fork, S.S.W. 4 miles. Part of the way through a narrow stony gap.[2] Leaving the creek we strike southward across a very uneven country covered with sage, dust, rock, juniper and greasewood. 12 m. without water to a valley running south, in which several cool springs gush out close to the trail, at the foot of a pile of rocks.[3] Camp here for noon at 2:30, and halt till near sundown. Then down the valley six miles and camp at some cool but swampy springs. No. 12 was detained by breakage of harness and missed the way across the swamps to the camp. Got in at 9 o'clock. No supper. Total today 24 miles. Brewster today lost my French book.[4]

Wednesday, August 15. Kept up the valley southerly three miles —then by a cut-off across two low ridges into a valley connecting with the one we left. 8 miles farther, halt for noon on bank of a stream now dry except a few holes where water stood. This whole valley looks like a desert. Dust, like new fallen snow, lies 6 inches deep on the roadside. Sun hot today. Afternoon kept along the valley. Sage gives place to pretty grassy lawn like the Platte bottom. Stopped to graze pony. Camped for the night on the dry bed of the stream. Water in wells. Pretty good grass. Total today 19 miles.

Thursday, August 16. Lay by all day. Turner proposes to divide the train and send the passengers ahead with the best mules. Discussion. Counter-proposition to cache 5 or 6 wagons. Talk with Turner. Camp seems to settle down on the first plan.[5]

Friday, August 17. Off at 5:30 a.m. Keep up the valley (Hot Spring Valley). At 2 miles, some running water in bed of stream. A little above it is found to be warm. 4 miles from camp several

---

[2] Little Goose Narrows, in present-day Nevada. The train is now moving along the valley of Little Goose Creek, a branch of Goose Creek (a tributary of the Snake River) that it has been following since August 12.

[3] A spot called Rock Springs.

[4] The book may have been a remnant of *Télémaque*, by Archbishop François de La Mothe-Fénelon (1651–1715). Reid found time to study his French. After abandoning so much of his baggage, he told his sister, he kept the copy of Fénelon "*un*bound in my pocket, and read when I could as we journeyed on. When I read a leaf I tore it off, and left it behind to edify other 'voyageurs.'" See Reid to Mary Reid, March 12, 1852; and Reid, journal, July 20, in which he recalled that he read Fénelon along the trail.

[5] No plan is resolved on this day.

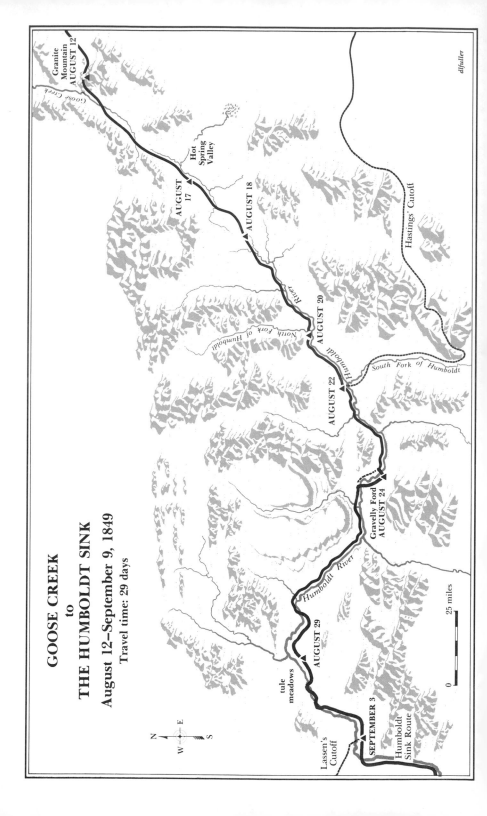

GOOSE CREEK
to
THE HUMBOLDT SINK
August 12–September 9, 1849
Travel time: 29 days

Granite
Mountain
AUGUST 12

Goose Creek

Hot
Spring
Valley

AUGUST 17

AUGUST 18

River

North Fork of Humboldt

AUGUST 20

AUGUST 22

Humboldt

South Fork of Humboldt

Hastings' Cutoff

Gravelly Ford
AUGUST 24

Humboldt River

AUGUST 29

tule
meadows

Lassen's
Cutoff

SEPTEMBER 3

Humboldt
Sink Route

0   25 miles

dfuller

N
W—E
S

hot springs in the bed of the stream,—so hot that emigrants now camped here cooked beans in them.[6] Further up are cold springs and good water. At 10 miles we leave the valley and bear S.W. to a gap in the range on our right.[7] Some springs in the ravine but hardly any grass. Ravine winds southwardly and gradually ascends to summit. Descent quite gradual on the other side, and we kept on southerly till fairly in the valley,—then turn down valley S.W. and at 3 p.m. camped on a small clear grassy stream, fringed with water cresses and willows. Leads into the Humboldt or Mary's River. Hard to wash off the dust of driving. Fray between Updyke and Andrews.[8] Total today 20 miles.

In a letter to his brother James, dated November 27, 1849, Reid recalled the grueling travel on these hot August days: "The immense clouds of dust continually attending the train made it extremely unpleasant either to walk or ride, for the thick clumps of snarly and jagged wild sage most generally prevented both man and horse from taking any but the beaten track. Suppose dry ashes and fine sand were thoroughly mixed together, and I should take a shovel and toss a large pile of the mixture against your face, head and whole body—suppose then you should run up and down a steep hill in a hot August sun till the perspiration oozed from every pore almost in streams. Let me then give you another coating of dust and ashes; and your appearance would then be a pretty good sample of that of every one of us, at every noon and night halt."

Saturday, August 18. Two miles down the valley came to a cañon through which the trail passes for four miles, crossing the run nine times,—often with scarcely room for the wagons, it was so narrow. The cañon rocky and rough. High rocky crags here and there overhang the road. Midway in the cañon was a large clear basin of rock,—like a bath tub—filled with warm water from springs on its margin. Water more than bloodwarm. Bathed hands, face and feet in it.[9] Beyond the cañon the valley widens,

[6]Cf. Perkins, Aug. 24: "Passed this morning a real boiling spring, the water being at a temperature of 212 & answering well for cooking purposes. A fish put into this spring by an emigrant was well-cooked in two minutes."

[7]The range is Summer Camp Ridge, the divide between Thousand Spring Creek and the Humboldt River, Nevada.

[8]R. J. Updyke and M. O. Andrews, both passengers.

[9]There were two roads leading from here to the Humboldt Valley—the other by way of the Humboldt Wells. The Pioneer Line chooses the more difficult route through Bishop's Creek Canyon. The two trails converged near present-day Deeth, Nevada.

and we follow it down, leaving the mountain range behind us and another high snow topped range on our left.[10] Camped for noon on the bank of the small stream we were following, at a place where two good springs issue from the bank. Sage for fuel. Afternoon kept on down the run and camped for night before sundown. Total today 19 miles. Pretty good camp ground. Willow fuel. High volcanic looking peak on our left.

Sunday, August 19. Our blankets white with frost this morning, and ice an inch thick in the wash basin. Quite wintry. Up at dawn. Kept on down the bottom, white in places with alkali. 7 miles crossed another small stream, nearly dry in spots. Other small streams converge with it in the valley. 2 or 3 miles lower down we camp for noon on the creek or river, supposed by some to be the Humboldt or Mary's River.[11] The channel 30 or 40 feet wide from bank to bank. Water clear, but almost motionless. Fish small. Saw none over 6 inches. Clusters of willows, roses and sweet briar. At 3:30 kept down the right bank of the stream— S.W.—10 miles camped in high rich grass. Good willow fuel. High rough mountains to the left and others in the distance looming up on the horizon. All assume a blue tinge in the twilight air. Road very dusty. Total today 19 miles.

Searls: "Another week is numbered with the past and finds us toiling down the Humboldt or St. Mary's River. . . . Our men are becoming emaciated and querulous. Luxuries in the way of foods are among the things to memory dear. Rancid bacon with the grease fried out by the hot sun, musty flour, a little pinoles and some sacks of pilot bread, broken and crushed to dust and well coated with alkali, a little coffee without sugar—now constitutes our diet. The men need more and must have it or perish. Yet at our present rate of progress, even these supplies must fail long before we can reach California.

"A deep gloom prevails in camp. The men know we must all inevitably starve unless relieved and yet feel like cutting the throat of him who would remind them of it. . . . But what of the sick? How are they to be cared for when the emergency arrives and disorganized, as we must inevitably become, each seeks his own safety? God only knows what fate awaits them. . . .

"We have discussed the question of dividing the train and pushing

---

[10] The mountain range behind is the Independence Range; the snow-topped range on the left is the Ruby Range.

[11] The river was first known as Ogden's, then called Mary's or St. Mary's, and then rechristened by Frémont in honor of Baron von Humboldt. The Pioneer Line now enters the Humboldt Valley; cf. Geiger and Bryarly, July 25, for the same uncertainty about the beginning of the river.

ahead with the sick and such others as choose to walk, leaving the heavy wagons and remainder of the men to come on at a slower pace, but as usual cannot agree upon any course of action, hence I conclude we shall go on as before."

Monday, August 20. Started after cacheing the "Prairie Bird" wagon, which broke a wheel last evening. Course of the river S.W. 3 or 4 miles a branch[12] comes in from the S.E. about as large as the one we were on. 3 or 4 miles farther the river sweeps around in a large bend, turning first west, and then N.W. to double a mountain point. It then receives from the N.E. another tributary or fork as large as the first.[13] This we cross near the junction. The river then flows through a cañon to the left, and the road keeps to the right over a dusty ridge covered with sage. We soon re-enter the valley where the river again cañons southward and the road passes over another ridge of sage and dust into the valley once more, where we camp on the river bank. The river here is more than twice as large as where we saw it first, and swifter. Plenty of willow fuel and pretty good grass. Lay by the balance of the day to make arrangements for dividing the train. Total to-day 15 miles.

Tuesday, August 21. Kept on down the river. At 10 miles camped on the river bank and lay by the rest of the day to complete arrangements for dividing the train. Had a good bath and washed clothes. Meeting called at corral at 2:30 p.m. Great farce. Rumsey's Preamble.[14] Limits of baggage to be allowed each man 20–25 or 30 lbs proposed. 30 carries the vote. Reported to Capt. Turner. He gets angry. Exercises the veto. Some talk on the question. Says he'll be boss in the future. No more voting. Threatens to let *hunger* bring us to reason. Edict goes forth—the line not to be divided, for the present. Saw Petreville this evening on his way packing along with Col. Gratiot.[15]

Wednesday, August 22. Started as usual about 7. At about 7

[12] Trout Creek, which rises in the East Humboldt Range.
[13] The North Fork of the Humboldt River, which actually comes in from the northwest.
[14] Apparently, Colonel Rumsey is still president of the passengers' "association" formed in the Sweetwater Valley, but the men's apathy here contrasts with their determination on July 11 and 12. The train is encamped on the Humboldt Meadows below present-day Elko, Nevada.
[15] These may be acquaintances from St. Louis, since the Gratiots were one of St. Louis's distinguished families, and Charles Gratiot, a Mexican War veteran, was a forty-niner.

miles a fork as large as the river itself comes in from the S.E. through a steep rocky cañon some distance above the junction.[16] The river is now much wider and somewhat deeper. On the way this morning we passed the camp of a Kentucky train that had lost 7 oxen last night—they thought the digger indians had stolen them.[17] A miserable looking indian, old, shrivelled and scarred, and almost naked had come into their camp this morning. They took it for granted he knew all about their loss, and while I was there—having stopped behind our train to see what they were going to do, they proceeded to tie him, preparatory to torturing him by whipping to compel him to confess and return the stolen cattle. They attempted to declare their purpose by signs, and he in like manner gesticulated and jabbered in digger language, most likely declaring his innocence. They however gave him the alternative of returning the oxen or being tortured—perhaps killed—in their vengeful fury. I ventured to plead for the poor old wretch,—reminded them that they had no proof of his guilt, and that, if guilty, he would not have voluntarily thrown himself into their hands by coming to their camp,—and that they ought to reflect well before proceeding to torture a defenceless old man whom all human laws would presume to be innocent till proven guilty. As against the crowd of angry accusers I was alone and unarmed, and my remonstrances would most likely have been unheeded,—but they proved not altogether thrown away, for while we were parleying, and the old man was being led about with a rope—his hands tied behind him—a cry was raised that the cattle were found among the willows of an island near by. The intended victim was at once unbound and one of the party generously took him into the camp and gave him a hearty meal. At 11 miles halted for noon on the river bank. Here one turns to the right over a succession of hills

[16] This is the South Fork of the Humboldt; Hastings' Cutoff across the Great Salt Lake Desert met the California Trail at this spot. Hastings' Cutoff was traveled by few emigrants in 1849, since most knew that the ill-starred Donner party had suffered dangerous delay in 1846 by taking this cutoff with its ninety-mile waterless stretch.

[17] The Paiute and Shoshoni Indians inhabited this region, but emigrants called them all Diggers because they dug for roots and plant food; they were small, undernourished people, living at a subsistence level. Emigrants detested the Diggers because they were adept at stealing stock, and wagon trains resumed guard duty along this stretch.

to avoid a cañon a mile or so below us. The other road follows
the river bank.

Rations issued today—*of flour only*. Which was the same as last
previous issue. But today we got some of a fresh beef bought
and killed last evening. Took the river road through the cañon.[18]
Odd looking rocks like statues and turrets jutting out of the sides
of the flanking hills. Cross the river 4 times in the gorge, which is
about 5 miles long. Some pretty spots in it. The valley now gradually widens. Poor grass. Camp for night in a thick patch of sage.
Scarcely room for lying down. Total today 19 miles.

Thursday, August 23. Off at 6 a.m., down the valley. At six miles
a clear cold stream comes in on the right. Water much better
than in the main river. Some warm springs a little below. 8 miles
to the head of a cañon [19] where the road strikes off over hills to
the right. Halted here for noon. Grass all eaten off. Sprinkled
a few drops of rain. Rolled out at 1:30 over some hills and hollows, and then climbed a high range of mountains, and a little
beyond the summit camped for the night near two good springs
near the trail on the downward slope in a narrow ravine. Two
other trains camped near. Much sage but little grass on this
mountain. Rained briskly after supper, and after our beds were
spread. They got quite wet on the upper side. Crawled in between the blankets and let it rain. Stuck my nose out for breath
and it got the full benefit of the shower. Continued raining more
or less till near midnight,—the only real rain we have had since
the last of June. Total today 16 miles.

Friday, August 24. Slept well considering the rain. It did not
soak thru the blanket. Train started at 6 a.m. Sun came out clear.
Tarried awhile behind the train. Passed several other springs
on our gradual descent of 9 miles to the river bottom. A mile
further crossed the river and halted for noon. Dusty, dirty,—
greasewood. Camp on stubble of scanty grass. Dinner of rice
and "pap."[20] After dinner kept down left bank, course here west-

---

[18] Frémont's Canyon.

[19] Emigrant Creek Canyon, near present-day Carlin, Nevada.

[20] The "pap" probably was pinola mush. Reid recalled that "the pinola was
miserable stuff. We could not make palatable or nutritious food of it, cook it as
we might." See Reid to James V. Reid, Nov. 27, 1849. The wagon train crosses
the river at Gravelly Ford, near present-day Beowawe, Nevada. Both Bruff (September 1) and Middleton (October 6) noted the grave of W. Maxwell, a teamster

ward, at 2 miles the river turns nearly north through a narrow gap in the end of a mountain range jutting close in on our left. On each side of this range is a valley extending to the left as far as the eye can reach. Camped close to some willows. Total today 17 miles.

Saturday, August 25. Grew cold before morning. Went northward 5 miles, where the river turns first west then S.W. At the bend the trail crosses the river and keeps down right bank. Camped for noon at 10 miles. Bo't [bought] a pair of coarse boots from ox train for $3.95. Had a good swim. Afternoon, kept down the river. Picturesque mountains on either side. Towards sundown the air becalms and the dust after rising a few feet high overspreads the plain like a lake of smooth muddy water. Along our line of wagons some are completely submerged in it. Others show only their tops, which seem to go floating along like little boats in the water. Here and there the heads of the men on foot stick up and glide along in rows and groups like ducks on a pond. Passed the grave of Melinda, wife of Henry Cain, of Platte County, Mo. Total today 18 miles.

Sunday, August 26. Our week to cook. Out of breadstuffs entirely. Breakfast on rice. Trail at times today diverges from the river to cut-off bends,—the river sometimes running south and then northwest. The wide plains passed over today are quite desert like, whitened with alkali and covered thinly with tufts of greasewood and sage. The dust was terrible. Camped on river bank. Total today 18 miles. Passed grave of Henry H. Robinson, of Union County, Ohio.[21]

Monday, August 27. Course today N.W., bottom very wide and level. At 9 miles nooned on river bank. Hot work baking. Saw Lamalfa.[22] Fire among the willows near us. Wattles' baggage all burned. Explosion of powder flask and pistols. Afternoon the

---

on the Pioneer Line who died on August 24. Since this grave was in the Hot Spring Valley, it was probably a teamster on the second train, though a W. Maxwell from Alabama was listed as a crew member of the first train in the *Missouri Republican*, May 17, 1849.

[21] Cf. the description of this terrain in Bruff (September 11), who noted that Henry Robinson, aged twenty-six, died of "dysentary" on August 13.

[22] Joseph Lamalfa may have left the Pioneer Line by this time. On August 13, James Wilkins met Lamalfa at the foot of Granite Mountain. Lamalfa said, according to Wilkins, that "the privation and hardship of the journey are such that he would not undertake it again for 5000$."

river makes another bend southward and runs through a cañon, which we avoid by keeping on westward around the hill, crossing only some low ridges. Some low regular shaped hills on the plain before us. On passing to the right of one of them we were struck with wonder at a scene that burst suddenly on our sight. It was the most beautiful and gorgeous sunset I have ever beheld. No pen can describe or pencil paint a picture of such extraordinary beauty—made still more beautiful by the mountains underlying the picture and by its contrast with the dreary desolation reigning in the desert around us. The wondrous scene was one of the bright spots on our long and tiresome way. Total today 19 miles.

Tuesday, August 28. Beautiful sunrise this morning. Kept down N.W. Windy and dusty. Halted for noon on the river bank considerably to left of the trail. Afternoon doubled the point of the bend in a tornado of dust and a labyrinth of ox teams,—and turned S.W. to where the road goes through a pass in the hills to avoid another river bend and cañon. Camped for night in the main river valley. Total today 20 miles.

Wednesday, August 29. Cold morning. Kept down 9 miles and halted for noon near point of bend. After dinner crossed two channels of the river. In crossing the first some mules fell in the harness. 6 miles farther camped on the river bank near a murmuring waterfall. Camped by a small stream tumbling in on the opposite side.[23] Total today 15 miles. Saw Wardlaw tonight.

Thursday, August 30. Lay in camp all day, recruiting the mules and making hay for a stretch of 75 miles of desert which we are told begins a little below our camp,—30 miles of the desert being in this valley and the rest in a new road leading off to the right and entering Sacramento Valley some 150 miles above Sutter's Fort.[24] Turner had gone on yesterday to get some information about the road. Returns this morning and decides to take the new road. Had a big job today mending cap and gray trousers. Took a swim and put on fine frock coat and black casimere[25] trousers, and had my hair and whiskers trimmed. All this change

[23] The train is at a tule meadow near present-day Winnemucca, Nevada.

[24] The new road is Lassen's Cutoff. The first train entered this cutoff on August 11, with only a vague notion of where it was heading.

[25] A soft woolen cloth often used for making men's trousers; also spelled cassimere.

capped by the new head-piece, so altered my appearance that the train hardly knew me.

Cold night. Saw Dr. Pitts—great change in his appearance.

Dr. G. F. Pitts, a passenger from Louisiana, is suffering from scurvy. In a letter to his brother James, dated November 27, 1849, Reid wrote about the ominous decline of a number of the passengers: "Soon our bad food began to do its work—symptoms of scurvy began to appear among the passengers—the disease spread and grew until our people presented a pitiable spectacle—stiffened in all their joints, swollen and discolored, full of pain—and rotting to death by inches!"

Friday, August 31. Lay by till noon gathering up the hay. Helped carry it. Reminded me of old harvesting times.[26] Finished my mending. Last night Capt. Reed, Elder and Bearce started ahead on foot. This morning Pearks and Brogden and Cody and Coleman started off also on foot.[27] Train moved at 1:30 p.m. Kept on left side of river. 10 miles camped in good grass. Plenty of water and prairie fowl. Started a deer from the willows just as we began to corral. Stood guard 3d watch. Pretty moonlight. Total 10 miles.

Diarist James Wilkins recorded on September 19 a conversation he had with Augustus O. Garrett, a passenger on the Pioneer Line. Garrett observed that he had seen Captain Turner "drop asleep as he stood. With watching thro' the night, as he was in continual fear some of the men would steal his mules, and been harassed during the day, he must have had a hard time of it." But the passengers and teamsters did not attempt to requisition the Pioneer Line's property.

Saturday, September 1. Kept on down the river 5 miles to a bend bringing it close up against a precipitous bluff, requiring us to climb and immediately descend a steep hill. Heavy sandy road— hard pulling, at 10 miles halt for noon. Good willow fuel, no grass. Met this morning an ox train from Oregon City—to Fort Hall, sent to meet the troops with flour and beef.[28] Brought news

[26] Cf. Perkins, Sept. 1: "Hundreds of wagons were here . . . making hay. . . . Everything was done as at home, some mowing & others tossing and drying."

[27] Cody and Coleman are teamsters; the others leaving the train are all passengers.

[28] See Wilkins, Sept. 4; Lord, Sept. 5; and Bruff, Sept. 8. They also noted this wagon train, on its way to Fort Hall with supplies for the Mounted Riflemen. Wilkins wrote that the train came "by what is called the South Oregon route," that is, the Applegate Cutoff, the eastern section of Lassen's Cutoff, opened in 1846. This is the same supply train mentioned by Reid on July 26.

from California and some account of the new Northern road, part of which they passed over. In the afternoon kept on down the river and camped on its bank. No grass for the mules. Atmosphere very hazy. Sun went down large and red behind a mountain peak invisible through the haze. Had the effect of an eclipse. Total today 18 miles.

Sunday, September 2. Our week to drive. Start at daybreak. Cross the river at our camp, where one road leads off over a sandhill. We follow the river down its right bank about 2 miles, where turning south about a mile around a bend we found a little grass and halted to let the mules graze. Started again at noon, crossing to the left bank for about a mile—then recrossed to right bank. Three miles further left the river and went over sand hills for some distance,—then back to the river and camp early on its bank, having found some good grass just across the river at this point. The air is still full of misty smoke, and the sun shines hot through it all. Evening pleasant.

Met Cope of Wisconsin—formerly of Greensburg, Pa.[29] Quite a chat about old acquaintances. Total to-day 10 miles.

Monday, September 3. Keep on down the valley, sometimes on the river bottom—sometimes on the sand hills. At 7 miles noon halt on river bank. Very hot sun. Turner has changed his mind and will now keep the old or left hand road. The new road is some 200 miles farther. Proceeded down to the forks of the road, where the new road leaves the river and bears off N.W. across an immense plain. The river and old road bend southwardly. At the forks many sticks and pieces of boards are stuck up as bulletin boards bearing letters, cards, notices and the like—telling of Mr. So and So, or Company so and so passing, and which road they took and advising their friends to follow on the same road.[30] Camp half a mile below the forks. Joseph Cooper, of No. 10, of Washington, Pa. died of chronic diar-

[29] Greensburg is a town in Westmoreland County, near Reid's childhood home.

[30] The Pioneers were lucky that Turner changed his mind here. By taking the new road to the northwest, Lassen's Cutoff, emigrants hoped to avoid the hardships of the Humboldt desert that lay ahead. But it was a long and difficult trail, and many of the forty-niners who chose it were saved only by a relief expedition sent out from California. Diarists who traveled via the cutoff included Bruff, Goldsmith, Middleton, Swain, and Webster. See also Morgan's chart of travel for many wagon trains in Pritchard, appendix.

rhoea, and was buried at noon halt. Lovely moonlight night. Full round moon—dimming the neighboring stars and shedding effulgence over the quiet earth. Lay there on my lonely bed with sleepless eyelids, contemplating the calm beauty of the scene. The gorgeous heavens—the majestic mountains, the extended plains—the silent, flowing river—the camp, just sinking to repose—the solitary camp fire still burning with a small group clustered around it, chattering and singing. All served to furnish food for contemplation and keep off slumber for some time. Total today 15 miles.

Diarist Douglass Perkins passed "the famous 'Pioneer Train,'" on which he had contemplated taking passage. "They have travelled no faster than ox wagons," he wrote; "in fact many of the latter have passed them. Their mules were overdone by fast driving the first two weeks . . . since taking provisions for sixty days they have been several times on the verge of starvation & have been relieved by ox trains, making purchases or borrowing flour, crackers, bacon etc. . . . They number some 35 wagons & make quite a show with their mules and spring coaches. The latter are a very neat and comfortable article & had their mules held out the passengers might have travelled very comfortably. Turner & Allen must lose considerably by the operation 40 mules have died or were left from inability to proceed & in consequence some 8 or 10 carriages have also been left. These losses in addition to the outlay for provisions at the enormous prices at which all such articles are held on the plains must entirely eat up the profits & draw on them considerable besides. I can but congratulate myself on my fortunate escape in not paying them 200$ for such passage. . . . Camped this evening opposite Pioneers they having crossed Humboldt to find grass for their Enormous herd of mules."

Tuesday, September 4. Started early. Five miles down we crossed to the right bank and kept up over sage hills to avoid a "narrows" caused by white sand buttes between which the river runs. About 11 o'clock camped on the sage for noon. Half a mile to water. Rice dinner. Carried a dish of it to Mr. James of No. 5.[31] Let the mules graze on a small patch of grass a couple of hours, and then gave them some hay at the corral. Afternoon kept on over the same barren sage plain, and finally after crossing with difficulty a deep ravine with perpendicular sides, we reached the river again after dark and camped on its bank. It was so dark

[31] Passenger John James is suffering from scurvy.

we could hardly see what we were doing. Greasewood in great plenty. Made bonfires of them. Picketed pony and fed him some hay. Made our beds on a smooth sand patch. Moon rose beautifully about 10 o'clock revealing the wild scenery around us. Total today 22 miles.

Wednesday, September 5. Trumpet called us up at 3 o'clock. Off before day in the bright moonlight. Soon regained the sage table land, then bore southward, past the point of a range of mountains jutting in on our right. Made noon halt in narrow river bottom—some willows and rushes, but little or no grass. Off again at 5 p.m. regaining the sage and greasewood plain. Until the moon rose our way was illumined by brilliant bonfires of fields of greasewood, lit at intervals as we marched along. Moon rose in cloudless splendor about 9. At 10:30 camped on the bank of a slough in the great plain, entirely destitute of vegetation as far as we could see and covered by a fine light dust like dark ashes. Had a cup of coffee and slept on the ashy bed. Near us was a mound or butte which seemed to be the extremity of a mountain range jutting into the plain on our right. A spring of clear water in the bank of the slough near our camp. Total today 22 miles.

Thursday, September 6. The matin trump called us up at a little after 3, and we moved at day-break. At about 2 miles came to the river, wide, full, almost motionless, and looking more like a lake than a river. It was fringed with willows and reeds. The grounds around had patches of salt or alkaline incrustations and damp exudations as if the soil had been watered in spots during the night. Just before we reached the river the soil for some distance was nearly black and was baked and cracked wide open in blocks like tile work. In about 5 miles halted for noon on a plain with a little grass and some water near the surface, for which we had to dig shallow wells. Half a mile to our left is the river, with its reeds and willows and a good margin of rich grass. We made the early halt to feed our hungry mules and horses. So ravenous was their hunger this morning before hitching up that they ran about wildly in the corral, picking up chips and sticks and crunching them like pipe-stems. They gnawed at the wagon boxes, tore the canvas covers, chewed ropes and driving reins, ate up a hat and some clothing of the teamsters. And all this after having had a feed of hay last night. They were about exhausted when we halted at forenoon today. I had a swim in the river here. Found it far beyond my depth. And infested with snakes, rats and a variety of insects. Some indians came over to our camp. Some of them claimed to be Shoshones and others Pah-utes, but all seemed to be of one tribe. They all wore tolerably good and well-fitting garments. No trinkets except that one young fellow wore around his neck a string of pearl oyster shells. One had a good gun. They understood no English,—but would repeat, with great readiness, parrot-like, anything we said to them or ask of them. One had been to California and described by signs and one or two English words the process of washing gold. In the same way they said it was 10 days over for horses, 20 for teams. In camp they coveted our fat bacon, raw or cooked, and ate the gravy of it up like honey or milk. One of them had a curious fishing line and hook of [space left blank] teeth. Brewster swapped something for it. At 4 p.m. started again down stream southward about 4 miles along a pleasant, level, verdant river bottom, much like that of the Platte,—in marked contrast with the sage and dust of the last few marches. Camped at a good spring some distance to the right of the river. Here we are to recruit our mules and prepare a supply of hay for the great desert before us.[32] Pretty camping ground, near other camps. Total today 9 miles.

Friday, September 7. In camp all day. The train hands mowing hay. I found a small scorpion. Indians in camp today again. They readily run two or 3 miles for fuel for us if offered a small piece of bacon. I feel nearly overcome by the heat of the day. Dunning almost shot today by accident. At night a man in one of the camps close by entertaining a ring of spectators by a series of excellent performances on the violin. Really fine music. A large bonfire in the centre, and the crowd circled around it as in a circus. I stood guard till 11 p.m.

Saturday, September 8. Chilly damp morning, followed by a hot day. Prepare to move on after dinner. Mr. James has high fever. Get some medicine for him from Dr. White. After starting a

[32] The train has reached the Great Meadow of the Humboldt, near present-day Lovelock, Nevada. Wagon trains "recruited" here before crossing the Forty-Mile Desert beyond the terminus of the river.

passing cloud sprinkles a little rain. Dust soon flies again. Keep down stream 6 miles and camped for the day. Gathered more hay. Some lightning and thunder and a light sprinkle of rain. Poor fuel. Poor water. Turn in to sleep till morning for another march.

Sunday, September 9. The reveille sounded at midnight, the moon just up. All ready and off a little after 1 o'clock, our course bearing south of west. In 2 or 3 miles the plain became a bare desert, looking like an old brick-yard, but white; almost like a winter snowscene. In some places the surface is like low heaps of fresh ashes in which one sinks to the ankle. No sign of vegetation in sight except here and there a bunch of coarse grass or a small cluster of greasewood. The odor given out from the ground is like that of fresh cinder at a glass factory. The mountains in the distance dimly visible in the pale moonlight seemed scarcely real. At length day dawned, and a little after sunrise we turned off to the left of the trail and camped at the foot of several wide marshes and pools of water terminating on a bank of ashy earth. This we understand to be the sink of the Humboldt or Mary's River. Scarcely any fuel here, and the water is strongly drugged with salt and alkali.[33] The coffee made with it is undrinkable. Bad bread. Poor breakfast. Lay down on the ground for a short nap. Started again at 10 o'clock, after giving the animals a feed of hay. Went 4 miles farther S.W., where we found some wells dug, from which we watered our animals. Water sulphurous and a little saltish but more drinkable than that of this morning. These 4 miles were over a flat desert of whitish crusted surface, except here and there a gentle swell tufted with river grass or stunted greasewood. Here we rested and hayed our mules till an hour before sundown. While resting here I baked some dough-nuts. We then moved on S.W. over a sand hill and at 2 miles we came to a fork in the road. On our left most of the way was a deep slough of stagnant water, probably an outlet or inlet to the

[33] The Sink proper is actually beyond the wells that Reid notes four miles after passing this spot. All diarists on the route wrote feelingly about the famous Sink of the Humboldt, though they were frequently confused about its exact where-abouts. See Shaw (p. 172): "A veritable sea of slime, a 'slough of despond,' an ocean of ooze, a bottomless bed of alkaline poison, which emitted a nauseous odor and presented the appearance of utter desolation." The distance traveled from the City of Rocks to this spot was approximately 480 miles.

sink. The right hand road is the old trail to Truckee Lake and Pass.[34] The left hand is said to be "Chiles Trail" crossing the Sierras some distance south of the Truckee Pass.[35] It is said to be 20 to 40 miles farther but a better road. Dr. White here leaves us going the old road with Waldo's train. We take to the left. Turner has a guide book giving the distance to "Pilot River" 25 miles from the sink. And on this road we expect less desert.[36] Kept on for an hour or two after dark, and on passing a point of mountain on our left,[37] we turned south. About 10 o'clock the mules gave out and we halted for the night. Total 27 miles. Our bed on a crust of whitish sand or clay.

Searls, whose diary entry is incorrectly dated August 26, writes: "Sink of the Humboldt—sink of everything that is human and humanizing!

"We have absolutely used up a good-sized river! Have run it into the ground! It is gone! . . . The thermometer indicates 140 on this arid plain. I never felt the heat till now, as reclining under the wagon, I look out over an arid, burning waste.

"The whole atmosphere glows like an oven. The water is bitter and nauseous. Off to the southwest, as far as the eye can extend, nothing appears but a level desert. This we must cross! Through its burning sands we must toil! Fate decrees it! A hundred dead animals around us admonish haste! Not a particle of food for our stock! We only pause here until night, to start for the Carson."

[34] The Truckee River was also known as the Salmon Trout, the name given it by Frémont in 1844 (*Report of the Exploring Expedition*, p. 316). Moving west on the Truckee route, emigrants could fill their kegs halfway along at the Boiling Springs, but their trail over the Sierra through Donner Pass was more difficult than the Carson route. The forks of the trails are near present-day Parran, Nevada.

[35] The Carson route, opened by Joseph Chiles in 1848; there was no good water at all on the forty miles of desert crossing.

[36] The river is the Carson River. The guide most commonly used was produced by a Mormon, Ira Willis, at Salt Lake City in 1849 and sold along the trail. See Ira J. Willis, pp. 193–207. Turner probably was not using the Willis guide, however, since Willis did not mention "Pilot River," and spelled Chiles as "Childs." Chiles, however, did state incorrectly that there was less desert on this crossing. The train Dr. White joins here almost certainly has William Waldo of Missouri as its captain.

[37] The Mopung or Mosquito Hills.

Across the Sierra Nevada to California

September 10–October 7

On the final stage of the journey, the Pioneer Line begins the trek to the Carson River. Halfway across the Forty-Mile Desert the wagon train breaks down, and the unharnessed mules are driven across the waterless stretch to the river. Like most of the able-bodied passengers, Bernard Reid leaves the Pioneer Line at the river to trudge on foot across the Sierra Nevada. On September 18 he reaches the summit of the great granite barrier. Descending the Sierra, he passes well-known landmarks like Tragedy Spring and Camp Creek, and reaches Pleasant Valley in California on September 21. The diggings at Weber Creek, near what is now Placerville, are only a few miles beyond.

A remnant of the Pioneer Line rests at the Carson River until at least September 23, when a few of the carriages leave to cross the Sierra Nevada. Bernard Reid waits at the diggings until the train arrives on October 10, carrying sick and dying passengers. Thirteen men had died by the time the Pioneer Line reached the Humboldt Sink; another nine die of scurvy on the final leg of the journey or soon after their arrival at the goldfields. The skeleton train sets out for Sacramento on October 12 and arrives two days later. In Sacramento only eight Pioneers, including Reid, board a schooner for San Francisco, the destination on the Pioneer Line's tickets. On October 21, 1849, Reid arrives in San Francisco, 160 days after leaving the campground outside Independence.

The Pioneer Line spent 35 days (September 10–October 14) on the journey from the Humboldt Sink to Sacramento. On October 7 Bernard Reid concluded his diary at Weber Creek, 28 days after he left the Humboldt.

Monday, September 10. Called up and ready to start at dawn. At daylight saw a large plain before us stretching southward and eastward, without any appearance of vegetation. Just before entering it we passed through a region of mounds and little conical hillocks rising up all over the plain like hay-cocks, each crowned by a tuft of greasewood. This barren plain is bounded by a chain of mountains on our right bearing S.E. by S. and by another behind on our left bearing E.S.E. and terminating near where our trail passed. A third chain is dimly seen in the distance through the haze bearing apparently N.E. and S.W.[1] In 5 or 6 miles the mules were so weak and broken down we had to rest them. We had no breakfast this morning, having no water to make coffee and no bread but the bad bread of yesterday. After taking a short nap, Bonnell, Brewster and I started off ahead of the train to reach the river. Talked of an arrangement to leave the train and push on to Sutter's Fort on foot. A little farther on we found some abandoned wagons. On one is written "20 miles to Salmon Trout River."[2] Road becomes very deep and sandy. As we advance we find dead oxen, remains of wagons, carts, harness and baggage strewn along the trail in profusion. Panic had evidently overtaken the emigrants ahead of us. In their distress, panic, loss of cattle, hunger, thirst and fatigue, they seem to have cast everything away to save life.[3] We begin to fear our guide book has deceived us, and that we have made a fatal mistake in the road. Farther on we met a courier from Turner, who was in advance, directing Moses [the wagon master] to leave everything but the carriages, the passengers, and their necessary bedding and provisions for a few days and push on with all the stock to the run to save them from total destruction. Bonnell and Brewster propose that one of us go back for our baggage and the other two to go on to the river and all three get ready to strike out tomorrow for Sutter's Fort. I propose to Brewster to divide our effects before starting and cease to be partners, but still travel in company as was proposed. We still move on hoping to find some wells of drinkable water. We had passed some that

[1] The chain of mountains on the right is the Hot Springs Range. On the left is Trinity Range; it appears to run east-southeast because Reid is looking head on at the tip of the range, but actually it runs from north to south. The range in the distance is the Stillwater or Sink Range.

[2] The Salmon Trout was another name for the Truckee River. The emigrant who wrote this information on the wagon most likely was using the Ira Willis guide, which mistakenly called the Carson River the Salmon Trout.

[3] Cf. Harker, pp. 58–59; and Wilkins, Sept. 12, who wrote: "I counted 163 head of dead stock oxen mules and horses, 65 wagons, some of them entire, others more or less demolished, about 70 ox chains, yokes, harnesses, trunks, axes and all minor things I did not count."

were very salty. We soon met another courier from Turner telling of a well a little farther on, which, if cleaned out, might do for watering the stock if the whole train could be forced to that point. We moved on to it, and although the water was a little salt and sulphurous, I got down in it (it was as deep as a grave) and drank copiously. This was about 6 miles from the last halting place. Several half dead oxen were lingering around the well. Soon other passengers began to come up, and some of them dug another well. Then one by one the carriages and wagons came up at long intervals, hauled by mules half dead. The last came in late in the afternoon. Made some slap-jacks and had something to eat. Was very hungry as well as thirsty. Turner returned with word that it was still 18 miles without water to the river! Fearful prospect for the train. At dark the best mules were hitched to the carriages. Bedding and provisions were put in. Every one able had to walk, and the mules were all taken on,—leaving the baggage train with Green [the teamster boss] and 4 or 5 teamsters to guard it.

Brewster and I remained to arrange our affairs—select what we wish to take with us and pack away the balance. Slept well all night in the silent corral. Seemed desolate and forsaken. Tied pony to a wagon and fed him hay,—giving him sparingly of water. Total today for us 12 miles.

Tuesday, September 11. Up at dawn. Watered pony with water drawn from the well last night and allowed to settle. Filled canteen with same,—tastes tolerably well. Mr. Hawxhurst and [son] Robert kindly invited us to breakfast with them. They, with Major Van Wight and Mr. Updyke, are the only passengers left with the [baggage] train,—being unable to walk on last night. They feel disheartened. We get our baggage and begin to assort it. I have an explanation with Brewster.[4] I propose to value the pony and his equipment at cost and draw lots for them,—the winner to carry some 20 lbs for the other. Brewster won. We cast lots for

[1] In his journal on this day Reid recalled telling Brewster of his conclusion that the arrangement made in St. Louis for the two men to form "a sort of companionship" while in California would have to be given up, as they were not "sufficiently congenial." See also Reid, "California Gold Rush Letter," p. 228; and Reid to James V. Reid, Nov. 27, 1849. Reid told his brother: "Our relation to each other is still friendly—nothing more. I became better acquainted with him [Brewster] than I was before, and concluded we would not do for partners or intimate associates as was at first our idea. The trip is the best 'developer' of human nature that could be invented."

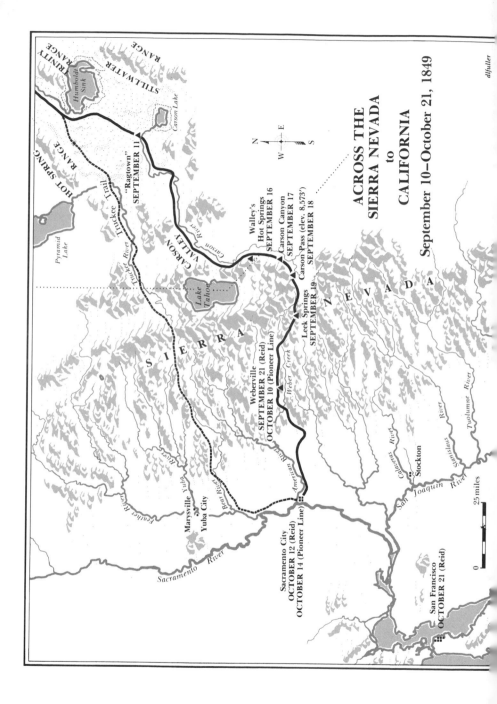

ACROSS THE
SIERRA NEVADA
to
CALIFORNIA

September 10–October 21, 1849

TRINITY RANGE

STILLWATER RANGE

Humbolt Sink

Carson Lake

HOT SPRING RANGE

Pyramid Lake

Truckee Trail

Truckee River

"Ragtown"
SEPTEMBER 11

CARSON VALLEY

Carson River

Walley's
Hot Springs
SEPTEMBER 16

Carson Canyon
SEPTEMBER 17

Carson Pass (elev. 8,573')
SEPTEMBER 18

Lake
Tahoe

N E V A D A

S I E R R A

Leek Springs
SEPTEMBER 19

Weberville
SEPTEMBER 21 (Reid)
OCTOBER 10 (Pioneer Line)

Weber Creek

American River

Feather River

Yuba River

Marysville
Yuba City

Bear River

Sacramento City
OCTOBER 12 (Reid)
OCTOBER 14 (Pioneer Line)

Sacramento River

Calaveras River

Stockton

Stanislaus River

Tuolumne River

San Joaquin River

San Francisco
OCTOBER 21 (Reid)

0   25 miles

dfuller

some other articles also—and made lists of the results. Packed away in the wagon the balance of our baggage. Packed on the pony what we had selected. Got something to eat from Mr. Hawxhurst. Bade them all good bye and started off about 2:30 p.m. Passed on our way many dead cattle and deserted wagons. Trail still bears south. In 6 or 7 miles we were surprised to find all our carriages and about 20 passengers either sick or attending those who were sick. The mules and other passengers had gone on to the river, still 12 miles away. Here was a well of clear water, but strongly impregnated with salt. Made tea of it but it was very bitter. Dr. Speer and Mr. Woolley kindly gave us some bread,— took a piece along. Remained here an hour or two making some further arrangements. Saw poor Mr. James delirious and nearly dead. He could hardly live anywhere,—*here* he must soon die. All, but the sick especially, suffer extremely for water. Mr. Bonnell having gone on ahead without blankets or any baggage, I take his bedding on my back. Got an ox team to carry his carpet bag to the river. Bidding all good bye at dusk we took to the road again. The road becomes terribly heavy with sand. No wonder the exhausted mules could not drag the train along. The stench of dead oxen still assails us at frequent intervals. We soon met Andrews on horseback going back to the train to prepare for packing. He had good water for the sick at the carriages. I was very thirsty but abstained for their sake. He told us that Turner, Rogers and others were coming with water and with mules to haul down the sick. In an hour we met them but did not drink. My load was heavy,—but even without a burden the toil of wading in the sand would be great. We passed some ox teams doing their utmost to reach the river, but in spite of the drivers' shouts and blows the poor animals were falling one by one in their tracks. Farther on we overtook and passed Squire [David] McCollum. He told us he could not stand it much longer without water. At about 10:30 we caught sight of trees that denoted water and soon came to the river bank.[5] Oh, how grateful to man

[5] The campsite at the Carson River would become known as Ragtown, apparently because emigrants hung their washing there after the desert crossing; it was about seven miles west of present-day Fallon, Nevada. The men carrying water to those stranded on the desert were passengers, with the exception of Turner.

and beast those clear delicious waters. The desert was past at last and we were in paradise. While we were resting on the bank McCollum struggled up crying "water! water!" I called him to come to us, took our large canteen to the water's edge, filled it and brought it up to him. He grasped it convulsively—and to my caution to drink judiciously he replied—"Yes, I will drink judiciously, *but I will drink it all*,"—and he did. We left him to enjoy his draught and guided by a light in a grove of cottonwoods, we found the advanced "Pioneers," bivouacked and mostly asleep. We waked up Bonnell, who was very glad to get his bedding and to hear of his carpet bag. He had intended to walk back for them in the morning. Got some hard bread, broiled a slice of bacon on the coals and ate a slight repast. Then spread our blankets under the trees near the fire, and slept soundly, with fatigue for an effectual opiate.

Total today 18 miles.

Searls, whose entry in his diary is incorrectly dated September 3, writes: "Left sink of Humboldt . . . and journeyed steadily but slowly all night, and . . . encamped on the barren desert to avoid travel during the excessive heat of the day. I was attacked with a light fever and have only a kind of dreamy recollection of the silence and the heat. Started again at sundown and by 3 a.m. had reached a point within eight or ten miles of the Carson, where we had struck deep, loose sand in which the animals floundered for a time and then, overcome by exhaustion, gave up and could be urged no further. A few fell and died in their harness and the rest were turned loose and started for the river. Our passengers soon abandoned the train also and, on foot and as best they could, made their way to the Carson. Five or six of us were sick in the wagons and were perforce compelled to remain.

"Charles [Mulford] stayed with me and a few other friends of the sick also remained. We remained without water until daylight . . . when Rogers came out with water in canteens, and on Friday, eight of the best mules having been sent out, we were all placed in a single wagon and hauled in."

At dusk on September 11, James Wilkins "came up with the pioneer wagons left on the road, their mules being unable to drag them further. they had taken them out and drove them on to the river to recruit. the passengers those that were able walked on. but there were a great many sick, and unable to walk. these had to stay with nothing but salt water to drink. amongst them a Mr. James was expected to die with the scurvey. they like us had nothing left but bread and bacon, and for these they were indebted to the ox teams on the road. three dollars a pint was offered for vinegar.[6] A soft heavy deep sand commenced here, and continued to the river . . . here we met Turner going back with a few mules to fetch one of the wagons containing those most severely sick."

Wednesday, September 12. Got breakfast for 50¢ at Wilcox's train, close by. It was spread at the root of a big tree. Had sugar in our coffee and pretty good bread. Ate heartily,—having experienced no bad effects from our late bad water which had sickened so many. Took a good river bath before breakfast. The water clear and cool on a bottom of sand and pebbles. This, as I anticipated from our southerly course across the desert, is Carson River instead of Salmon Trout. It flows from the Sierra Nevada range eastwardly into Carson Lake,—which has no outlet. Willows line its banks and groves of cottonwood flank the willows. Good grass two miles below. Got a copy of a guide, across the mountains following up the river some 90 miles.[7] At 8 o'clock Turner brought in a wagon load of sick. They were carried into shady places, and supplied with water and wholesome food. Employed the day preparing my pack for an early start tomorrow. Pack 17 lbs of clothing & traps [belongings] in my india rubber bag, and blankets 8 lb,—making 25 lb, which with my blanket coat are to be put on the pony. My provisions and gun I shall carry on my back. Got some hard bread from the commissary and a small piece of bacon. We got the cook where we breakfasted to bake up about 20 lb of flour for us. It made 69 nice light biscuits, which we divided among four of us,—Capt. Jack O'Brien having joined us. In the evening Dr. Pierson also volunteered to go with us. We 5 cooked supper together after dark. The night was warm and my slumbers were broken.

On September 16 James Wilkins noted in his diary that "Mr. James of the pioneers died and was buried yesterday, 'with a blanket wrapt

---

[6] Vinegar was one of the preventives against scurvy. Writing from Sacramento, McCollum said that "nearly half the passengers in the Pioneer Line . . . have had the scurvy." See McCollum to J. H. Lund, Oct. 20, 1849, in Bidlack, ed., *Letters Home*, p. 34. In his journal (pp. 113–14) Reid described the symptoms of scurvy: "The principal symptoms of land scurvy are a yellowish discoloration of the skin, the gums shrink and the teeth loosen; the joints contract and stiffen,—and a sort of dry rot sets in, whose duration is longer or shorter according to the constitution of the victim."

[7] Judging by Reid's identification of landmarks ahead on the trail, he is using the Ira Willis guide.

around him.' what a tale of suffering and neglect he could tell, if the dead could speak. Turner offers 500$ to any one that will fetch in his provission wagons 3 in number and about 16 miles out, but no emigrants have teems enough to do it."

On September 19 Wilkins continued: "It has been observed on this road that a man may have travelled to Santa fee and Chiwawa, and yet derive no information necessary for a trip to California. Of this I suppose Mr. Turner can bear witness. speaking of Turner, Mr. Garritt of the Planters house Peoria told me that he offered 3000$ to any one that would take his receipts and pay his expenses for this trip, that he had done all that a man could do for the comfort of his passengers, but what could a man do in a desert.[8] he has purchased provissions from the emigrants at an enormous price, that the order passed for reducing every mans baggage to 75 lbs was from a committee of 12 and not from him, that his own private stores that he had laid in to emeliorate the ruggedness of the route, went in the general wreck."

On September 23 Searls, still resting at the Carson River, writes: "We have remained at this point . . . to recruit our teams which have come to be mere wrecks; to procure as best we can provisions from passing emigrants and to give rest to the sick.

"I am suffering from an attack of what promises to develop into a case of scurvy. Dr. Hutton is down with the same disease. Mr. James died from a like attack the other day and unless we move soon or obtain relief in the way of more suitable food and medicines, a first class cemetery would be a paying investment at this point."

Thursday, September 13. Got up at dawn and went to work getting breakfast and completing our preparations for the journey. Then adjusting the pony's pack and strapping on my own and slinging my rifle, we bade good bye to all around and filed off— a nice little party of 5, with the pony to bring up the rear.[9] Kept up the left (or north) bank of the river—here and there cutting off bends. At 12 miles (estimated), we halted for noon, where the road leaves the river for 12 miles. At this point Brewster and I finally adjusted our affairs, he giving me eight dollars cash and his due bill for $128.00.[10] Pushed on again at 3 o'clock. The next

[8] "Mr. Garritt" is passenger A. O. Garrett.

[9] Reid, his messmates A. C. Bonnell and John Brewster, and Capt. J. J. O'Brien and Dr. O. H. Pierson, all passengers.

[10] Reid had paid for the pony and the two men's equipment in St. Louis; now Reid and Brewster adjust the sum owed by Brewster, who had given his note for 100 dollars to Reid for equipment on June 14. Reid apparently received only 50 dollars in payment from Brewster, and that only some weeks before he sailed for home on September 1, 1852. See John A. Brewster to Bernard Reid, July 16, 1852; and notes at end of Reid, diary, 1851–52.

12 miles of sandy road among the hills made hard walking. On the way we passed over half a mile of beautiful smooth white level basin,—looking like a fairy lake surrounded by steep rough hills. Reached the river after sundown. Found a placard put up by P. W. Thruston, of Kentucky, describing a new road along the river above this, instead of the 20 or 25 miles drive across the desert.[11] Half a mile further halted at the camp of an emigrant party of two wagons from Livingston County, Mo. They furnished us utensils and we cooked our supper at their hospitable fire,—rice, chocolate, bacon and our excellent biscuit. Such was our first supper on our march, and our keen appetites did justice to it. After supper Capt. O'Brien sung some songs assisted by Dr. Pierson. Turning pony loose among the willows and short grass we spread our blankets and slept soundly till daylight. Passed 17 wagons on the way. Total distance 24 miles.

Friday, September 14. Bade our Livingston County friends good bye at 6:30 a.m. and took the new or left hand road. Two miles up found a train in which was Capt. Ankrim, of Pittsburgh, who left home the Captain of a party of nearly 300 men. They are now all scattered and he is now the hindmost man of his whole company on the road.[12] The first 9 miles are heavy sand—then enter river bottom and find meadows of beautiful rich grass. At 10 miles we rested an hour under a spreading cottonwood, and the course of the river all along is marked by a line of these stately trees. On starting again Bonnell, O'Brien and Pierson stumble on a sack of clothing, mostly new. The sack was marked "David Taylor." They helped themselves to coats, trousers, etc., but I declined to share in the find. Some distance farther we crossed to the south bank of the river. Passed several patches of good grass, and halted at sundown at a camp of Irish miners and their families from Dubuque, Iowa,—who extended to us the

---

[11] Cf. Wilkins, September 19, who wrote that on September 17 he saw the same notice put up by "a philanthropic Kentuckian" who had returned along the trail to pass the information; one of the men in Wilkins' party thought the man "a fool for his pains." The philanthropist was probably a member of the prominent pioneering Thruston family of Kentucky.

[12] On March 24, 1849, the *Missouri Republican* reported that a steamer had arrived from Pittsburgh, Pennsylvania, carrying a company of 250 men led by Ankrim, a Mexican War veteran; the newspaper believed that it was the largest company to leave for California in 1849.

same hospitalities we had met with at our last night's camp,— and gave each of us in addition a cup of coffee with cream and a piece of good light bread before our own supper was ready. Turned pony into a patch of good grass along with another pony already picketed there, believing that he would not leave his good fare and good company; but about bedtime the other pony was removed and ours started down the road at a trot. Brewster and I started after him on the run and at the end of three miles gave up the chase in despair. The night was very dark, and willow thickets were abundant. We expected to have to lose a day searching for him tomorrow, when all at once we heard him sniff and found him. The night grew cold, and I slept poorly. Passed 13 wagons to-day. Total distance 26 miles.

Saturday, September 15. Up before dawn. Breakfasted and off at 6. The morning chilly till after sunrise. In a little distance we found in a grove Rumsey, Treadwell, Davidson and eight others, all on foot. They had travelled all night and had just halted. At 10 miles we crossed back to the north bank of the river and made a short halt. Here we strike the right hand road which had come down to the river a short distance back. The trail now ascends a pretty steep hill and crosses a juniper and sage plain of 10 miles, then strikes the river again at a bend. In a cottonwood grove 2 miles up we found a train from Mercer County, Mo. We bought of them 5 lbs of bacon, and prepared our supper in their cooking utensils. Trees are growing rarer on the river's bank. Total today 22 miles.

Sunday, September 16. As the river comes through a cañon here the trail turns northward through a gap leading into a side valley, which we follow five or 6 miles and come to the river again, where the valley widens into an immense level meadow of high grass intersected here and there with small rills of clear cold water gushing from the foot of the mountains and irrigating the plain.[13] The borders of some of the rills are quite boggy. Very few trees appear in the valley, but clumps of willow are abundant. At the noon halt I bathed my feet and found them swollen. In the afternoon passed some very hot springs near the foot of the mountain.[14] Their waters uniting some distance below form

[13] Reid is moving up the Carson Valley in Nevada.
[14] These springs now are called Walley's Hot Springs, a mile or so south of present-day Genoa, Nevada.

a sulphur lake or bayou. The mountains in view today begin to be clothed with pines and other evergreens.[15] When it was near dark the pony mired badly in a boggy slough. Had difficulty in getting him out. Halted for the night in the plain, and gathered a large pile of sage to keep up a fire through the cold night. Capt. Jack gave out half a mile back and had to be helped to our camping place. Picketed pony near us. While at our supper of crackers and tea a stranger without a coat presented himself,— with a gun on his shoulder and a fawn that he had killed across his back. He was a Mr. Sanford from Boston, attached now to the Rough & Ready train from Missouri ahead of us. He was out in the mountains hunting—got benighted, saw our light and in coming towards it got bemired in the same slough that our pony got into. We shared our tea and crackers with him and he remained with us till morning. We stood guard tonight by turns, as several notices have been stuck up, warning emigrants of indian depredations in this valley.[16] False alarm towards morning. Total today 26 miles.

Monday, September 17. Last watch called us at 4 a.m. Start before breakfast in order to overtake Sanford's train to buy provisions and borrow their cooking utensils. Rumsey's mess passed us as we were getting rigged up. Kept along near the base of the mountain, crossing several more mountain rills. At 7 miles overtook the Rough & Ready train just about starting. Got some of their bacon and flour and the use of their tea pot and frying pan, and had Sanford with us for breakfast. We had good pancakes. The river[17] forks about opposite to us, and pine trees displace the cottonwood on both branches. Heretofore we have been bearing a good deal south of west. We now follow the north fork in a westerly course. The valley is now much narrower. We soon ascend a hill and turn down into a romantic glen. There were the stately pines—the steep mountain sides—the subdued sunlight—the foaming torrent tumbling and roaring over its rocky bed. Here begins a cañon, of which the first mile or two is pretty and shady, with a good road,—but presto, what a change!

---

[15] Reid is viewing the Sierra Nevada.

[16] The detested Digger Indians are again the source of concern; all diarists on this route wrote about them. Cf. Decker, July 24; Pritchard, July 30; Tiffany, Aug. 8; and Wilkins, Sept. 21.

[17] Still the Carson River, near the present-day Nevada-California border.

A gold rush drawing of Pass Creek or Carson Canyon shows why Bernard Reid described it as a "hell-gate" for wagons. One of the two "rude wooden bridges" he crossed can be seen in the foreground. *Courtesy: California Historical Society.*

Steep pitches up and down—appalling rocks,—stumps and logs, —sudden bends—all make the worse piece of road I ever saw or could dream of. How will our wagons ever get through such a hell-gate?[18] But it is grandly romantic. The lofty crags overtopping our way on both sides—almost shutting out the sky— the stately trees—the cool seclusion of the spot, could not fail to excite the admiration of the lover of nature. In 7 miles of hard toiling we get through the cañon, having on the way crossed the roaring torrent three times—twice on rude wooden bridges. We emerged into a valley, still narrow, but nearly level, with a good road and some patches of grass.[19] Six miles more brought us to the camp of the Rough & Ready train. We camped near them, bought bread of them and had a good supper and a blazing fire to keep us warm. Capt. Jack gave out again this afternoon, and I carried his pack in addition to my own, while the others helped

[18] This is Carson Canyon, then called Pass Creek Canyon; the west fork of the Carson River flows through it. Woolley (p. 7) recalled that it took the Pioneer Line wagons two days to negotiate six miles of the rocky pass. Cf. Hixson, July 29; and Tiffany, Aug. 16, who described the canyon as "a frightful chasm."
[19] The bridges in Carson Canyon supposedly had been built by Mormons in 1848; see Decker, Aug. 2; Pritchard, Aug. 4. The trail emerges from the canyon into Hope Valley.

him along. Some of the R. & R. train had gone back to the cañon with pack mules to assist a Frenchman, with his wife and sick boy, whose team of two horses gave out in the pass, returned with them sometime after dark—but the whole party were nearly frozen with the bitter cold since sundown. Boaz and Candie overtook us today.[20] Total today 26 miles.

Tuesday, September 18. The summit of the great sierra looms before us and must be passed today. Keeping up the mountain stream three miles brought us to a small lake nestled among high precipitous crags. The margin of the lake, called in some guide books "Red Lake," is fringed by a growth of rich grass. Passing around on the left or south side of the lake we began the ascent of the first mountain or main dividing ridge.[21] It was steep and rocky, so much so as to make me doubt whether the pioneer wagons can ever be dragged over it. The ascent is between one and two miles. From the summit the eye takes in a stretch of country extending westward in a succession of mountain peaks, hills and ravines far toward the Pacific Ocean. I could not help feeling joy at the thought that the great barrier was passed at last and we could now look down into the land of promise. But another high mountain was yet to be climbed,—a spur of the main dividing ridge. Descending 3 or 4 miles by an easy slope brought us to a small valley gemmed by another mountain lake having an outlet to the west.[22] Here we made a short noon halt, then turned southward up a high ravine ascending considerably. 3 or 4 miles brought us to the foot of the crest of the ridge. In some places it was covered with snow to the depth of 10 or 15 feet. Another mile or two of steep climbing brought us to the summit.[23] We were now on a very high point. Much higher than the

[20] In his journal Reid rewrote this incident, stating that he and his party met the French family on September 17 and helped them, though they were unable to provide them with animals. On September 18, according to the journal, the Rough and Ready train went back along the trail to rescue the family. Boaz and Candie or Candee are Pioneer Line passengers.

[21] The first summit (Carson Range) of the Sierra Nevada; this ascent is made over Kit Carson Pass, more than 8,000 feet above sea level. The first summit was more difficult to ascend than the second. See Pritchard, Aug. 5; Wilkins, Sept. 28.

[22] Emigrants called this spot Lake Valley. One much larger artificial lake (Caples Lake) now fills this valley.

[23] The final ridge of the Sierra Nevada. Wilkins (September 28) wrote that though the second summit was higher, the road was not so rocky and their wag-

dividing ridge of this morning. The air was rare and chilly although the sun shone brightly, and the prospect in every direction was one of great extent and sublimity. Very few peaks of the whole range towered above us, and the whole country to the east and to the west seemed spread out, like a map at our feet. Two beautiful lakes of limpid water lay in deep recesses a little to the right of our trail as we descended. Our road now lay over rough, winding steeps—sometimes up—sometimes down, till at length in the dim twilight we reached what is deservedly called Rock Valley. Finding a very small patch of it free from rocks and covered with grass cropped very short, we pitched our camp near a rill running through the middle of it. Gathered our pile of wood, cooked our simple meal, and prepared to rest our weary bones. Finding no train here as we expected, it was necessary to keep watch by turns all night for protection against indians that are said to infest this wild region. Capt. Jack and I sat up the first half of the night and Bonnell and Brewster the last. Total today 20 miles.

The Pioneer Line's wagons crossed the first summit of the Sierra Nevada on September 30, and the second the following day. In his diary entry of September 30, Searls writes: "I breathe more freely. We have traversed the Carson River to the mouth of the worst cañon opening into the valley and that, of course, we turned into to find our way to the Summit. For eight miles we literally climbed and hauled the wagons by ropes and mules over the jagged rocks which in places were higher than the wagons and perpendicular. At the west of the cañon, we emerged into Hope Valley—rested a day and spent another in getting to the first Summit and were caught in a storm of sleet by which forty mules were frozen to death. We are now in camp by a snow bank under the 2nd Summit, with a prospect of reaching it tomorrow and looking down on California!

"I am deathly sick and must get better soon or *play Moses* by looking at the Promised Land and never entering therein. Hutton is dying. Royer is down with scurvy and a score of others are showing the effects of starvation or, what answers the same purpose, the effects of spoiled provisions that do not nourish. Judging from the effect of scurvy on others, I am good for about three weeks—and then—and then—

"Well, at the end of a week if no better progress is made, I will, if able, confiscate a mule and ride for life.

"October 1st, 1849—The Summit is crossed! We are in California!

---

ons reached the top in only five hours. The summit's elevation is 9,500 feet. See also Hixson, July 31; Hutchings, Oct. 10.

Far away in the haze the dim outlines of the Sacramento Valley are discernible! We are on the down grade now and our famished animals may pull us through. We are in the midst of huge pines, so large as to challenge belief.

"Hutton is dead. Others are worse. I am better."

Monday, September 19. Started at daybreak. 3 or 4 miles came to a small lake in the woods with a steep cavernous bluff on one side. Stop here to get our breakfast.[24] 4 miles further Tragedy Spring beside the trail. Here is a kind of cairn or large tomb walled up and roofed with stone. On a tree near by was this inscription—"To the memory of Daniel Brouett, Ezra H. Allen and Henderson Cox, who are supposed to have been murdered and buried by the indians on the night of the 27th of June 1848."[25] These men were mormons and were at the time of their massacre engaged in exploring and laying out the road on which we are now travelling. Eight miles further over rough hills (the same all day), brought us to Lake or Leek Spring, where we nooned and got dinner for 50¢ each at a wagon from St. Louis travelling with the Holt County, Mo., Company. Scarce any grass here for pony, and a placard on a tree informs us that it is still 50 miles to the diggings and no grass at all on the way. 10 miles further came to Camp Creek, good water but no grass. I had walked on ahead to hunt grass here. Found oak bushes along the road—a sign of leaving the mountains. Found also some strange shrubs and berries on the slope of the hill above the creek.[26] On this slope a splendid forest of pines and firs. Beautiful clouded sunset seen through the tall trees like colored lights breaking through the windows of some vast gothic cathedral,—trees forming the aisles, columns and arches—huge rocks the altars—the hum of bees the only chant. Really impressive. Brewster being behind with the pony, I waited while Bonnell and Pierson went up the hill to find trains that we expected to camp with 3 miles

[24] Reid is at Mud Lake.

[25] Tragedy Spring and Tragedy Creek are sources of the Bear River, one of the headwaters of the Mokelumne River in California. Dale Morgan, editor of the Pritchard diary, writes (p. 170) that the dead Mormons' names were David Browitt, Daniel Allen, and Henderson Cox.

[26] Wilkins, on October 2, noticed at this well-known campsite "a great many new kinds of shrubs and wild fruit"; in 1850 McKinstry (p. 309) identified soap root, the common name for the yucca plant.

further. Capt. Jack, having again given out, stretched himself to rest till Brewster came up with the pony,—when we all started. It was now dark—the hill was very long and steep. I carried Jack's pack—he at first refused to walk—wanted us to leave him to die and go on without him,—we had to drag him along at first by force.—At last we saw the light of a camp fire and were at a camp of Missourians from Jackson county. It was so late we got no supper. Turning pony loose among the bushes we spread our blankets around the fire and slept soundly. Total today 28 miles.

Thursday, September 20. Got enough flour, coffee and bacon from the Missourians for our breakfast without charge. Kept on down the dividing ridge—rather rough road. Pony getting very thin and weak. 3 or 4 miles watered him at a spring a little off the road to the left. 12 miles farther a camping ground to the left of trail near a spring. Here found a Michigan train, with no provisions to spare. They were driving their animals 3 miles down the hill to the left of the road to graze on a patch of grass. The other 3 went on while Brewster and I took the pony down to the grass spot to give him a taste of it. We got a little rice from one of the train. We took our blankets with us to the grass patch. The grass was not plenty but better than none. Cooked our rice supper and spread our blankets at a big pine fire. Total today on the trail 15 miles

Friday, September 21. At daylight climbed up the hill to the trail, cooked our rice breakfast and moved on over the same kind of up and down road we have had for several days. Oaks gradually take the place of cedar, pine and fir. 12 miles to the head of pleasant valley at a spring, where we halted two hours and cooked our dinner, and then started for the gold diggings, 10 miles distant.[27] This valley is narrow, nearly level and timbered with fine large branching oaks. The bluffs and rolling hills that border it frequently present picturesque views,—and altogether it deserves its name, especially in contrast with the rough regions we have lately traversed. Occasionally a spring would rise in the side of the road, but the water is not yet of the best quality. The road crosses some ridges and hollows. At 10 miles we came to several camps of emigrants—then the forks of the road and imme-

---

[27] Pleasant Valley was near two forks in the trail: one led to Sutter's Fort (Sacramento), and the other to Sutter's Mill (Coloma). Reid takes the right-hand fork toward Coloma.

diately below on the right hand road was the *"town,"* at the diggings.[28] It was after dark when we arrived and the camp fires on both sides of the road as we kept along the ravine—the tents and rough log huts scattered here and there among the trees—the busy sounds of hands gathering in from work to their evening meal, was something so different from our daily routine for months back that I could hardly realize the change. We met a good number of our fellow "Pioneers" who had come in advance of us, and at the "Round Tent Tavern" we rejoined our late travelling companions, Bonnell, Pierson and O'Brien. Supper was over but we had one set for us at $1 apiece. B[rewster] got 2 quarts of barley for his pony for $1.00. Supper was of bread, coffee, sugar, molasses, fried ham, and stewed potatoes. Ate very heartily. Table under an awning supported by trees and poles. Landlord's name McNeely. Pony nearly done for. All very tired. Spread our blankets on a parcel of pine chips beside some hewed timber and went to rest. Total on the trail today 22 miles.

Though not at our journey's end [29] we at least are at a place of rest and refreshment. And the balance of our way will be short and easy compared with the long, tedious and difficult route behind us.

Saturday, September 22. Breakfasted at the round tent. Took a walk among the diggings. Some of the miners are making good wages—others barely paying expenses. All seems a lottery. Mended up my old clothes. Bought a pick for $6.50,—wood for a handle for 50¢. Made the handle myself. Got a second hand wash bowl or pan for $1.00,—the selling price of new tin bowls being from $4 to $7.50.[30] Had not money enough left to buy a shovel. I borrowed one from the old emigrant from whom I bought the pan. Selected a spot on the creek bank (this is Weber

[28] At another fork in the trail, the left-hand road led to Hangtown (to become Placerville), and the right-hand road, which Reid took, to Weberville or Weaverville on Weber Creek. Weberville was named after Charles Weber, who made his fortune mining gold at the site in 1848, and founded the town of Stockton. See Edward Gould Buffum, *Six Months in the Gold Mines*, pp. 92–93. The distance traveled from the Humboldt Sink to Weber Creek was approximately 230 miles.

[29] Reid means, of course, that the Pioneer Line's destination is supposed to be San Francisco.

[30] The prices Reid quotes are similar to those in other accounts; new arrivals in California were amazed at the inflated prices for food, equipment, stock, and lodging. Cf. Chamberlain, Aug. 20; Perkins, Sept. 19; Pritchard, Aug. 13; and Wilkins, Oct. 5.

Miners at Weber Creek, the spot Bernard Reid reached on September 21. *Courtesy: Bancroft Library.*

Creek, a tributary of the American River), and began to dig about an hour before sundown. I first cleared away a large pile of rubbish. Then dug down to the rock, and filled the bowl once to pan out just for an experiment. I did not expect I had reached any gold, yet I was surprised to find when I "panned out" at twilight, nearly a dollar's worth of gold dust in the pan. Engage boarding for a week at $18.oo and conclude to remain that long to continue the experiment, hoping to dig enough to take me on to San Francisco. Ferguson and young Cottrel come in the evening and bring word of the death of old Mr. James.[31] Our baggage has lain all day outside by the hewn timber. There is no

[31] Ferguson and Cottrel are other Pioneer Line passengers.

such thing here as putting things away under shelter or lock and
key. Everything seems as safe out of doors as if locked up. There
are very few cases of theft known—probably because they are
summarily dealt with.[32]

Sunday, September 23. A few straggling miners about the round
tent not at work remind me that it is Sunday. A few others are at
work as usual. I walked down the creek valley to try to find some
clear water to bathe in. Rocky cañon. Rich diggings here last year.
Yankee doctor, and two Kentuckians. Found but few miners at
work. Most of them spend Sunday washing clothes, prospecting,
visiting friends, going off to other diggings, loafing about dram
shops, etc. etc. Crossed the hills. Felt lonesome. Hard to realize
my present condition.

Sunday, September 30. —Have been at work all the past week,
and still am $8 in debt for boarding. I dug 50¢ worth on Mon-
day, $1.00 Tuesday, Wednesday $1.70, Thursday $2.00, Friday
$2.00 and Saturday $6.00. Bought a spade on Tuesday for $4.00.
Paid $10 last night in gold dust in account of my week's board. Am
not discouraged yet, but find it very hard work for a little filthy
lucre. Am anxious to get enough to take me to San Francisco to
get letters from home and answer them. Hope to go in one week
more. Mr. Bonnell returned last night from Sacramento City—
boards at the round tent. Spread our blankets together in the
new house. Very airy apartment.[33] Visited the monte room
yesterday. Americans and Mexicans all mixed up in gambling
eagerly.[34] Americans as great gamblers as Spaniards and more
profane while engaged at it. Sick old Mexican. Dirty place. Heard

---

[32] Hangtown, a few miles from Weberville, received its name from the lynch-
ing in January 1849 of three men accused of robbery and attempted murder.
Reid's comment about security is typical of new arrivals' accounts; all seemed to
think that "lynch law" was the reason for the good order. Cf. Lord, Jan. 5, 1850;
McCall, Oct. 13; Parke, Sept. 18; and Wistar, p. 123, who wrote: "The general
honesty . . . is usually attributed to the prompt and severe punishment always
ready for the offenders. . . . The miners are anxious to get back to their work
and the prisoner is not long kept in suspense."

[33] In his journal on this day Reid recalled that the "apartment" was "a new
hewed log hotel, which is to take the place of the tent. . . . The doors and windows were not yet in place and our only roof was the star spangled sky."

[34] Gambling tents and halls were common in all mining camps; cf. Wood,
Nov. 4; and Perkins, p. 195: "There is a bar or gambling house at every step, and
no law to restrain these things." See also Reid, "California Gold Rush Letter,"
p. 231.

the voice of a preacher in the woods. Went to hear him. Very commonplace preacher.[35] Small congregation sitting on the ground. In the afternoon Bonnell and I took a walk among the ravines.

Sunday, October 7. I have worked steadily all week and it has been but a little more productive than the last. I dug—

An unfinished sentence concludes Bernard Reid's overland diary. But in a letter to his sisters, written on October 24, 1849, from San Francisco, Reid recalled his experiences following those first discouraging weeks as a gold miner, and his emotions upon greeting the bedraggled Pioneer Line when on October 10 it arrived at the diggings on Weber Creek:

"Shall I tell you of the journey or of this far-famed land? Of the latter I know but little yet; of the former I know too much, almost, to tell. When I now look back upon it, it appears like a long, dreadful dream from which I have just awakened. As to the 'Pioneer Line' we were all grievously deceived (unintentionally perhaps), by the press and the leading merchants of St. Louis. It proved an infamous imposture; its proprietors swindlers and worse than that, criminals of the deepest die,—for the deaths of several men and the tears of widows and orphans are the consequences of their bad faith, cupidity and inhumanity. . . . The worst came last. The wayside over the deserts of the Great Basin,—the rugged passes of the Sierra Nevada,—and the descent into the valley of the Sacramento, are marked by the graves of the wretched victims of the 'Pioneer Line.' . . . After my leaving the train was the worst time on the passengers. When I went to their camp at Weber's Creek I saw a great change. The well were sick,—the sick were worse,—several were dead. Two of my messmates died.[36] It made my heart sick to see the condition of the train. They had no flour, nothing

---

[35] Cf. Johnson, Dec. 18: "Religion and religious services, like everything else in California, is singular and unnatural. There is preaching occasionally by some Doctor of Divinity or gold-hunting minister; but . . . it is a kind of mongrel preaching, a little of everything and not much of anything."

[36] Dr. C. C. Hutton and W. W. Wattles died on the road over the Sierra; John James had died at the Carson River. Dr. C. H. Wesson, J. C. Hunt, H. Kilburn, I. P. H. Verden, J. D. Royer, W. or J. Bacon, and Andrew Duhring died after arrival at the goldfields. All died of scurvy and all were passengers. Wattles and Duhring were Reid's messmates. Hutchings (p. 193), who saw Wattles's grave, noted that he died on Oct. 3. See lists of dead in the *Missouri Republican*, Dec. 24, 1849; in the Reid Papers; and in Searls, p. 64. See also Reid, journal, p. 113; McCollum to J. H. Lund, Oct. 20, 1849, in Bidlack, ed., *Letters Home*, p. 35. McCollum wrote: "Many on arriving here cannot walk or stand and but few are really healthy or able to walk at present. . . . I advise all men to stay home and not come here." Woolley (p. 7) recalled that he had scurvy and was "too weary and worn out" to mine for gold. For this excerpt, in which some of the paragraphs are rearranged, see Reid, "California Gold Rush Letter," pp. 224–30.

but miserable pinola (parched corn) and bacon—and Turner, with inhuman stinginess procured nothing for the passengers,—nothing even to relieve the sick. One of my messmates had managed to walk from camp to the village, to get something to relieve him, but was too weak to walk back again in the evening. He found no shelter and his bedding was at Camp. In his condition he was much worse in the morning from the exposure. When I found him there for the first time he was very much reduced; his limbs were stiff and painful, he could scarcely move and was little more than conscious. Touched at his pitiable condition I applied to Turner (whose carriage was in the village to take out provisions for himself) and begged of him to take out Mr. Duhring in his carriage to camp where his bedding was, and where his mess would take care of him. Turner refused to do so. I implored him for the sake of the man's life; he still refused, with curses! With difficulty, I got him taken out in an empty wagon the same day,—went out with him,—fixed his bed about him, and stayed awhile till he said he felt better and his messmates promised to take care of him. I found a friend of his at the diggings who undertook to carry out some food that would be good for him and, hoping to see him again at Sacramento, where he could get proper food and attention, started for Coloma.[37] When his friend went out to camp early in the morning poor Mr. Duhring was no more. This is only one of many such scenes that have taken place in our ill-fated train."

Two days after the Pioneer Line reached the diggings, Bernard Reid walked to Sacramento to await the arrival of the passenger train. Sacramento, he told his sisters, "is a large place doing an immense business, and only a few months' growth. It is on the east bank of the Sacramento River, just below the mouth of the American, and two miles from Sutter's Fort, which is now turned into a hotel and hospital. On the river bank is a strip of timber nearly a mile wide, chiefly of large branching oaks, the noblest I ever saw. Right in the timber is the city, few of the oaks being cut away. Their trunks are far apart but their branches interlock, forming a delightful shade. Beneath and among these trees are the houses, sheds and tents composing the city, ranged in regular streets, blocks, etc. 'The St. Louis Exchange,' the best hotel in the place, at which I put up while there, was under an arm of one of these oaks and the sign swung from a limb.[38] But the oddest sight was the shipping at the wharf which, to an observer at a little distance, seemed to mingle its many masts and spars with the living timber on shore. It was a novel

[37] Coloma, on the outskirts of Sacramento, was the site of Sutter's Mill, where gold was discovered in 1848. Reid visited there to find the two sons of Dr. and Mrs. Samuel Merry, friends from St. Louis. See Reid, journal, p. 114; and Dr. Samuel Merry to Bernard Reid, April 28, 1849.

[38] The St. Louis Exchange Hotel had been built only a short time before and was kept by the "brother of Commodore Garrison." See Bancroft, *Works*, XXIII, 449. Commodore C. K. Garrison was a steamship owner and banker who became mayor of San Francisco in 1854.

This sketch of Sacramento City in 1849 shows the ships' masts and spars that, to Bernard Reid, seemed to mingle "with the living timber on shore." *Courtesy: New York Public Library.*

sight, at any rate to me who never saw any shipping before. Barques, brigs, schooners, sloops and all sorts of small craft came to this port,— being at the head of tide-water. Two or three small steamboats also ply between there and the port of San Francisco. The place has had a wonderful growth since Spring but 'the oldest inhabitant' says the site overflows every May,—and if the overflow should come everything would go afloat."[39]

Upon meeting the passenger train in Sacramento on October 14, Reid insisted that Captain Turner fulfill the Pioneer Line's contract to transport him to San Francisco. Seven other passengers joined him in demanding passage to the Pioneer Line's original destination. Captain Turner reluctantly agreed to their claim and bought tickets for the group on a schooner sailing from Sacramento. More than half of the

[39] Reid, "California Gold Rush Letter," pp. 228–29. Sacramento (called Sacramento City in 1849) was settled in 1839 by John A. Sutter (1803–80). With the discovery of gold nearby in 1848, the settlement became an instant city, serving as a port and supply center for nearby mining regions. Spring floods were commonplace and winter floods were not unusual. One of the worst occurred in January 1850, only a few months after Reid's arrival, when about four-fifths of the city was submerged. See Taylor, *Eldorado*, chap. 21; Gray, Nov. 9; Johnson, Sept. 9; and Lord, Dec. 22. For the famous flood see Bancroft, *Works*, XXIII, 453–54; Delano, pp. 290–91; and Morse (1850), p. 62.

"Pioneers" accompanying Reid were suffering from scurvy, though improving with proper diet. Reid recalled in later years that one of them, Dr. G. F. Pitts, had arrived at Weber Creek in "the last stages" of the disease. Another, Walter Hawxhurst, was "by the contraction of his joints, drawn up into a kind of ball, and could have been rolled over and over like a bale of carpet."[40] Embarking from Sacramento on October 16, Reid wrote: "We glided down the beautiful, blue, still Sacramento River till we entered the bay, the first salt water I ever was on. The scenery was pretty and my impressions were new and interesting. The bay was not very rough; the wind was ahead, but we made the port by 'beating and tacking' after a pleasant voyage of five days. The harbor was full of shipping of every size and from nearly all nations; and there on the hill-side before us lay the far-famed town of San Francisco, whose streets were said to be paved with gold. It is a more picturesque than eligible site for a city; a portion of the bay dips into the land in the shape of a crescent and circling around this curving beach is the business portion of the town, the back part of which rises by a rapid slope until it runs up into hills of considerable elevation. The buildings now extend some way up these hillsides and, when viewed from the bay at night, with their windows all illuminated, it looks like a vast and beautiful amphitheatre."[41]

Upon reaching journey's end, Bernard Reid felt little more than relief that he had arrived safely and in good health. The community in "the far-famed town," he continued, "is peculiar, unique and unequalled in any age or clime. It will require years to temper it down and give it a feeling and tone like settled society elsewhere, but I am not qualified to tell you much about it now. I am too new a comer yet to be sufficiently acquainted either with the people or the country. . . . I have hardly yet awakened from my dream to see my position clearly and realize my situation and my feelings. It will require a few weeks of *real life* to bring me to. . . . I enclose you a specimen of gold dust,—the first that I dug. . . . I enclose also a cactus-flower, plucked on the wayside on the Great Prairie; it is a memento of the trip; its hues are yet bright, though it seems an age since I plucked it. I have many more such mementoes. Of the journey, I have yet a thousand things in store to tell you."[42]

[40] See Reid, journal, p. 113; and notes at the end of Reid's overland diary, Reid Papers. Those who accompanied him to San Francisco, in addition to Walter Hawxhurst and Dr. Pitts, were Robert Hawxhurst, A. C. Bonnell, John Davidson, and two other passengers; Brewster remained in Sacramento.

[41] Reid, "California Gold Rush Letter," p. 232. For San Francisco at this time see Bancroft, *Works*, XXIII, chap. 10; Taylor, *Eldorado*, chaps.6, 20; Soulé et al., *Annals of San Francisco*; Gray, Nov. 18. The gold rush turned San Francisco from a village into a cosmopolitan boom town. Its population rose from fewer than 2,000 in early 1849 to an estimated 30,000 by the end of 1850.

[42] Reid, "California Gold Rush Letter," pp. 231, 235.

Editor's Afterword

Editor's Afterword

One of the purposes of this Afterword is to show something of
Bernard Reid's life in the decades following his arrival in California. Another is to enlarge on the claim made in the Introduction that in 1849 the Pioneer Line, the first commercial passenger train, would make a distinctive journey.

Despite its vaunted advantages, the Pioneer Line shared in the
ordeals of overland travel, and Bernard Reid's diary casts in
high relief that common struggle to reach the goldfields. But its
difficulties were compounded by the train's size and commercial
nature. With the Reid diary as the indispensable source, supplemented by other contemporary accounts of this first passenger
train, it is possible to focus here on a neglected aspect of overland emigration: the early experiments with commercial transportation to the West after the discovery of gold.

When Bernard Reid arrived at the Pioneer Line's campground
outside Independence, he was "elated in spirit," like Niles Searls,
"only pitying those less fortunate in their choice of conveyance."[1] His realization that basic mistakes were made preparatory to the journey came only with hindsight.

In the preindustrial West essentials for safe travel across the
plains were reasonable loads, careful selection of animals for
their stamina, and proper care of the stock along the trail. Despite his responsibility toward his dependent passengers, Captain Turner, in the interest of profit, violated two of the princi-

[1] Notes to the Editor's Afterword are on pp. 214–25.

ples for safe travel. The Pioneer Line's "remarkably fine" mules
turned out to be small and unbroken—cheaper on the market
than seasoned mules. A supposedly experienced staff loaded the
wagons with mail and kegs of liquor (presumably for the proposed trading post), as well as baggage and supplies. The wagons became so heavy that extra mules were transferred from the
carriage teams. With just two mules to each carriage, the messes
nevertheless were increased at the last minute to accommodate
additional passengers.

Lumbering along the trail "with all the solemnity of a funeral
procession," the Pioneer Line, as we know, immediately encountered a rain-soaked prairie and the fearful reality of cholera.[2]
Yet when it reached Fort Laramie on June 27, it was only a few
weeks behind the first wave of caravans. Considering its size and
a journey "unfortunate all the way," the train had made fair
progress.[3]

But time was money to the train's proprietors, and the passengers had paid for "a quick trip." Spurred on by "all sorts of
abuse" from impatient gold seekers promised that they would
reach California in no more than sixty days, Captain Turner
drove his mules relentlessly.[4] Even before the train reached Fort
Kearny, some 300 miles along the trail, a number of mules gave
out, their shoulders badly galled. Thus, on the first leg of a long
journey, Captain Turner violated the third prerequisite for safe
travel.

An obvious remedy for the poor condition of the mules was
drastic unloading. Here again the commercial nature of the Pioneer Line affected decisions. Turner had a contract to deliver
baggage and a pecuniary interest in his company's cargo and
equipment. His passengers in turn grumbled about the slow
pace of travel, yet valued their personal effects. The majority
had paid extra for excess baggage, even though the limit of 100
pounds of free baggage was double the weight recommended by
veteran overlanders. As members of such a superior wagon
train, they apparently never contemplated losing their belong-
ings so early in the journey. Turner, therefore, preferred to
sacrifice his passengers' comfort rather than their (and his) be-
longings. After the train left Fort Kearny he urged able-bodied
passengers to walk rather than ride in the carriages, having un-

loaded only a small store of provisions. At Fort Laramie, called "Camp Sacrifice" because of massive unloading by most wagon trains, Turner chose to replace five heavy freight wagons with five lighter ones bought from other gold seekers, unload some articles like lead shot and tents, and discard more provisions, keeping enough for only sixty days.[5] With these modest measures, the passengers seemed confident that henceforth the wagons would move with relative ease.

Within a few days they knew better. West of Fort Laramie overlanders encountered their first really rough terrain. Wagons still carrying excess baggage hastily unloaded on this stretch—but not so the Pioneer Line. As we have seen, the mules faltered under "their hard fare," and passengers no longer grumbled about the train's slow pace or placed such high value on their personal effects. Now they worried about their chances of ever reaching the goldfields at all. Clearly, as Bernard Reid observed, the Pioneer Line was on its last legs and needed reform.[6]

The issue of reform raised perplexing questions for the Pioneers. Because size as well as weight affected mobility and the chances of finding adequate water and forage, most large wagon trains divided on the trail; by the time emigrant trains reached Fort Laramie a dividing "fever" raged. As John P. Reid has demonstrated in a legal study, nineteenth century overlanders clearly understood the principle of concurrent property, and they dissolved their unwieldy organizations according to the rules of property law rather than by force. On disbanding, members divided joint property, and new, smaller groups became owners in partnership of their shares of wagons, animals, and supplies.[7] But the passengers on the Pioneer Line owned only their baggage. One course already adopted by a few disgusted men had been to leave, sacrificing passage money, food, and baggage, and walk or make arrangements to travel with other trains. That was a risky step—too risky for most of the urban Pioneers, who decided to stay with the train. When the Pioneer Line reached the banks of the Sweetwater River on July 11, however, its passengers took matters into their own hands.

Bernard Reid tells us that Captain Turner had induced his wagon master and teamster boss to threaten desertion unless the train unloaded. Turner apparently hoped thereby to persuade his passengers to abandon their baggage voluntarily, as protection against possible future litigation. With the train "unable to budge another inch," the passengers needed no such threat.[8] Emulating members of conventional wagon trains, they convened a meeting, elected officers and an executive committee— and went beyond Turner's expectations. Voting unanimously to cut each man's baggage to 75 pounds, they also applied the restriction to the captain and his staff. They voted as well to discard eight of the wagons, and appointed a committee to "assist" Turner in the future management of the train. Furious at this usurpation of his authority and the loss of valuable company property, Turner nevertheless complied with his passengers' demands—undoubtedly because he was greatly outnumbered by determined adversaries.

Such assertive action by the passengers was the result of peaceful assemblage and majority vote. In a critical situation, with few precedents to guide them and no recourse to the machinery of law enforcement, a heterogeneous group behaved like participants in a town meeting, gathered together to resolve a community problem. Although heavily armed, angry and fearful, the passengers did not resort to violence among themselves or against the captain and his staff. Nor did they commandeer wagons, animals, and supplies and divide into smaller groups. They forced the abandonment of some of the Pioneer Line's property in the interest of the general welfare, but respected the laws of property. Their social behavior vindicates the recent claim by John P. Reid that, because the principles of self-government and law were accepted by nineteenth-century overlanders, there was "less need for violence in the American wilderness" than popular legend has assumed.[9]

Despite such massive unloading at the Sweetwater River, the mules continued to falter. Dozens gave out or died along the trail, and the rest were so jaded that other forty-niners, their own animals weakened by hard travel and inexpert care, exclaimed at their condition. Another critical problem was a shortage of food. Turner had unloaded provisions rather than baggage at Fort Laramie on June 28, allegedly keeping enough for sixty days. But on August 2, when the train reached Soda Springs, supplies were almost exhausted. The "routine of fatigue and exposure" in the weeks that followed increased the passengers' dependence on the captain and crew, and dangerously lowered their morale. By the time the Pioneer Line reached the headwaters of the Humboldt River, its passengers exhibited few traces of their former initiative. There was no resistance on August 21 when Captain Turner vetoed a plan to divide the train and reduce the load, and warned that he would brook no further interference in the management of the train.[10]

Yet even as the hardships assumed nightmarish proportions on the trail along the Humboldt, the passengers clung to their belief in property rights and the rule of law. Although Turner lived in "continual fear" that the men would steal his mules and pack to the goldfields, the steady trickle of passengers and crew who left the train continued to take their chances on foot.[11] And even though the Pioneers remained armed and in the majority, they still refrained from violence against Turner and his staff. As a group, they demonstrated to the end that the frontier did not lead necessarily to lawlessness. The restraints of their social conditioning in the East carried over into the wilderness.

Some of the train's problems might have been avoided if Captain Turner had won the loyalty and cooperation of his passengers after it became clear that the company could not fulfill its contract. David Potter has concluded that the wisdom and character of Captain Frank Smith were the major reasons for the superior performance of the Charlestown Company, a large joint-stock wagon train that reached California in 110 days.[12] But Turner based key decisions on his determination to salvage company profits, and despite one observer's comment that he seemed a man of energy with an almost impossible job, he was obstinate, callous, and frequently drunk. His presence became "obnoxious" to the men, whose resentment increased as they observed that Turner and his staff enjoyed adequate rations and good health. The passengers in turn were a sore trial to Captain Turner. They never let him forget that they had paid for service and a quick trip, constantly complained, and frequently dodged heavy duty.[13] The commercial nature of the Pioneer Line thus hindered the emergence of the wise leadership and cooperative effort essential on the overland trail and characteristic of all efficient and successful wagon trains.

On the banks of the Sweetwater the passengers acted assertively, exercising good judgment and showing firmness of purpose. But that was an isolated incident, too late in its execution. For the most part, the Pioneer Line passengers were ill-suited to frontier life, a fact they had recognized when they joined the Pioneer Line rather than a more conventional wagon train. Because they had no choice, they did learn (with ill grace) to drive, cook, and help the crew, but they never became efficient or ingenious overlanders like so many "city men" in other wagon trains.[14]

But if the Pioneer Line's passengers and management failed to cooperate sufficiently to form a successful wagon train, the passengers did forge strong fraternal bonds among themselves. Historians like John Faragher, Howard Lamar, David Potter, and John Reid have emphasized the importance of institutions and values that promoted social order on the overland trail—the ties of family, religion, or region, and the deeply rooted belief in property rights and the rule of law. The Pioneers lacked those familial, local, or religious ties seen by scholars as the most cohesive bonds. Yet this "incongruous" group of passengers developed a social unity and camaraderie exemplified by Bernard Reid's telling reference to other passengers as "our people."[15]

The Pioneer Line passengers set out for the West at a time when anti-Catholic feeling had intensified, when sectional tensions were aggravated by the Wilmot Proviso and national debate over the extension of slavery, and when abolitionist and temperance advocates had become organized and uncompromising crusaders. Among them were Protestants and Catholics, abolitionists and natives of the deep South, temperance men and a small "hard set" of drinkers. Particularly sensitive in this regard, Bernard Reid noted no instance of anti-Catholic sentiment, and he shared a mess amicably with Protestants; the Pioneer who would become his closest friend, Walter Hawxhurst, was a Quaker. Northerners and Southerners lived in harmony throughout the journey, and in a number of carriages they messed together.[16]

One passing emigrant who observed the Pioneer Line, Dr. Israel Lord, portrayed the "hard set" as "men without character and perfectly reckless." All the passengers who left records of the journey were temperance men; yet none excoriated the sinners in their midst. Bernard Reid and Niles Searls—the former a Catholic and the latter a Protestant—both emerge as genteel, serious young men with prejudices that included displeasure over indulgence in drink and gambling. Yet both were tolerant of the rowdier element in the train. Unlike many overland diaries, theirs are free of religious and regional slurs or diatribes against uncouth companions. Reid writes of "family" tiffs among messmates and of the irritability common among overlanders facing hardship and stress. But throughout the journey there apparently was only one serious quarrel, and that between a passenger and a member of the crew. With fistfighting among male emigrants a characteristic of life on the trail, as John Faragher has observed, the camaraderie among the Pioneer Line passengers was remarkable.[17]

The hardships endured by the Pioneers revealed that their social bonds went far beyond surface amity. Messmates who were strangers in Independence tenderly cared for their sick companions. Niles Searls, who watched two of his young messmates die, expressed concern and compassion for his unfortunate new-found friends. Younger passengers were especially solicitous toward their ailing elders; Bernard Reid was only one who prepared food and helped care for aging Pioneers like John James, dying of scurvy as the train moved along the Humboldt Valley. Passengers did everything in their power to smooth "the pathway to the grave" for the dying, and they buried their dead with simple dignity. Friends stayed on the desert beyond the Humboldt to care for those unable to walk, and the first passengers to reach the river trudged back across the sand with canteens of water for the men stranded in the carriages. Those who left the crippled train at the Carson River—their departure "a sad leave-taking" of their "comrades in travel, toil, and suffering"—were not motivated solely by self-interest. They knew that the surviving mules ("mere wrecks") could carry only the desperately sick passengers and a few healthy men to care for them. Bernard Reid was not the only man who waited several weeks at the diggings in order to help his sick and dying friends as the last few wagons straggled in.[18]

The Pioneers were middle-class men, and the majority apparently held traditional American attitudes toward religion, social order, and acceptable behavior. Any conflicting views about issues central to their lives back in "the States" undoubtedly were submerged in the crucible of shared hardship and the recognition of their frustrating dependency. Their emerging sense of unity most likely was enhanced by a common enmity toward the Pioneer Line's captain. Nevertheless, such social harmony was unusual on a large wagon train. The evidence of community among these men, "tumbled in together" to form a company, seems stronger than that found in wagon trains formed by emigrants with familial or regional ties. Lifelong friendships among the passengers were born along the trail. Surviving Pioneers always felt that they were a special group, forever touched by the shared ordeal of passage on a disastrous pioneering enterprise.[19]

After 1849 no more was heard of the Pioneer Line and the ambitious scheme to establish permanent transportation to and from California. Although apparently less agonizing, the journey of the company's second train proved to be yet another unhappy experience. Originally scheduled to leave Independence in late May, the train finally set out one month later with Mr. Allen, co-owner of the Pioneer Line, as the captain. It made good time across the prairie, carrying lighter loads and approximately seventy-five passengers, and on August 1 reached Fort Laramie. The train arrived one month later at Goose Creek, beyond the City of Rocks, but by then its food supply was almost exhausted. It lost thirty mules in an Indian raid on the Forty-Mile Desert, and when a government relief expedition met the train along the route over the Sierra Nevada on October 15, it was in "a crippled condition." Evidently members of the company struggled on to California so dangerously late in the season with the help of the relief forces.[20]

Despite its failure in 1849, the Pioneer Line was not the only commercial transportation company to emerge as a result of the gold rush. In the following year at least eight entrepreneurs sent out trains from Missouri River towns. A subdued editor of the *Missouri Republican* refrained from any enthusiastic endorsement, but the newspaper hopefully predicted that "the trials of last year" would serve as a lesson and help promote the success of new ventures. Another five companies emerged in 1852, and a few optimists even sent out trains at the tail end of the gold rush, in 1854 and 1856. Only two of these passenger trains—one in 1850 and another in 1854—reached the goldfields intact. All others broke down along the way or abandoned their wagons on the desert. None ever repeated a maiden journey.[21] After the gold rush subsided, overland passage reverted to the "family system" of wagons wending their way west with settlers.[22]

Passenger trains were a phenomenon of the gold rush. In retrospect they were perceived as a "humbug" by their disillusioned customers.[23] But in 1849 the Pioneer Line was hailed as the best scheme ever devised to reach California by wagon. None of the later passenger trains ever received the promotion given to the Pioneer Line's first train. None has left such rich records that contribute to our understanding of the diversity of overland experience.

For the Pioneer Line, California was journey's end in 1849. But what of Bernard Reid, about to begin another adventure in the land of promise? The historian Kevin Starr has written that, as epic experience, the gold rush was both Iliad and Odyssey—an Iliad to the emigrants who suffered hardship and defeat, an Odyssey to those whose western pilgrimage brought hope and exhilaration. For Bernard Reid a long "exile" in "a beautiful prison" became his Iliad.[24] By the time he sailed for home in 1852, Reid was more than ready to embrace a life with stability, roots, and membership in the tribe.

Within a few days of his arrival in San Francisco, Reid found work as a "rodman" for the city surveyor, no mean feat in a seaport teeming with unemployed men returning from the mines in the rainy season. Writing to his sisters on October 24, Reid had exulted in his good health. But he "boasted prematurely."[25] After four days at work he became seriously ill for the first time since he had left the East. As he told his brother James:

Exposure and bad food (the latter more especially) had sown the seeds of sickness in my system, and these needed but the presence of exciting causes to develope them. The sudden change of weather was a sufficient case. I had I hardly know what. I had chills and fever—but not "*the* chills and fever" [cholera] and my fever raged almost to delirium. I never knew before what fever was. I had also some sort of irritation or

San Francisco in about 1849. This idealized drawing conveys the beauty
of the setting that greeted Bernard Reid when he sailed into the harbor
from Sacramento on October 21. It omits, however, the flotilla of deserted ships in the harbor and the "tent city" that housed the gold-
seekers. *Courtesy: Bancroft Library.*

inflammation of the skin that was extremely severe. The Doctor said
these were things I was obliged to suffer, in some shape or other, *to get
cured of the trip*—and to enable nature to get rid of all its bad effects.—
Fortunately for me 3 or 4 of my fellow passengers (one of whom,
Mr. Bonnell, had been my mess mate all the way through; a fellow "voy-
ageur" on foot ahead of the train for nearly 300 miles over the great
Sierra) were boarding at the same House and gave me every attention
and assistance in their power. Without them I would have been bad off
indeed. It is a hard thing to be sick in this country—particularly if you
are penniless and friendless. Let me give you an idea. Sick and without
money, if the hotel would admit you at all you would stand a chance of
dying for want of attention. Everyone is too busy and time is too pre-
cious. Well what resource have you?—the hospitals? Ah, yes, there you
may get medical attendance, food, and nursing—*provided* you can pay
for a fortnight in *advance* at the rate of 5, 10 or 16 dollars a day, according to the kind of accommodation you want![26] This is consolatory to the
poor suffering, destitute vagabond who is turned out or left to die neglected! Well now let me give you an idea of my situation. . . . Our
Hotel, the "Revere," one of the best, quietest and cleanliest in town, con-
sists of a one-story *frame*, about 20 by 60 all in one apartment, with a
front at both ends. This frame is *weatherboarded and roofed with cotton
sheeting*, and floored with a rush-mat spread on terra firma. The roof

was *pitched* since my recovery. However pleasant this kind of house might be in fair weather, you can guess what sort of shelter it would afford to sick or well amid continual rains! It generally rained 12 out of 24 hours—either all night or all day. Our lodgings are on the floor. During the day I had to spread my blanket in one corner, among the baggage, and throw my india rubber cloak over me when the rains began to come down through the roof and ceiling. The doors at both ends continually opening, admitted every other moment a current of damp, chilly air and we were strangers to the luxury of a fire. If, in daylight, I was obliged to go out, for want of the ordinary conveniences, it was necessary to crawl down a steep bank about one square to the beach. On more than one occasion, when there, through excessive weakness I would have to lie like a drunk man for half an hour or an hour on a pile of boards or a bale of hay,—and on my way back to the Hotel perhaps cling to a post or sit down on a muddy wheelbarrow to avoid falling down in the mire. During the stages of the fever, which generally was on me half the time, I was entirely helpless. My hosts and the doctor were kind enough to wait on me for their pay till I should get employment after my recovery. On the 15th [of November] I was better and able to go about, gaining strength rapidly,—but it was not until the 22nd that I succeeded in getting anything to do. I then got into another surveyor's party under the City Surveyor, at the same per diem, and it is likely that we will be kept employed for a fortnight at least, perhaps much longer.[27]

Reid held this job, earning eight dollars a day, until January 1850, and moved to a tent in order to make ends meet in the booming city. Seeking to establish some semblance of his ordered life in the East, he began attending a Catholic church founded in 1849 by two French-Canadian priests, Fathers Langlois and Brouillet; he also studied Spanish in the hope that it would be "of service" in the former Mexican province. Reid frequently saw other Pioneers who drifted to San Francisco from Sacramento, and he cemented his friendship with Walter Hawxhurst, an upright Quaker who had been a prosperous storekeeper in Fort Madison, Iowa.[28]

In February 1850 Reid joined Walter and Robert Hawxhurst and a former acquaintance from St. Louis in a "trading and digging" expedition to the "southern" mines near Stockton, in the San Joaquin Valley. Walter Hawxhurst furnished the capital for goods, and Reid hoped to make a quick profit so that he could realize his hopes of returning to the East in the spring. His hopes were dashed, however, by the venture's failure and a new burden of debt. When the trading partners settled accounts in May, Reid found that he owed Mr. Hawxhurst over five hundred dollars, to be repaid at 15 percent interest.[29] That obligation would shadow his life for nearly two years.

Following his unhappy experience as a trader, Reid turned to panning gold at nearby Woods Creek, a branch of the Tuolumne River (all the time religiously studying Spanish). Finding that the best week of this "slavish" work yielded only thirty dollars, he accepted an invitation to join a mining association formed by forty men who planned to build a dam on the Stanislaus River. Such a scheme was common by 1850. With the flood of newcomers to the goldfields, the best sites were already worked over or preempted, and "placer" mining no longer sufficed. Thus prospectors had begun experimenting with ways to extract gold from untapped sources like riverbeds.[30]

The men in the association "worked like Turks" on the dam. They worked in the water and out of it, Reid wrote, "among rocks and bramble, and lizards, and snakes, and scorpions and tarantulas, and fleas. . . . The sun glared down on us like a hard taskmaster till the sweat would pour and the limbs totter."[31] The venture proved to be yet another failure. Plagued by legal problems over the claim and unable to "turn" the river, the association disbanded in October. Reid resumed panning gold at Woods Creek, but meeting with meager success, he decided to return to San Francisco to seek "more congenial" work. In a letter that echoed the sentiments of many other frustrated gold seekers, the disillusioned Reid allowed his bitterness to surface: "Oh! how bitterly do many curse the day they left home, and swear vengeance upon the whole tribe of editors who deceived them! They come here with high hopes and bright gold dreams —and alas when the charm vanishes they find themselves in the condition of convicts condemned to exile and hard labor. . . . You perhaps have seen in the newspapers that apt etymology of the word California—from the Greek [meaning] *beautiful moonshine!*"[32]

In November 1850 Bernard Reid arrived back in San Francisco "lame, ragged and penniless." His career as a miner, which he had never liked, had ended. But more congenial work failed to materialize. Reduced at first to shoveling sand for four dollars a day, Reid moved on to work as a "roller boy" in a newspaper office. "Who ever heard of an 'Editor and proprietor' becoming a roller boy? Sic transit gloria!" he wrote to his brother James.[33] Yet despite his poor prospects, he declined an offer to teach in a parochial school founded by his pastor, Father Antoine Langlois, because of a continuing "aversion" to teaching.[34]

His "old friend Poverty" drove him in the new year to Santa Clara, a small settlement located near a Franciscan mission of that name and adjacent to the new state capital of San José. Walter Hawxhurst, "friend and partner in journeys and disappointments," had bought land there, opened a store in a frame house near the mission, and sent for the remaining members of his family from Iowa. Hawxhurst offered the younger man a share in the profits in return for help in the store and on the farm.[35]

Reid's drooping spirits revived for a time in Santa Clara. He was "more comfortably fixed" keeping "bachelors' hall" with the two Hawxhursts than at any time since leaving the East, and his descriptions of the domestic round in the neat white house are almost sensuous in their delight with the order and comfort.[36] Reid became intoxicated, too, with the beauty and serenity of the valley he called "the garden spot of All-America":

Winter *here* seems not to hush a note in all that lovely harmony that elsewhere only comes from birds of summer. To the right and to the left, at a goodly distance, rise the blue-tinted Sierras that hem in the valley like a street. These with their varied outline, majestic height, and dark foliage relieve the level sameness of the valley and add a feature of quiet grandeur to the scene. There is no gradual rising and swelling of the plain into hill and mountain, such as we always see at home, so that it is hard to tell where the one ends and the other begins; but the mountain starts up abruptly from the level greensward like a vast barrier intended by nature to defend the lovely Eden at its base.[37]

Reid's euphoria did not last. By the summer of 1851 his life in "so pleasant a Siberia" had become one of "anxious toil." The store failed to prosper, a dry spring had ruined any chances of a good harvest, and he had succeeded in repaying only 154 dollars of his debt to Walter Hawxhurst.[38] Once again he decided that chances for more profitable employment lay in San Francisco, and once again he met with disappointment. After returning to shoveling sand and working part-time in a printing office in the city, he finally accepted a teaching post in the parochial school opened by his pastor, Father Langlois.[39] From September 1851 until he returned home a year later, Bernard Reid would find security, and a measure of contentment, in working for his church.

He remained at the school in San Francisco only four months, returning to the Santa Clara Valley in the new year.[40] In 1851 Reid had become friendly with Father John Nobili, a Jesuit missionary and the founder of Santa Clara College on the site of Mission Santa Clara. Nobili had arrived from Oregon in 1849 with Father Michael Accolti to investigate the prospects for a college in the former province of Catholic Mexico. Accolti, the driving force behind the mission, found the prospects discouraging and returned to Oregon in 1850 on orders to become superior of the Jesuit missions in the Northwest; Nobili remained as assistant pastor of the San José parish church. But toward the end of 1850, an ally emerged in the person of the new Dominican Bishop of Monterey, Joseph Alemany. As head of the Catholic community in California, Alemany was determined to found religious schools in the fast-growing state. In the spring of 1851 he offered the crumbling mission in Santa Clara to the Jesuits. Within a few months, in May 1851, Father Nobili opened the first college in California.[41]

Santa Clara College was "the germ only" of an institution of higher learning. In reality it was a preparatory school for boys from privileged families, including the sons of Peter Burnett, California's first elected American governor and a convert to Catholicism; the school would remain an academy until 1854, when the Jesuit order could spare enough priests for college instruction. In 1851 Father Nobili operated the school with the help of two sickly Jesuits and two lay teachers, and had been forced to turn away prospective students for lack of sufficient faculty. He needed a competent and devout English-speaking teacher like Bernard Reid, whom he offered a position teaching mathematics, English, and Spanish.[42]

With the blessing of Father Langlois (about to leave his order to enter the Society of Jesus as a novice), Bernard Reid arrived at the college on January 3, 1852, as boarders were returning from their Christmas vacation.[43] To his amazement, Reid came to "like

Santa Clara College, on the site of a former Franciscan mission, as Bernard Reid saw it in 1852. The open space in front of the college was a public plaza. *Courtesy: Archives, Univ. of Santa Clara.*

the teaching part . . . very well." But he had "a busy time of it" at the school. After supper each evening he "engaged in familiar scientific conversations" or "exercises in the languages" with the boarders, and on "free" afternoons twice a week he accompanied them on "a pleasant ramble." Since Father Nobili accepted boys from the age of six, promising their parents "affectionate care" under the eye of the faculty, "day and night," Reid found "the responsibility of governing, watching and regulating the boys a pretty heavy and irksome charge." Nor did his duties end there. Though fluent in a number of European languages, the Italian-born Nobili "distrusted his command of good English," and Reid became his private secretary, handling much of the English correspondence.[44] Father Nobili was a busy man in 1852. Mission Santa Clara resembled "Augean stables" after years of neglect and mismanagement. Moreover, an "army of competitors"— squatters and claimants to land and buildings—challenged the Jesuit title to all but the church, cemetery, and a wing of rooms. Much of Nobili's energy was devoted to securing title to all of the mission, and in Reid's words, converting "dark and dingy" rooms "blackened by the smoke and obscured by the dust and cobwebs of centuries" into classrooms and dormitories.[45]

Despite all the activity within the college, few local events disturbed the "peaceful atmosphere," for Father Nobili deliberately sequestered his young scholars from the rude California society he considered a moral wilderness. Isolating the students was not easy, since "swindlers and squatters" milled around the mission, and the "local culture" encouraged periodic revelry on the public plaza outside the college.[46] Despite his Catholicism and new knowledge of Spanish, Bernard Reid expressed little understanding of the customs of "native Californians." Intrigued by the colorful dress of the Mexican men and women who came to the mission for mass on Sundays, he nonetheless thought they made an "odd appearance," and lamented that "not a bonnet is seen in church." Lively pageantry like an Easter celebration in which Mexicans attacked "a *stuffed Judas*" with clubs and swords, seemed irreverent "spectacles" to a conventional product of Anglo-American culture.[47]

In the spartan atmosphere of the college, Reid spent his final months in California. One of the few diversions, besides regular visits to the Hawxhurst family, was an experience that proved to be his "first and last." On June 2, 1852, an earthquake struck Santa Clara, provoking Reid to write a vivid description of the event: "The earth was not jarred or shaken merely, but actually *moved* as though it possessed life and muscle. The motion was from West to East and back again, and resembled the twitching of a horse's flesh when he feels himself annoyed by a fly."[48]

After February 19, 1852, Reid could make plans to return to the East. On that day he made the final payment on his debt to Walter Hawxhurst and received his cancelled note. With free board, a salary of $100 a month, and few expenses at the schools in San Francisco and Santa Clara, Reid had made regular payments to his friend for nearly six months. He continued to save for passage home and for a nest egg, and even taught a class on mnemonics in order to earn extra money. Despite urgent pleas from Father Nobili to remain at the college, Reid was determined to leave California.[49]

As "the privations of a long and weary exile" persisted, Reid had become increasingly homesick—and "home" was Clarion,

Pennsylvania. He wrote long letters to his family, and eagerly awaited letters and newspapers from his brothers and sisters. Moreover, he had decided to finish reading law upon his return, as "a means of earning in some permanent spot a competent livelihood." Sad experience, Reid wrote, had convinced him that it was important to "choose a calling and a settled home and stick to them, in order to get along and be useful in the world." Having decided to end "five years of wandering," he also began making occasional allusions to matrimony.[50]

In California, where the population by 1852 remained predominantly male, Reid had met few young women. So ascetic did he appear to Father Antoine Langlois that his old pastor was "truly unbelieving" when Reid wrote from Clarion about his impending marriage in 1854. Years later Langlois joked to Reid that he thought it would be "a mystical union rather than [a] real marriage," but was reassured when informed of the ensuing birth of children.[51]

Despite his ascetic life, Bernard Reid was ready for marriage. When Walter Hawxhurst's family arrived in Santa Clara in 1851, Reid became "fascinated" with his daughter Jane, a young schoolteacher. But there was one flaw in Reid's warm relationship with the Hawxhursts—they were not Catholic. Since all of the members of the Quaker family refused to be drawn into any religious discussions, Reid despaired of ever leading them back to the "true fold," and was "afraid of falling in love" because Jane was unlikely to convert. He remained smitten with Jane, writing her a sentimental poem and a farewell letter before boarding his ship in San Francisco. But he consoled himself by reasoning that an "unseen hand" had guided him, for Jane's heart was not mellowed by "the touch of true religion" and her expression lacked "a gentle, subdued Catholic look." Having emerged unscathed from the temptations of a misalliance, Reid nonetheless fretted that, back in "the States," no suitable young woman would "unite her destiny with that of a poor, brokendown, unfortunate, returned California adventurer."[52]

Reid was present at the first commencement of Santa Clara College on June 2, and remained in Santa Clara until July 28 to help Father Nobili prepare for the coming year. Returning to San Francisco, he booked passage to New York via the Isthmus of Panama. He sailed as a deck passenger on the *Winfield Scott* on September 1, cheerfully maintaining that the trip across the plains and life in the mines had inured him to exposure.[53]

The ship made good time to Panamá, but its deck passengers spent six nights huddled in wet blankets and unable to sleep because of driving rain; the smell of unwashed bodies and dirty clothing added to their misery. Reid relived, too, the "great fear" engendered by an outbreak of cholera. He retained his robust health, but ten men had died by the time the ship reached Panamá on September 19.[54]

Reid crossed the Isthmus on foot as far as Cruces (a "wretched looking place" about eighteen miles from Panamá), arriving with boots worn to shreds and feet blistered and peeling. At Cruces he took a canoe or "bungo" along the Chagres River to Barbacoas. There Reid transferred to the new railroad, "whizzing along" the river bank through "the dense tangled forest of strange and luxuriant vegetation, flowers and vines." At Aspinwall he boarded his connecting steamer on September 23, with only moments to spare.[55] The manners of the passengers on the *United States* were "swinish," but the "fare and attendance" better than on the *Scott*. After one stop for fuel at Kingston, Jamaica, and a fast but rough voyage with the seas at times like "moving mountains," the steamer reached New York on October 3, 1852.[56] Reid spent four days exploring the city, carrying messages to families of California exiles, and buying a wardrobe suitable for a dignified return to Clarion. Arriving in Pittsburgh ("awfully black looking") on October 9, he greeted his family two days later in "a joyful meeting."[57]

Upon returning to Clarion, Bernard Reid resumed reading law, supporting himself with savings and occasional work as a surveyor. He began, too, the courtship of his first love, Letitia Farran, who by then was twenty-five years old and no longer unreceptive to his suit. Reid's sisters, whose attitude toward their favorite brother was proprietary, believed that Letitia was not the right choice for "our Bernard." His older sister Mary thought Letitia had "plenty of amiability" but was "wanting in 'gumption' and independence," exhibited "dilatory" habits, and lacked spirit and energy. Brother Bernard remained undeterred. His

Bernard Reid as paterfamilias. This photograph, most likely taken early in 1859, shows Reid at the age of 35, his wife Letitia at 31, and three of his children—Anna, close to four years of age, Ambrose at two, and the infant Mary Agnes. *Courtesy: Archives, Univ. of Santa Clara.*

earlier "sentiment" for Letitia had been "cherished fondly" for years, and the very qualities his sisters scorned appealed to a man who favored "a gentle, subdued Catholic look." Letitia also satisfied his desire for a heart mellowed by the "true religion," for she displayed "a deep-seated and active piety." The sister of a priest and a nun, she was even more devout than he. The couple married on February 21, 1854, a few months after Reid was admitted to the bar.[58]

The "thousand cares" of a new law practice and a growing family absorbed Reid's energies for a number of years after his marriage. He estimated that two-thirds of Clarion's population were Know-Nothings and was convinced that his Catholicism harmed him professionally; for some time most of his slender income derived from surveying.[59] His prospects improved when

he formed a partnership in 1857 with one of his former precep-
tors, as firmly Protestant as Reid was Catholic. In 1859 he could
afford to buy a house from his brother John, who was prosper-
ing as a druggist and landowner, and hire domestic help for his
harried wife. By 1861 Bernard and Letitia Reid were the parents
of five children: Anna, Ambrose, Mary Agnes, Charles Vincent,
and John. Reid did find time during this period to help found
the first Catholic church and parochial school in Clarion and to
become, for the only time in his life, active in politics.[60]

Reid had leaned toward the Whigs in the past and had admired Henry Clay for his strong nationalism. After returning to
Clarion he switched to the Democratic party but became increasingly disturbed by political division over the slavery issue.
He did not join the new Republican party, perhaps because of its
sectionalism or its Know-Nothing wing. But in 1858 Reid joined
a minority of local Democrats in a public censure of their party's
acceptance of the Lecompton Constitution for Kansas, a pro-
slavery document that exacerbated the sectional tension gener-
ated by the Kansas-Nebraska Act in 1854. Reid supported Stephen Douglas in the presidential election of 1860, but when
Lincoln won the election he became a "Union man" who admired the president and scorned the "copperhead" Democrats
who opposed civil war.[61] Immediately after the Northern defeat
at the Battle of Bull Run in July 1861, the ardent Unionist recruited volunteers from Clarion County to form Company F of
the Sixty-third Pennsylvania Regiment. Reid was commissioned
a captain and left with his company in September for Camp
Hays, near Washington, D.C.[62] His departure for the battlefield
became the second great adventure of his life.

After months of training in Virginia, the regiment moved under General McClellan to engage in the Peninsula Campaign between March and August 1862. In August Bernard Reid resigned his commission. He was weakened by dysentery, anxious
about his large family, and perturbed about his law practice,
stagnant because his partner had resigned to enter the Pres-
byterian ministry and a replacement had decided to move west.[63]

Dozens of Reid's letters to his wife from camps in Virginia
have been preserved. They reveal him as a paterfamilias with a
loving concern for his wife and children. There is no question

Bernard Reid as a Union officer in the Civil War. His gaunt appearance suggests that the photograph probably was taken in 1862, after Reid served in the Peninsula Campaign in Virginia. *Courtesy: Archives, Univ. of Santa Clara.*

that he was content with his "dearest Letitia," his "true wife," dear companion, and the mother of his "cherubs."[64] The letters are more remarkable for their revelation of Reid's metamorphosis from company commander behind the lines to weary soldier on the battlefield. Those written during the months of training are filled with anecdotes of camp life, accounts of sightseeing

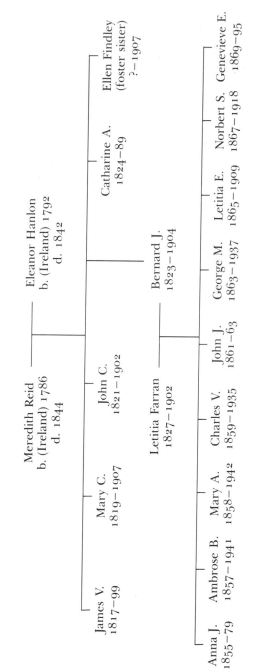

Bernard J. Reid's immediate family.

trips to the capital, or "geographical explorations" of the Virginia countryside.[65] When the regiment finally moved into action, the adventure was over. Reid's letters from the battlefield are filled with anguish and shock.

He did not fear death. Always sustained by his deep faith, Reid serenely believed that if he were killed in battle it was God's will. But he was badly shaken by the terrible casualties, the sight of another soldier shot down by his side, and the ordeal of writing to the families of the dead and wounded young men he had come to know so well. Begging his wife not to be "horror-stricken" by the news that he had killed his first rebel, Reid "shuddered" when writing of his part in taking human life.[66]

After resigning his commission, Bernard Reid settled back for a time into the routine of life as a small-town lawyer. He became disturbed, however, by the extent of "copperhead" and anti-Lincoln sentiment in Clarion during the dark days of 1863. On the "urgent occasion" when Gen. Robert E. Lee invaded Pennsylvania in June, Reid reenlisted in the Fifty-seventh Pennsylvania Militia.[67] His regiment was not dispatched to the East but pursued Gen. John Hunt Morgan, the Confederate raider, through West Virginia and Ohio. When the regiment mustered out after a three-month tour of duty, Reid returned once more to Clarion. He had been promoted to major and served for a time as regimental commander.[68]

Bernard Reid remained in Clarion for the next eight years, building up a practice principally involving land law and litigation over oil production. Between 1863 and 1869 four more children were born—George, Letitia (Letta), Norbert, and Genevieve.[69] In 1871 Reid moved his family to Titusville and in 1874, to Erie, both towns being centers of the Pennsylvania oil industry. After three years in Erie the family returned to Clarion, by then an important oil production field, and in 1883 Reid could write that he enjoyed a comfortable income.[70] In 1900 Bernard and Letitia Reid moved to Pittsburgh, where at the age of seventy-seven, Reid became a consulting lawyer in his son Ambrose's law firm. During the decades spent in Clarion he had been active in civic affairs and in county and state bar associations, and presided at the center of an extended family. His unmarried sisters, who shared a house in Clarion with their bachelor brother John, depended on Bernard for counsel and companionship. Descriptions of Bernard Reid in these years by family, colleagues, and friends include such expressions as "high-minded," "straight as a string," and possessed of "saint-like" patience.[71] He remained a devout Catholic all his life, actively practicing, fostering, and defending his faith.[72]

In 1883 Reid boasted of his "true good wife" and "a family of dutiful and exemplary children."[73] Ambrose and George read law with their father and entered his law firm. Ambrose went west in 1891 for a short time but returned to practice law in Pittsburgh; he eventually became the president judge of the court of common pleas of Allegheny County. Charles Vincent, who also went west as a young man, and Norbert, the youngest son, followed Ambrose to Pittsburgh and settled down as businessmen. Given the piety of Bernard and Letitia Reid, it is hardly surprising that three of their children entered religious life. George abandoned law and in 1893 was ordained as a priest; a decade before Mary Agnes and Letta had become Sisters of Mercy.[74]

But his life had been "not without vicissitudes," Reid wrote to a California friend, Peter Burnett. Three of the nine children died young: John as an infant in 1863; Anna in childbirth in 1879 at the age of twenty-four (her daughter, the first grandchild, died nearly a year later); and Genevieve in 1895 at the age of twenty-six, from heart disease.[75] Bernard Reid had a severe financial setback when a Titusville bank in which he was a stockholder failed in 1877; the family suffered "pinching experiences" for some years as Reid struggled to pay off his share of the debt. Both Charles Vincent and Norbert had difficulties establishing themselves in business. They finally achieved some measure of success, but in 1895 Bernard Reid observed that of his three sons out in the world, only Ambrose was self-supporting.[76] By 1900 Letitia Reid, stout and in poor health, suffered from "nervous tension"; her husband and children were convinced that, on certain subjects, "Mamma's" mind was unbalanced. The gentle, pious matron, with no interests beyond her family and church, quarreled with her sister, a succession of "servant girls," Ambrose's wife Lucy (whom Bernard Reid dearly loved), and any friends and relatives who visited the large family house in Clarion. To the modern mind it could appear that the model wife and mother allowed sternly repressed hostility or jealousy to surface in her old age. Her uncharacteristic behavior caused so much consternation that George, Mary Agnes, and Letta said special prayers, the local priest held a mass for the family, and a protesting "Mamma" was moved to Pittsburgh in 1900 so that she could be nearer some of her children and Mercy Hospital, where Letta nursed as Sister Mary Alphonsa. Letitia Reid died in Pittsburgh in 1902 at the age of seventy-five.[77]

As Reid advanced in age, his participation in two profound national experiences—the gold rush and the Civil War—assumed increasing significance. The tour of duty in the Pennsylvania Militia appears to have left no imprint, but his service in the Sixty-third Regiment of Pennsylvania Volunteers became a source of intense pride. Reid corresponded for decades with former officers and troops of Company F and attended their annual reunions. He joined the Society of the Potomac, was a post commander of the Grand Army of the Republic in Clarion, and in 1896 was appointed judge advocate for the department of Pennsylvania. Reid delivered patriotic addresses for the GAR and wrote letters to local newspapers on his regiment's participation in the Civil War. From 1863 until his death the zealous patriot was known as Major Reid. Two decades after the war he seriously contemplated writing a history of Company F, having collected records on the beloved corps for many years.[78]

The full meaning of his western experience, however, eluded Bernard Reid for a number of decades. Those three years spent in California had remained for him "a time and place possessed in memory." But unlike another aging forty-niner, Howard Gardiner of New York, who recalled that his years in California had been "the happiest in the whole course of his experience," Reid found his memories painful.[79] He had kept in touch with "cherished friends" from the old Pioneer train and from the years spent in San Francisco and Santa Clara. But he remembered the overland journey as a long and dreadful dream, and his exile in "a mercenary and hardened land" as years of weary privation.

With the death in 1856 of Father John Nobili from tetanus, which Nobili contracted after stepping on a nail while supervising construction, Reid "grieved exceedingly" for his "best of friends," and wrote that henceforth the college for him was no longer Santa Clara.[80] It was not until he returned to California in 1886 at the age of sixty-three that Bernard Reid began to comprehend the historical significance of his youthful adventure.

Reid returned alone to California, since Letitia Reid disliked traveling, and his trip on the "iron horse" through some of the country he had crossed by wagon 37 years before was a powerful experience.[81] In San Francisco, a city changed almost beyond recognition, he found some "familiar spots and faces" and spent much of his time visiting the Hawxhursts, the family of former governor Peter Burnett, and men who had been his pupils at Santa Clara College.[82] From San Francisco he moved on to the Santa Clara Valley, living "in clover" with the family of a former pupil, Bernard Murphy, the grandson of Martin Murphy, whose wagon train had been the first to cross the Sierra Nevada in 1844. Writing to his wife from San José, Bernard Reid exclaimed: "O what a change in the valley since my time! Were it not for the everlasting mountains on each side I could not believe it the same I toiled in a generation ago!" Even more startling was his first sight of Santa Clara College. The changes there seemed so remarkable that Reid confessed he felt like Rip Van Winkle. New buildings had been constructed, the number of students had risen to over 250, and the former preparatory school had become a full-fledged college. Only the mission church was "much like itself," and Reid's emotions on entering it were "overpowering." But his visit to the college was "more sad than joyful" because all "the fathers, professors and attachés" he had known in 1852 were dead.[83]

After his first visit the siren call of California became so strong that Reid returned in 1890, 1892, and 1903; only his wife's poor health prevented a visit in 1901.[84] His ties to California were strengthened by the warm hospitality of "true and dear friends" who took him into their homes and "honored and fêted him."[85] But Bernard Reid developed a proprietary interest in the state after recognizing the importance of his participation in two pioneering enterprises—as a member of the first passenger train

Bernard Reid in old age. *Courtesy: Archives, Univ. of Santa Clara.*

to cross the plains in 1849, and as a faculty member of the first college to open in California. He began a collection of records for the college after discovering that its archives contained few records of the "foundation year." He sent to Santa Clara a list of students and faculty present during that first year, a newspaper account of the first commencement, and a brief description of the college that he wrote in 1894. In 1901, when Santa Clara awarded him an honorary degree on the occasion of its golden jubilee celebration, Reid wrote a lengthy memoir of the college as he remembered it years before, proudly signing his reminiscences as "the last survivor of the first faculty." This memoir provides an invaluable account of forgotten events, and vivid descriptions of the men who participated in the founding of California's first college.[86]

On his first visit to the west in 1886, Reid promptly joined the Society of California Pioneers in San Francisco. Over the years he reminisced with fellow survivors of the Pioneer Line like A. C. Bonnell, Robert Hawxhurst, and Dr. R. H. McDonald about the "trying time" they had experienced as passengers on a commercial wagon train. Learning that Reid had kept a diary of the overland journey in 1849, these aging survivors apparently expressed intense interest in its contents. In fact, Reid wrote to his wife from California in 1890, Dr. McDonald's brother "almost fell on his knees to worship me" after discovering that Reid had preserved his overland diary.[87] Reid sent copies of a passenger list he had compiled in 1849 to some former Pioneers after his second visit to California in 1890, but did nothing about the diary until he returned to Pittsburgh in 1903 from his fourth western journey. The lingering illness of his youngest child, Genevieve, culminating in her death in 1895, followed by the onset of Letitia Reid's sickness and "nervous tension," may have been instrumental in the postponement of any plans to circulate his diary.[88] Toward the end of 1903 he made a fair copy of his tattered original diary and in the process evidently decided to flesh it out by writing a narrative journal of his overland trip. Letters and memorabilia of 1849, which Reid had carefully preserved through the years, and information he obtained on men like Dr. Sylvanus Goheen, the physican whose brother had died of cholera in Independence, enabled him to write the introduction incorporated in this volume as a prologue to the overland diary.

Reid apparently completed writing the journal based on his diary sometime after March 1904. He probably intended to distribute copies among his friends and family, and may have planned to give a copy of his overland diary to the Western Pennsylvania Historical Society, which he had joined after moving to Pittsburgh in 1900. But Reid's life was a busy one in 1904. Hale and hearty and "looking forward to years of usefulness," the indefatigable traveler set out in May to attend a reunion of the Grand Army of the Republic in Hartford, Connecticut, visiting Philadelphia and New York on the way.[89] He had hardly returned, much "revived" by his excursion, before he was off again, this time to the St. Louis Exposition with his son George. In a sprightly letter to his eldest son, Ambrose, Reid wrote of visiting "old haunts," attending mass in the cathedral where he had gone so often in "the forties," and spending an evening with surviving friends of those days. He returned to Pittsburgh in early November with a severe cold. It developed into pneumonia, and on the afternoon of November 15, 1904, Bernard Reid died at the age of eighty-one.[90]

Appendixes

This list of passengers was drawn up by Bernard Reid at the campground outside Independence. The names in boxes are those of the men who died. The page numbers placed beside some of the names were added by Reid in 1904, when he began writing the journal based on his overland diary. *Courtesy: Archives, Univ. of Santa Clara.*

Biographical Information on Persons Mentioned in the Text

The names of passengers, staff, and crew of the Pioneer Line mentioned in Bernard Reid's text or in excerpts from other diaries are indicated by asterisks. Unless otherwise noted, passengers are included in a list published in the St. Louis *Missouri Republican*, May 17, 1849, and in another compiled by Bernard Reid in 1849 and preserved in the Reid Papers. The carriage or mess numbers of 120 passengers are given in Reid's list.

* Alden, I. F. From Lewistown, Illinois, Alden presumably joined the Pioneer Line with two others from his home town, M. O. Andrews and S. D. Reynolds, who were his messmates in Carriage No. 2. He is listed as S. F. Alson in the *Missouri Republican*.

Allen, ———. Allen was coproprietor with Thomas Turner of the Pioneer Line. He, with Turner and two other men, had been in charge of ten supply wagons during Col. Alexander Doniphan's expedition in 1847 to Chihuahua, Mexico, during the Mexican War. Allen was captain of the Pioneer Line's second train, which left Independence at the end of June 1849 with about 75 passengers. The train made good time, but ran out of provisions along the Humboldt River Valley and was found in a crippled condition on the route beyond the Carson River, where it received aid from a California relief expedition. See Barry, *Beginning of the West*, pp. 703, 875–76; Dewolf, Sept. 3; Hutchings, Oct. 10; *Missouri Republican*, Sept. 6, 1847, June 21, Aug. 5, 1849; U.S. Senate, *Executive Document 52*, pp. 111, 112; and Unruh, *The Plains Across*, p. 102.

* Andrews, M. O. From Lewistown, Illinois, he shared a mess with two friends from his home town, I. F. Alden and S. D. Reynolds, in Carriage No. 2. Andrews is one of the few men, according to Reid, who had tiffs with other passengers; he quarreled with R. J. Updyke, also from Illinois, on August 17. Andrews was also one of the Pioneers who returned to the Humboldt desert on September 11, carrying water for stranded passengers.

Ankrim, William J. A former lieutenant in the Mexican War, Ankrim, a Pennsylvanian, was the captain of a wagon train from Pittsburgh, believed by the *Missouri Republican* to be the largest company to set out for California in 1849. This "Pittsburgh Enterprise Coy.," with some 250 men, was a quarrelsome one that divided early along the trail. See Barry, *Beginning of the West*, p. 804; Bruff, II, 447; Decker, April 24; Hamelin, May 9; Heitman, *Historical Register*; Hutchings, June 27; and *Missouri Republican*, March 24, 1849.

* Beadles, Robert. Bernard Reid identifies him as a passenger, a newspaperman from Iowa and one of three members of the train who died of cholera in Independence in May 1849. The *Missouri Republican*, however, listed him as a member of the Pioneer Line's crew from Orange County, Virginia. Beadles's death is noted by Reid in the margin of his passenger list; by the *Missouri Republican*, Dec. 24, 1849; and by Searls, p. 64. Searls also identified him as a crew member, known as "California Bob," and wrote on May 15 that he died on that day. Perhaps Reid did care for a dying passenger from Iowa but forgot his name, and over fifty years later decided that it was Beadles; see Hafen, ed., *The Mountain Men and the Fur Trade*, p. 117, for a letter from "Gerald" (Bernard J. Reid) to the Independence *Daily Union*, May 14, 1849, in which Reid wrote that in Independence he witnessed three deaths, the number he recalled in 1904.

* Bearce, ———. This passenger is listed only by Bernard Reid, and was a member of Carriage No. 15. On July 14 he joined Niles Searls's mess in Carriage No. 17. Searls spells his name "Bierce," as does Reid in his passenger list. He may have come from Virginia, since he is listed with two others from that state in No. 15. He left the train on August 30 with R. Elder and Henry J. Reed to pack to the goldfields.

* Boaz, E. D. From Appomattox County, Virginia, Boaz was a member of Carriage No. 7, which he shared with a man from Missouri, three from the Midwest, and one from Maine.

* Bonnell, A. C. From Indianapolis, Indiana, Bonnell was Bernard Reid's messmate in Carriage No. 12 from Independence to the Humboldt desert, and accompanied Reid on foot over the Sierra. He lived in the same hotel as Reid in San Francisco for a few months in 1849, and the two men saw one another occasionally until Reid left California. Bonnell was a clerk in San Francisco and evidently had private means. He was listed as one of the "monied men" in San Francisco in 1851 (though low on the list with an estimated wealth of $6,000). By 1854 he had left for Oregon, sent for his family, and invested in a lumber business in Portland, where he lived for the rest of his life. In 1890 Reid visited Bonnell, by then a commission broker with the firm of Coffin, Bonnell and Co., in Portland, where the two men reminisced over the "trying time" they had spent together in "No. 12." See Reid, "Diary, 1850" (1937), Feb. 2, 1850; Walter Hawxhurst to Bernard

Reid, Sept. 15, 1854; A. C. Bonnell to Bernard Reid, n.d. [1890]; and *A "Pile," or, A Glance at the Wealth of the Monied Men of San Francisco and Sacramento City.*

* Brewer, W. T. From Eberton, Georgia, he is absent from Reid's passenger list. Brewer may have shared a mess in Carriage No. 14 with two other men from Eberton, B. E. Henry and I. A. S. Jones.

* Brewster, John A. The physican from Philadelphia whom Reid befriended while the two were traveling by steamer to St. Louis. Brewster and Reid agreed to travel west together, sharing the expenses for traveling gear and a pony. They became messmates in Carriage No. 12. Brewster arrived in San Francisco in January 1850, after the Sacramento flood, and lodged for some weeks in Reid's tent. By 1852 Brewster had moved to Sonoma, California, where he was appointed county surveyor, practicing medicine only as an "avocation." In 1856 he became surveyor-general of the state for one term, and for the rest of his life he was known as General Brewster. Apparently he and Reid never met again after 1850, and Brewster repaid only 50 dollars of his debt to Reid of 128 dollars for his share in the cost of equipment and the pony bought for the overland trip. Walter and Robert Hawxhurst agreed with Reid that Brewster did not wear well on the trail; on hearing a rumor in 1859 that Brewster had married, Robert Hawxhurst wrote, "I pity the wife." But Brewster never married. A dedicated Mason, he spent his life in Sonoma as a member of the surveying firm of Brewster and Peabody. See Reid, "Diary, 1850" (1937), Jan. 16, 31, Feb. 2, 1850; John Brewster to Bernard Reid, July 16, 1852; Walter Hawxhurst to Bernard Reid, June 1, 1854, and Robert Hawxhurst to Bernard Reid, Oct. 17, 1859. See also Celeste G. Murphy, *The People of the Pueblo, or, the Story of Sonoma*, p. 172; and Bancroft, *Works*, XXIII, 700.

* Brogden, H. W. Apparently a Canadian, Brogden or Brogdon joined the Pioneer Line with a friend, Fred Pearks; both men were in Carriage No. 1, where one of their messmates was Lell H. Woolley. On July 14 Brogden and Pearks joined Niles Searls's mess, but they left the train on August 31, according to Reid, to pack to the goldfields along the Lassen Cutoff.

Bryant, Edwin. A newspaper editor from Kentucky, Bryant traveled overland in 1846. Many emigrants, including Reid and Searls, used his guide, *What I Saw in California* (1848). Bryant led a pack party to California in 1849.

* Burns, ———. A member of Capt. Turner's staff. Reid recalled in his journal (p. 28) that Burns was known as "Indian Bill."

Campbell, ———. A sutler or merchant traveling with the Pioneer Line and selling goods and liquor at high prices to the passengers. He was dismissed from the passenger train on July 11 after the Pioneers discovered that his wares were owned by the Pioneer Line. See Searls, July 11.

* Candee, S. Reid spells this passenger's name as either Candee or Can-

die. Bidlack, the editor of *Letters Home* (p. 18), gives his name as
S. Camden. From Monroe, Michigan, he was a member of Carriage
No. 7. Candee apparently did not know the trio from Ann Arbor,
Michigan—Cranson, McCollum, and Sinclair—who messed together
in Carriage No. 17.

Chenie, ———. A fellow surveyor of Reid's in the surveyor-general's
office for the districts of Illinois and Missouri, St. Louis. Chenie gave
Reid a letter of introduction to Dr. Victor Fourgeaud, a former
St. Louis physician who had become a rich and civic-minded San
Franciscan. Fourgeaud helped Reid obtain work as a rodman in a
surveying party in 1849. See Reid to James V. Reid, Nov. 27, 1849;
and for Fourgeaud, Soulé et al., *Annals of San Francisco*, pp. 191,
558, 678.

*Cody, ———. In his journal (p. 97), Reid recalled that Cody was one of
the train crew.

*Coleman, ———. In his journal (p. 97), Reid recalled that Coleman
was one of the train crew.

Conway, Frederick R. Surveyor-general for the districts of Illinois and
Missouri, based in St. Louis, Conway employed Reid as an examiner
of surveys from 1847 to 1849. Conway was relieved of his post in
1849. See S. P. Lalumière to Bernard Reid, Aug. 23, 1853; F. R. Conway to Bernard Reid, Dec. 6, 1853; and St. Louis *City Directory* for
1848.

*Cooper, Joseph. From Washington, Pennsylvania, Cooper joined the
Pioneer Line with four friends from his home town who shared a
mess in Carriage No. 10. On September 3 he died of dysentery.
See Forrest, "Forty-Niners from Washington County, Pennsylvania,"
pp. 5–6. Forrest erroneously writes that Cooper returned home. See
also *Missouri Republican*, Dec. 24, 1849.

*Cottrel, G. W. This passenger's name was also spelled Cottrell. From
Montreal, Canada, he shared a mess in Carriage No. 5 with G. Fer-
guson of Montreal, John James of St. Louis, and J. C. W. Cottrel or
Cottrell, a relative who was either his father or his son.

*Cottrel, J. C. W. Cottrel, or Cottrell as Reid spelled the name on his pas-
senger list, was the son or father of G. W. Cottrel, traveling in Carriage No. 5. He may have been the Joseph Cottrell listed in the San
Francisco *City Directory* for 1850 as a grocer.

*Cranson, Charles. The young son of a retired farmer, Cranson was one
of a trio from Ann Arbor, Michigan, along with David T. McCollum
and Charles Sinclair. They all shared a mess with Niles Searls in Carriage No. 17. For a description of Cranson's sickness, and his death
on June 19, see Searls, June 12, 17, 19, 20. McCollum wrote that
Cranson was "well and hearty" until June 10. See Bidlack, ed., *Letters
Home*, pp. 13, 20.

*Cunningham, ———. One of Captain Turner's "principal lieutenants,"
he almost certainly was Capt. Noble C. Cunningham of St. Louis,
listed as a passenger in the *Missouri Republican* but unlisted by Reid.

Noble Cunningham served in the Mexican War as a captain of Missouri infantry. In 1850 he was elected marshal of Sacramento. See Heitman, *Historical Register*; Sacramento *Transcript*, April 1, 3, 1850.

Damen, Rev. Arnold. Damen was a Dutch Jesuit who in 1848 organized the Young Men's Sodality at St. Francis Xavier church in St. Louis, to which Bernard Reid belonged. Father De Smet said that it was made up of "the best men in the city." Damen later moved to Chicago, where he became a popular preacher and evangelist, and died in 1889. Reid saw him again in St. Louis in 1886. See Conroy, *Arnold Damen, S.J.*, esp. chap. 4. See also S. P. Lalumière to Bernard Reid, Aug. 26, 1853; and Reid to Ambrose Reid, July 11, 1886.

*Davidson, John M. A young man of leisure from Maryland, and a member of Carriage No. 9, he was one of the seven men who accompanied Bernard Reid to San Francisco in October 1849, and lodged with him for some weeks there. Reid described him as from "an aristocratic family, bro't up in ease and luxury." Davidson became a drayman carting goods in San Francisco after his arrival and soon was "pocketing his 65 or 70 dollars a week." Ten years later another passenger, Robert Hawxhurst, remembered "the gentleman Davidson driving his mule cart through the mud." See Reid to James V. Reid, Nov. 27, 1849; Robert Hawxhurst to Bernard Reid, Oct. 17, 1859; and Reid, "California Gold Rush Letter," p. 233.

De Smet, Pierre-Jean. Born in Belgium in 1801, Father De Smet became a Jesuit missionary in the United States, with his headquarters in St. Louis. Father De Smet was a noted western explorer, writer, and authority on Indian populations, particularly the Flathead Indians. He died in 1873. See *Dictionary of American Biography*, V, 255–56.

*Dillard, R. S. From New Orleans, Louisiana, Dillard was a member of Carriage No. 4, and a messmate of the two Hawxhursts. Dillard was one of the few passengers, along with his messmate R. J. Updyke and M. O. Andrews, who engaged in open quarrels; Dillard quarreled with a teamster on June 8.

*Dodson, C.B. From Chicago, Dodson apparently came originally from Geneva, New York. He was attacked by cholera on May 30, and Searls wrote (May 31) that it was "feared he cannot recover." Dr. Israel Lord, who knew Dodson, saw him on July 5 and was shocked by his appearance. Dodson left the Pioneer Line on July 11 to join Lord's train. See Lord, July 5 and 11.

*Duhring, Andrew. Originally from Maine, Duhring was a jeweler in St. Louis in 1848 according to Bernard Reid. He was Reid's messmate in Carriage No. 12 from Independence to the Humboldt desert, where Reid left the train. He died of scurvy on October 11. Reid in his journal (p. 114) calls him Henry, but he is listed as Andrew or A. Duhring in both passenger lists and in the St. Louis *City Directory* for 1848, where his occupation is given as "clerk."

*Dunning, H. C. From Collinsville, Illinois, Dunning was a member of

Carriage No. 11. One of his messmates was Oliver Trowbridge, one of the first passengers to die of cholera (on May 17). The other passengers in No. 11 were Southerners except Trowbridge, a Canadian who apparently had lived in Utica, New York, prior to joining the train. See Searls, May 17, and p. 64. Dunning was almost shot by accident on Sept. 7.

*Eastman, J. J. From Pittsfield, New Hampshire, Eastman was the third man to die (July 31) from Niles Searls's original mess, Carriage No. 17. According to Searls's entry for August 5, Eastman was sick throughout the trip with tuberculosis. He left Carriage No. 17 at Ft. Laramie to join another mess.

*Elder, R. From Ottawa, Illinois, Elder was a member of Carriage No. 9, but on July 14 he transferred to Bernard Reid's mess in Carriage No. 12. Elder left the train on August 30 with his friend Bearce and another passenger from Ottawa, Capt. H. Reed, to pack to the goldfields.

*Falkner, Charles. Called "Charley" by Reid, Falkner was the Pioneer Line's commissary. Attacked severely with cholera at the Pioneer Line's first campground outside Independence, he was one of the few to recover from the disease. See Searls, May 12, and p. 68.

*Ferguson, G. From Montreal, Canada, Ferguson shared a mess in Carriage No. 5 with the two Cottrels, also Canadians. Two of his other messmates died—Richard Smith and John James.

*Flinn, ———. Reid spelled this name Flinn in his diary, but Flynn on his passenger list. There were two Flynns with the Pioneer Line, both from Zanesville, Ohio, and probably brothers. Both were members of Carriage No. 15, which they shared with a man from New Jersey and three men from Virginia.

*Foncannon, Reuben. A teamster on the train, Foncannon died of cholera on June 1, and was buried on June 2. Like his friend, Jacob Keller, he came from Bluffton, Indiana. In the Searls published diary his name is transcribed incorrectly from the Searls manuscript diary as Cincannon. See Searls, June 2 and p. 64; *Missouri Republican*, Dec. 24, 1849.

Fortier, ———. One of Bernard Reid's friends in the Young Men's Sodality of St. Francis Xavier church in St. Louis. A clerk in a large shoe store, he married in 1849. See Dr. Samuel Merry to Bernard Reid, April 1, 1850.

*Francisco ———. In his journal (p. 67) Bernard Reid recalled that Francisco was "the oldest of the Mexican vaqueros" who were teamsters on the Pioneer Line.

Garesché, Julius P. The fellow boarder of Bernard Reid's at Newman's in St. Louis, and an assistant adjutant general in the Union army, Lieutenant Colonel Garesché was killed at the Battle of Stone River (Murfreesboro), Tennessee, on Dec. 31, 1862. Reid saw Julius Garesché's family regularly in St. Louis in later years; prominent in the

city, the family had come originally from the French West Indies. See
W. Rosecrans to H. W. Halleck, Jan. 4, 1864, in *The War of the Rebellion: A Compilation of the Official Records of the Union and Confederate Armies*, XX, 185; Reid to Ambrose Reid, July 11, 1886, Oct. 30, 1904; *Encyclopedia of the History of St. Louis*; and Holland, "Saint Louis Families."

*Garrett, Augustus O. From Peoria, Illinois, Garrett was a long-time hotelkeeper who built the well-known Planters House in 1840. He sold the hotel before leaving with the Pioneer Line. Garrett returned to Peoria in 1858 and died that year at the age of seventy-five. Probably the oldest of the passengers at sixty-five, Garrett is listed as a colonel by Reid, but the title probably was honorific or from service in the militia. He belonged to Carriage No. 9. See Wilkins, p. 74, n. 14.

Gilmore family. Robert and Mary Gilmore, of Saline County, Missouri, died on the same day, July 18, 1849, at the Little Sandy River in present-day Wyoming, and were buried in a common grave. They were survived by two children, who were abandoned by their wagon train after their parents died. Bernard Reid discovered the children on July 20, and members of the Pioneer Line paid a Missouri ox train to carry the children to California. After Reid made inquiries about the children in Missouri and Sacramento newspapers in 1903, he received a response from B. B. Burgess, the young woman's nephew, who wrote to Reid three letters dated December 6, 12, and 21, 1903. Nellie Gilmore, Burgess wrote, was born in June 1832 and married his uncle, Henry F. Parsons, traveling with the Missouri ox train, in California in 1849. The couple returned to the East in 1874, and lived subsequently in Wisconsin, New York City, and Michigan. Henry Parsons died in Michigan in 1885, and Nellie Gilmore Parsons died in Howard, Wisconsin, in December 1903, according to Burgess; they had no children. The young son of the Gilmores was named Charles. Born in 1835, he died in Michigan in 1878 or 1879. Some of Burgess's dates are contradictory, and Nellie Gilmore Parsons's death cannot be verified, since records of deaths in Wisconsin were not required before 1907. I am indebted to Mary Jane Herber, Brown County Historical Society, Green Bay, Wisconsin, who unsuccessfully searched available records for me. See Bruff, Aug. 2; Reid to editor of the *Republican*, Marshall (Saline County), Mo., Nov. 13, 1903 (clipping), Reid Papers; Burgess-Reid correspondence, Reid Papers; and Mrs. Edwards of Sacramento to Bernard Reid, Feb. 16, 1904. See also the Pittsburgh *Gazette*, which published the Gilmore story in its editions of December 7 and 16, 1903.

*Goheen, Rev. Davis. Originally a passenger on the Pioneer Line, this Methodist clergyman, of Belleville, Illinois, died of cholera in Independence, probably on May 9, before the Pioneer Line set out across the plains. Reid and John Brewster helped Goheen's brother Sylvanus care for him, and another passenger, Dr. R. H. McDonald, helped Sylvanus bury him. The Reverend Goheen, a bachelor, was a graduate of McKendree College in Lebanon, Illinois. The president of the college told Reid in a letter dated February 4, 1904, that the two Goheens hoped to earn enough money in the goldfields in order to endow the college. See McDonald, *McDonald Overland Narrative*, p. 63; lists of deaths in the Reid Papers and in the *Missouri Republican*, Aug. 11, Dec. 24, 1849; and Folder 59, Reid Papers, containing correspondence on the Goheen brothers following Reid's letter of inquiry about the Goheens published in a number of editions of the Belleville *Advocate* in January 1904.

* Goheen, Sylvanus M.E. Originally a passenger on the Pioneer Line, Sylvanus returned to his home town, Belleville, Illinois, after the death of his brother Davis. Dr. R. H. McDonald and Dr. C. H. Swift took the brothers' seats on the Pioneer Line, which was sold out when the two physicians first tried to buy passage. Sylvanus, a physician born in 1813, was married with no children. He attended McKendree College in Lebanon, Illinois, and was an ardent temperance advocate. Dr. Goheen wrote a letter to the *Missouri Republican* from Belleville on May 15, praising the Pioneer Line as a train with "superior advantages" over more conventional wagon trains. The following year he traveled to California on another passenger train, and became speedily disillusioned with such a mode of transportation, calling it a "humbug." He died of cholera near Sacramento in 1851. See McDonald, *McDonald Overland Narrative*, p. 63; *Missouri Republican*, May 17, 1849, Jan. 23, 1851, letters from Dr. S. M. E. Goheen; Folder 59, Reid Papers, for correspondence from many persons answering a letter of inquiry about the Goheens from Bernard Reid, published in a number of editions of the Belleville *Advocate* in Jan. 1904. See especially the letter from Anna Goheen (widow), Jan. 29, 1904, who wrote that "two finer men" than Davis and Sylvanus never lived and expressed the wish that California had "never been heard of"; and a letter from Dr. J. F. Snyder of Virginia, Illinois, president of the Illinois Historical Society, Jan. 25, 1904, who was with Dr. Goheen when he died in 1851.

Gratiot, Col. Probably an acquaintance of Reid's from St. Louis, where the Gratiots were a distinguished family. Most likely he was Charles Gratiot, a Mexican War veteran (though only a lieutenant) who lived in Sacramento. Reid met him and another St. Louis man as the two packed along the Humboldt River. See Heitman, *Historical Register*; St. Louis *City Directory* for 1848; and U.S., *Bureau of the Census*, 1850 (Sacramento, Calif.).

Graves, W. J. The fellow boarder of Reid's at Newman's in St. Louis who became a county judge in California. Reid saw him occasionally in San Francisco in 1849 and in the mines during 1850. Graves practiced law in Santa Cruz, later settling in San Luis Obispo, where he became a county judge in 1852. He tried to find work for Bernard Reid, first as clerk to a judge in 1850, and later as county clerk in

San Luis Obispo in 1852. See Reid, "Diary, 1850" (1937), Jan. 31, July 12, 1850; and W. J. Graves to Bernard Reid, Jan. 23, 1852.

* Green, Robert. Green was the teamster boss for the Pioneer Line. He remained with the wagon train to the end.

* Harris, Moses "Black." A "monumental" figure in the fur trade of the Far West, Harris's origins are obscure, but it is believed that he came from South Carolina; the nickname was given because of his swarthy complexion. Harris had been the overland guide to Oregon for the Whitman missionary party in 1836 and for a train of settlers in 1844, and was painted by Alfred Jacob Miller in 1837 in the famous water-color "Trappers," now in the Walters Art Gallery, Baltimore. Harris arrived in St. Joseph from Fort Laramie on April 18, 1849, on his way to serve as the Pioneer Line's guide, but he died in Independence of cholera a few weeks later. A letter to the Independence *Daily Union*, May 14, signed "Gerald," told of Harris's death. Almost certainly Bernard Reid, a lifelong writer of letters to newspaper editors, wrote this letter; he used the same pseudonym in a letter to the editor of the Pittsburgh *Catholic* from Santa Clara, California, in 1852. Reid reported to the *Daily Union* that three men in his hotel in Independence died within 24 hours, the first being "Black" Harris, "chosen to lead us across the Rocky Mountains." As he lay dying, according to Reid's letter, Harris spoke of a wife and two children living in an Indian village "in the mountain fastnesses." This statement is the only evidence that Harris had a family. See Jerome Peltier, "Moses 'Black' Harris," in Hafen, ed., *The Mountain Men and the Fur Trade*, IV, 103–17, esp. p. 117 for the reprint of the letter signed "Gerald" in the *Daily Union*. See also copy of Reid's letter to the Pittsburgh *Catholic* signed "Gerald," Aug. 21, 1852, Nobili Presidential Papers; Searls, May 24; and Barry, *Beginning of the West*, p. 825.

* Hawxhurst, Robert. Fifteen years old in 1849, Robert Hawxhurst accompanied his father, Walter Hawxhurst, on the Pioneer Line and shared a mess with him in Carriage No. 4; he took care of his father as the latter became progressively weaker with scurvy on the last stage of the journey. The youth worked in a store in Sonora, California, from 1850 until he joined Reid and his father in Santa Clara in 1851. He served as a cabin boy-cum-passenger on a boat to the Society Islands in 1853, and after sundry odd jobs in California, became a partner of his father's in a store in San Francisco. In 1856 he and his father were members of the San Francisco Vigilance Committee, which was dominated by merchants. Hawxhurst corresponded intermittently with Bernard Reid throughout the years, and Reid stayed with him and other members of his family on all his visits to California after 1886. Robert Hawxhurst continued his father's business, married, and lived in Alameda, California. He always regretted the "passing of his best five years out of school" because of the journey to California, and regarded Bernard Reid, twenty-six years old when he was fifteen in 1849, as "a strong influence" in his life. See correspondence between Robert Hawxhurst and Reid, esp. Hawxhurst's letters of May 25 and Oct. 17, 1859; and Robert Hawxhurst to Ambrose Reid, Dec. 28, 1904, Reid Papers.

* Hawxhurst, Walter. Born in New York in 1794 of Quaker parentage, Hawxhurst in 1849 was a prosperous storekeeper from Fort Madison, Iowa, with a wife and six children. He never intended to mine but went west to investigate opportunities for trading. Barely surviving the trip across the plains, accompanied by his son Robert, he suffered early reverses in trading and farming in California, where the rest of his family joined him in 1851. In 1853 he moved to San Francisco, where he opened a general store. In 1859, soon after Robert joined him as a partner, he retired to a farm outside Martinez, California, where he died in 1883 at the age of eighty-nine. He was a strong temperance advocate all his life, joined other merchants on the 1856 San Francisco Vigilance Committee (whose brand of "frontier justice" troubled Bernard Reid), and with his wife and family remained devoted to Reid. Hawxhurst died leaving an estate of $50,000, having given his children "much more" a few years before his death. See correspondence between Walter Hawxhurst and Reid; Hawxhurst obituary (clipping), Reid Papers; and Robert Hawxhurst to Bernard Reid, April 7, 1883. The name Hawxhurst is garbled in the *Missouri Republican* passenger list.

Hayes, James M. The Jesuit priest who, before he entered the order, boarded wth Reid at Newman's in St. Louis. He was still alive in 1904, living in Chicago, and he remembered Reid well. Hayes became a well-known author of children's books. See S. P. Lalumière to Bernard Reid, June 28, 1849, Aug. 23, 1853; James M. Hayes to Ambrose Reid, Dec. 2, 1904, Reid Papers; and Faherty, *Better the Dream*, p. 123.

* Heath, Solomon. There were two Heaths, father and son, with the Pioneer Line. Solomon Heath, the father, was a seafaring man from Belfast, Maine, who shared a mess in Carriage No. 8 with other seafarers from Maine. See U.S., *Bureau of the Census*, 1840 (Maine).

* Heath, W. S. The son of Solomon Heath, from Belfast, Maine, who shared a mess with his father in Carriage No. 8. In the *Missouri Republican* passenger list the Heaths are listed as Solomon Heath and son.

Hooker, Joseph. In his journal (p. 55) Bernard Reid recollected that the Captain Hooker he met near Fort Laramie was Joseph Hooker, the general with whom he fought in the same army corps in the Civil War, and that in 1849 Hooker was with a company of dragoons en route to the Pacific Coast. Webster's *American Military Biographies* (p. 181) notes that Hooker (1814–79) was assigned to the Division of the Pacific from 1849 to 1851. Appleton's *Encyclopedia* (III, 249–50) states that Hooker was sent to the Pacific Coast on July 9, 1849; since Reid met Hooker on June 29, it appears that the July 9 date is incorrect. Hooker resigned from the army in 1853 and was a farmer in

Sonoma, California, from 1853 to 1858. See *Dictionary of American Biography*, IX, 196–98.

* Hoy, Alexander B. A physician from Louisville, Kentucky, Hoy was a member of Carriage No. 19. One of his messmates was John McKaraher, with whom he set out on July 22 to pack to the goldfields. In 1850 Hoy practiced medicine in Sacramento, and in 1856 he was living in San Francisco. See U.S., *Bureau of the Census*, 1850 (Sacramento, Calif.); San Francisco *City Directory* for 1856.

Hughes, Edward. A friend of Bernard Reid's from St. Louis, Hughes was a fellow member of the Young Men's Sodality of St. Francis Xavier church. Reid wrote Hughes a letter on January 23, 1850, describing his overland trip, that was published in the city's *Catholic Telegraph*. Hughes later became a partner in a wholesale jewelry business in Cincinnati. See Dr. Samuel Merry to Bernard Reid, April 1, 1850; and S. P. Lalumière to Bernard Reid, Aug. 23, 1853.

* Hutton, C. C. A physician from Chicago, Hutton originally shared a mess with another doctor, Alexander Hoy, and four Pennsylvanians. On July 14 he and two messmates, J. D. Royer and Horace Guth, transferred to Niles Scarls's carriage. Hutton was sick with scurvy at the Carson River and died shortly before the Pioneer Line reached the summit of the Sierra Nevada. See Searls, July 14, Sept. 23, and p. 64.

* James, John. Originally from Belfast, Maine, James was a "finisher" of fine furniture in St. Louis in 1849, and an elderly man. He was a member of Carriage No. 5, and two of his messmates, "young" Cottrel and G. Ferguson, gave Bernard Reid news of his death from scurvy on September 15 at the Carson River. See Reid, journal, p. 113, St. Louis *City Directory* for 1848; Scarls, Sept. 23; Wilkins, Sept. 16; and *Missouri Republican*, Dec. 24, 1849.

* Jones, Edward. A passenger from Maine in Carriage No. 7.

* Jones, I. A. S. A passenger from Eberton, Georgia, in Carriage No. 14.

* Keller, Jacob. A teamster on the Pioneer Line and a friend of Reuben Foncannon, another teamster. Both came from Bluffton, Indiana, and both died of cholera. Keller died on June 4. See Searls, June 4 and p. 64; *Missouri Republican*, Dec. 24, 1849.

* Kelsey, Charles M. From New Orleans, he shared a mess with George W. Kelsey, also of New Orleans, and certainly a relative. Both were members of Carriage No. 11, which contained two other men from New Orleans.

* Kelsey, George W. From New Orleans, he shared a mess with Charles Kelsey, a relative from New Orleans. George W. Kelsey was a member of the Society of California Pioneers in the 1850's, and a partner in the real estate and auctioneering firm Scooffey and Kelsey. See San Francisco *City Directory* for 1854.

Kewen, Achilles. A fellow boarder of Bernard Reid's at Newman's in St. Louis. Born in Mississippi, the brother of E. J. C. Kewen and pro-Southern, he served with General Lopez in Cuba in 1850, and was killed on the William Walker expedition to Nicaragua in 1855. Not all the men were killed, as Reid believed, and Walker became dictator of Nicaragua from 1855 to 1857. See Bancroft, *Works*, XXXV, 760; and Hittell, *History of California*, III, 772.

Kewen, Edward J. C. A fellow boarder of Reid's at Newman's in St. Louis, Kewen also traveled overland in 1849, though not with the Pioneer Line, and became attorney-general of California that year, at the age of twenty-four; he resigned in 1850. His title of Colonel apparently was honorific or from service in the militia. Bernard Reid disliked Kewen; he told his brother John that Kewen was one of those men "whom I would like to buy at *my* estimate of their worth and sell at *theirs*." Kewen married Fanny White, practiced law in Sacramento and San Francisco, and was a member of the Society of California Pioneers. Born in Mississippi, he and his brother Achilles were pro-slavery. By 1862 Kewen had moved to Los Angeles and was a member of the state Assembly. He was arrested that year for pro-Southern activities and sent to Alcatraz for a few weeks until he pledged allegiance to the Union. See Bernard Reid to John C. Reid, May 30, 1850; Bancroft, *Works*, XVIII, 314; Hittell, *History of California*, IV, 222; San Francisco *City Directory* for 1852; and U.S., *Bureau of the Census*, 1850 (Sacramento, Calif.).

*Kinsey, Charles. From Ewington, Illinois, Kinsey was a member of Carriage No. 18. His mess was composed of men from the Midwest (three from Illinois and two from Wisconsin). He may be the C. Kinsey, aged 35 and born in Pennsylvania, who was listed in the Census as living in El Dorado County in 1850; see U.S., *Bureau of the Census*, 1850 (California).

Knowlton family. A Mormon family, the Knowltons kept a boarding house at Fort Kearny. A number of emigrants besides Reid and Searls commented on this family. Decker, May 14, was impressed with the dinner he ate with them, and "bought of the old lady a large gingerbread for 30 cts." Both Decker and Long, May 19, remarked on the family's pretty daughter. Decker wrote that the Knowltons lost their stock on the way to "the brethren" at Salt Lake, and expected to move on in 1850 after "making something of emigrants." See also Bruff, June 17; Gould, June 16; Harker, May 31; and Staples, June 16, who wrote that some of the army officers boarded with the family.

Lalumière, Stanislaus P. A fellow boarder of Reid's at Newman's in St. Louis and deputy clerk of the circuit court. He became a Jesuit novice in 1849. He was attached to St. Xavier's College in Cincinnati for some years, and later became the first president of Marquette University in Milwaukee. See Reid-Lalumière Correspondence, Reid Papers; St. Louis *City Directory* for 1848; and Garraghan, *Jesuits in the Middle United States*, III, 383, 453.

Lamalfa, Joseph. Lamalfa was not a passenger on the Pioneer Line but traveled with the train for company and protection. A confectioner in St. Louis, he planned to trade in California. Bernard Reid saw him in San Francisco in 1850 and referred to him as the St. Louis "ice-cream king." See Reid, "Diary, 1850" (1937), Feb. 22, 1850; Woolley, p. 14; and St. Louis *City Directory* for 1848.

* Mallerson, Moses. From St. Charles County, Missouri, Mallerson was the Pioneer Line's young wagon master. He remained with the Pioneer Line to the end.

* McCollum, David T. From Ann Arbor, Michigan, McCollum was the only one of a trio of Pioneers from that town who survived the trip. He and his two young friends, Cranson and Sinclair, were messmates of Niles Searls in Carriage No. 17. McCollum was fifty years old in 1849, a devout Methodist, temperance man, and abolitionist. Having been a well-to-do businessman and local politician in Ann Arbor, he sold a farm for $2,000 to finance his trip west. His nickname was Squire, probably in reference to a former political post he had held as County Register of deeds. McCollum, who was sick for most of the trip, returned to Ann Arbor in 1851, and died in 1880. See Bidlack, ed., *Letters Home*, esp. pp. 13, 49; and Searls, esp. June 4, July 17, 18, 21.

* McDonald, Richard H. Born in 1820 in Kentucky, McDonald was a physician and a member of Carriage No. 13 until he left the train on June 16 with Dr. C. H. Swift and Louis Sloss. The *Missouri Republican* gave his address as Prairie du Rocher, Illinois. McDonald practiced medicine in Prairie du Rocher before joining the train. He traded in Sacramento for a time after arriving in California, and then returned to medicine, married a Sacramento widow in 1851, and moved to San Francisco, where he became a rich banker, a pillar of the Congregational church, and a prohibitionist. He ran unsuccessfully for governor of California on the Prohibition party ticket in 1882. McDonald and Reid saw one another frequently on Reid's visits to California, and corresponded in their old age. See McDonald-Reid correspondence, Reid Papers; McDonald, *McDonald Overland Narrative*; and Hittell, *History of California*, IV, 667.

* McKaraher, John. Born in Philadelphia, McKaraher was a member of Carriage No. 9 until he left the train on July 22 with his messmate Dr. A. B. Hoy. McKaraher and J. J. O'Brien, a friend from Philadelphia, had left their original wagon train in Independence to join the celebrated Pioneer Line. Called Major Jack, McKaraher evidently had served in the militia; he was not a veteran of the Mexican War. He became a clerk in San Francisco and a member of the 1851 San Francisco Vigilance Committee, which dispensed "frontier justice" in the disorderly seaport. In 1851 it was reported falsely that McKaraher had been murdered in a tavern. He was still in San Francisco in 1856. Reid delivered a letter from McKaraher to the latter's mother and sister in Philadelphia on his way home to Clarion in 1852. See *Missouri Republican*, May 1, letter from Independence dated April 21, 1849; Searls, July 22; Reid, diary, 1851–52, Oct. 8, 1852; Stewart,

Committee of Vigilance, pp. 304ff; San Francisco *City Directory* for 1852 and 1856; and Soulé et al., *Annals of San Francisco*, p. 575.

Mengarini, Gregory. Born in Italy (1811), Mengarini was a Jesuit missionary based in St. Louis who traveled in the West as Father Pierre-Jean De Smet's linguist and ethnologist. He later retired to Santa Clara College in California, where Bernard Reid taught in 1852, and died in 1886. See *Dictionary of American Biography*, XII, 535–36.

*Merrie, R. From Louisville, Kentucky, Merrie was a member of Carriage No. 16. All others in the mess were from Illinois.

Morrison, Robert F. A fellow boarder of Bernard Reid's at Newman's in St. Louis, and a graduate of the University of Missouri, Morrison became a chief justice of the California supreme court in 1880. A devout Catholic, he was born in Illinois in 1826 and died in California in 1887. Reid thought highly of Morrison, and visited him in California in 1886. See Hittell, *History of California*, IV, 645; Bancroft, *Works*, XXIV, 409; Reid to Letitia Reid, July 22, 1886; and Reid to Ambrose Reid, July 11, 1886.

*Mulford, Charles. Born in New York state, Mulford was a law school friend of Niles Searls in Rensselaerville, New York. It was Mulford who persuaded Searls, then unsuccessfully practicing law in Missouri, to join the gold rush; the two traveled together in Carriage No. 17. Mulford and Searls traded and mined together in California until September 1850, when they settled in Nevada City. Mulford opened a book and stationery store and gave up the law. His store was burned out in 1851, and he returned to the East. See Searls, pp. 1–2, 66–69.

Newman, Capt. Jonas. A former Mississippi river-boat captain, Newman operated the boarding house where Reid lodged in St. Louis from 1847 to 1849. He and his French wife, the former Susanne le Beaume died within a few days of one another in the cholera epidemic, July 1849; both lived little more than twelve hours after the onset of the disease. See S. P. Lalumière to Bernard Reid, June 28, 1849; Dr. Samuel Merry to Bernard Reid, April 1, 1850; and *Encyclopedia of the History of St. Louis*.

Newman, Socrates. The son of Jonas Newman and a graduate of St. Louis University, he was a good friend of Bernard Reid's in St. Louis from 1847 to 1849. After surviving a cholera attack in the summer of 1849, he left for California with his uncle. Reid saw him frequently in St. Louis on his way to California in later years; apparently Newman had spent little time in the goldfields before returning home. Newman became a rich man, president of the St. Louis Gas Company, and was a close friend ("Cousin Soc") of the family of Julius Garesché. See Socrates Newman to Bernard Reid, Dec. 15, 1848; Dr. Samuel Merry to Bernard Reid, April 1850; Reid to Ambrose Reid, July 11, 1886; Faherty, *Better the Dream*, p. 71; and *Encyclopedia of the History of St. Louis*.

*O'Brien, John J. From Philadelphia, O'Brien was a member of Carriage No. 14; one of his messmates was another former officer, Major McKaraher. O'Brien apparently earned his title of Captain in the militia. He accompanied Reid on foot over the Sierra. At first "Capt. Jack" enlivened the journey over the Sierra with his fine singing, but he became so sick that without the help of his companions he could not have survived.

Pasquier, Augustine. Pasquier was a St. Louis acquaintance Reid met at Fort Laramie on June 27. Pasquier most likely was a nephew of Charles Primeau from St. Louis, who was a partner with Alexander Harvey in the St. Louis Fur Company. Pasquier was not a gold seeker but was on his way to the Little Missouri River in present-day South Dakota. See Reid, journal, June 26; and Barry, *Beginning of the West*, pp. 875, 933.

*Patterson, J. R. One of the seafaring men in Carriage No. 8, Patterson came from Newcastle, Maine.

*Pearks, Fred. Pearks shared a mess with his friend H. W. Brogden in Carriage No. 1, and like Brogden, apparently was a Canadian. Lell H. Woolley was of one of their messmates. On July 11 Pearks and Brogden transferred to Niles Searls's mess, No. 17, but the two men left the train to pack to the goldfields via the Lassen Cutoff August 31, according to Reid.

*Perce, ———. There is no "Perce" in the passenger lists, but he could be H. E. Pearce or Pierce, one of the seafaring men from Belfast, Maine, in Carriage No. 8, since in New England "Pearce" or "Pierce" can be pronounced "Perce." See Reid, diary, July 11, where Perce is listed along with four other men, all seafarers from Maine.

*Peters, J. L. Peters came from Columbus, Ohio, and was a member of Carriage No. 3 with four other men from the Midwest and two from the South.

Petreville, ———. Probably an acquaintance of Bernard Reid's from St. Louis. Reid met him on the trail along the Humboldt River, packing with Col. Gratiot, another St. Louis man.

*Pierson, O. H. Pierson or Pearson was a physician from Peoria, Illinois, who shared a mess in Carriage No. 11 with two companions from Peoria. He accompanied Reid on foot over the Sierra and helped J. J. O'Brien enliven the journey with his fine singing.

*Pitts, G. F. A physician from New Orleans, Pitts shared a mess in Carriage No. 11 with three others from New Orleans. In the "last stages" of scurvy when the train arrived at Weber Creek on October 10, Pitts recovered with proper diet and was one of the passengers who accompanied Reid from Sacramento to San Francisco, arriving on October 21, 1849. See Reid, journal, p. 115; and notes at the end of the Reid overland diary, Reid Papers.

Point Nicolas. A Jesuit missionary, born in France in 1789 and based in St. Louis, Point was Father Pierre-Jean De Smet's illustrator; he died in 1868. Point's journals and paintings, produced during western trips with De Smet and Mengarini, have been published in Donnelly, ed., *Wilderness Kingdom*.

Pomeroy, Theodore. A former merchant from Lexington, Missouri, Pomeroy and his brother formed in 1849 a "mercantile train" of 33 wagons to sell provisions along the trail and eventually establish a trading post in California; the overland diarist Joseph Hamelin joined this train, which moved on to Salt Lake City after traveling near the Pioneer Line along the Sweetwater River. One emigrant, Charles Lotts, who bought cheese and liquor from the train near Pacific Springs, estimated that there were forty wagons in all. See *Missouri Republican*, May 13, 1849; and John P. Reid, *Law for the Elephant*, p. 105, for quotation from Lotts.

Porter, Andrew. Porter (1820–72) was the army officer whom Reid met on the plains on July 30. Originally from Pennsylvania, he was a lieutenant colonel (not a captain, as Reid wrote) with the Mounted Riflemen. Reid as an old man mistakenly recalled that Porter was Gen. FitzJohn Porter, with whom Reid fought in the Civil War. But FitzJohn Porter was an instructor at West Point from 1849 to 1855. When Andrew Porter's company reached Cantonment Loring, near Fort Hall in present-day Idaho, it remained there with Porter as commandant; other companies continued on to Oregon. Andrew Porter, like FitzJohn Porter, became a general with the Union army in the Civil War. See Appleton's *Encyclopedia*, V, 722; Bruff, Aug. 19, 22, 24; and Heitman, *Historical Register*, I, 798.

* Reed, Henry J. From Ottawa, Illinois, Reed was a former captain of the Fifth Illinois infantry in the Mexican War, arriving in Santa Fe about September 10, 1847. He belonged to Carriage No. 14, sharing a mess with four other men from Ottawa and two from Georgia. He left the Pioneer Line on August 30 with Bearce and Elder to pack to the goldfields. See Heitman, *Historical Register*; and Barry, *Beginning of the West*, p. 701.

* Rogers, William. From Danville, Illinois, Rogers was a member of Carriage No. 16, sharing a mess with three other men from Illinois. Known as "Uncle Billy," Rogers was a gambler. According to Lell Woolley, who saw him in California in the 1860's, Rogers "gambled all the way across the plains." Woolley said that Rogers did not drink and was "all heart," a man who took care of the sick; he was one of the Pioneers who walked back to the Humboldt desert on September 11 with water for stranded passengers. Rogers had $11,000 in 1860, but when Woolley saw him later in the decade in Nevada, he had lost it all. See Woolley, p. 35; and Searls, Sept. 3.

* Rowe, Cyrus. Rowe was a member of Carriage No. 8, composed of nine seafaring men from Maine, according to Bernard Reid. His brother Harrison, killed by Indians at Loup Fork, apparently was from Platteville, Wisconsin. Rowe, aged forty in 1849, was living in Sacramento in 1850 and had been joined by his wife Harriet, also from Maine.

See St. Joseph *Gazette*, Aug. 3, 1849; U.S., *Bureau of the Census*, 1840
(Maine), 1850 (Sacramento, Calif.); and Foster, May 25, who read a
note left by a wagon company on May 22 telling of the death of
H. Rowe, killed and robbed by Indians.

* Royer, J. D. From Montgomery County, Pa., Royer originally was a
member of Carriage No. 19. He and two messmates, Dr. C. C. Hutton and Horace Guth, transferred to Niles Searls's carriage on
July 14. Royer died of scurvy in Hangtown in Nov. 1849. See Searls,
July 14, Sept. 30, and p. 64.

* Rumsey, William H. From Madison County, Kentucky, Rumsey was a
former colonel, probably in the militia, who belonged to Carriage
No. 4; one of his messmates was John Davidson. He was still in Cali-
fornia in 1854, though he had been unsuccessful in the mines. Walter
Hawxhurst did not think much of him. See Walter Hawxhurst to
Bernard Reid, Feb. 16, 1854.

* Sackett, ———. This passenger is unlisted by both Bernard Reid and
the Missouri *Republican*.

* Searls, Niles. Searls belonged to Carriage No. 17 and, like Reid, kept
a diary of the trip. Born in 1825 in New York state, Searls moved
to Canada with his family in 1837, returning to the United States
in 1842 for his schooling. He was admitted to the bar in 1848 and
then moved to Missouri to practice law. He and a law school friend,
Charles Mulford, joined the gold rush and became messmates on the
Pioneer Line. In California Searls mined and traded with Mulford,
then both settled in Nevada City, where Searls became a lawyer.
Searls married on a trip East in 1853, and became chief justice of the
California supreme court in 1887, serving until 1889. He retired in
1899 and settled in Berkeley, Calif. Searls was a member and officer
of the Society of California Pioneers. See Searls, pp. 65–70.

* Sinclair, Charles. One of a trio from Ann Arbor (the others were Charles
Cranson and David McCollum), Sinclair, aged twenty-three, was a
clerk who had worked in his brother's store in Ann Arbor. All three
were messmates of Niles Searls in Carriage No. 17. Sinclair died on
May 30, the first of three men in the mess to die on the trail. See Bidlack, ed., *Letters Home*, pp. 13, 20; and Searls, May 21–23, 27–30.

* Sloss, Louis. Born to a German Jewish family in Bavaria in 1823, Sloss
emigrated to America in 1845 and opened a store in Mackville, Kentucky, the home town of Dr. R. H. McDonald, though the two men
first met on the Pioneer Line. He was at first a member of a large
mess in Carriage No. 1, but soon moved to Carriage No. 5. Sloss went
into business in Sacramento in 1849 with Dr. McDonald and Dr. Swift,
his companions when he left the Pioneer Line on June 16. The three
men were lifelong friends. Sloss later became a grocer in Sacramento,
then a stockbroker in San Francisco, and finally, in 1873, a founder of
the Alaska Fur Company, which became a great trading enterprise
after the discovery of gold in Alaska. Sloss was a millionaire, a philanthropist, president of the Society of California Pioneers from 1884

to 1885, and treasurer of the University of California, Berkeley, from 1885 until he died in 1902. See McDonald, *McDonald Overland Narrative*, pp. 102ff.; and *Dictionary of American Biography*, XVII, 219–20. The *Missouri Republican* passenger list mistakenly recorded Sloss's home town as Louisville, Kentucky.

*Smith, Richard. From Kentucky, Smith was a member of Carriage No. 5. Among his messmates were John James of St. Louis, the two Cottrels and G. Ferguson from Canada, and Louis Sloss, who moved to No. 5 from Carriage No. 1. The Oddfellows assisted the Masons in burying Smith, who died on June 6. See Searls, June 7.

*Speer, H. T. M. A physician from Chesterfield, Virginia, Speer or Spears was a member of Carriage No. 15, which he shared with two other Virginians and two men from Ohio. In 1854 he was a surgeon and a dentist in San Francisco. See San Francisco *City Directory* for 1854.

*Steele, A. H. Steele or Steel was a physician from Oswego, New York. He was a member of Carriage No. 6, and shared a mess with a companion from Oswego, Arza Crane.

*Stowe, J. B. Listed as L. B. Stow in the *Missouri Republican*, he came from Chicago. Stowe was a member of Carriage No. 6 at first but transferred to Bernard Reid's carriage, No. 12, on July 28. Beyond the Carson River, where Reid left the wagon train, what became of Stowe is unknown.

*Stoyell, R. S. From Moravia, New York, Stoyell was Bernard Reid's messmate in Carriage No. 12 from Independence to the Humboldt desert. Since Reid left the train at the Carson River, Stoyell's subsequent history is unknown.

*Swift, C. H. A physician from Turnbull, Monroe County, Alabama, Swift was a member of Carriage No. 1 until June 16, when he left the train. He entered business in Sacramento with two other Pioneers, Dr. R. H. McDonald and Louis Sloss, who packed with him to the goldfields; his son later married Dr. McDonald's sister. Swift had left his wife and grown children in Alabama and carried with him 2,200 dollars in gold sovereigns, apparently intending to trade in the goldfields. He financed the first business for the three men, all of whom became very rich. Swift's family joined him in Sacramento, where he opened a drug store in 1850. He became the county physician, a judge, and eventually mayor of Sacramento for two terms; he also founded the Sacramento Savings Bank. See McDonald, *McDonald Overland Narrative*, p. 63 and appendix.

*Tiffany, P. D. Originally from Maine, Pardon Dexter Tiffany practiced law in St. Louis; Reid apparently was mistaken when he recalled in 1904 that Tiffany came from New York. Dr. Augustus Heslep of St. Louis met Tiffany on the trail outside Independence and reported to the *Missouri Republican* that the St. Louis lawyer's health was much improved and he was enjoying the "sports of the prairie." Tiffany returned to St. Louis, where he died in 1861, "leaving a large estate." See *Missouri Republican*, July 4, 1849; *Encyclopedia of the History of St. Louis*; and St. Louis *City Directory* for 1848. Tiffany should not be confused with the overland diarist Palmer C. Tiffany of Iowa.

* Todd, S. One of Captain Turner's "principal lieutenants," Todd signed Bernard Reid's receipt for his passage money in Independence on May 5, 1849; the receipt survives in the Reid Papers.

Tooke, J. H. The enterprising huckster in St. Louis from whom Bernard Reid took lessons in the "searching, testing and smelting of gold," for a tuition of ten dollars. Tooke also gave lessons in St. Joseph, Missouri. See Tooke's advertisements in the *Missouri Republican*, March 9, 1849; and in the St. Joseph *Gazette*, April 20, 1849. In the St. Louis *City Directory* for 1848 he is listed as a jeweler.

* Treadwell, C. A seafaring man from Waldo, Maine, Treadwell was a member of Carriage No. 8, carrying nine seafarers in all from the coast of Maine.

* Turner, Thomas. The captain of the Pioneer Line's first train, Turner was also the co-owner with Mr. Allen of the Turner and Allen Company of St. Louis. Turner and Allen and two other men named Emerson and Teabout had been in charge of ten wagons under the escort of the Missouri Third Regiment of Mounted Volunteers, en route along the Santa Fe Trail to join Col. Alexander Doniphan's expedition to Chihuahua, Mexico, in 1847, during the Mexican War. Turner and Allen, both from St. Louis, organized the Pioneer Line in 1849. Turner was a heavy drinker, and his whereabouts after a remnant of the Pioneer Line reached Sacramento on October 12, 1849, remain unknown. In the St. Louis *City Directory* for 1848 a family of Turners, who were bakers, lived at the same address given for the Pioneer Line's office in 1849. See Barry, *Beginning of the West*, pp. 703, 875–76; *Missouri Republican*, Sept. 6, 1847, Feb. 6, 7, 1849; Wilkins, Sept. 19; Reid, journal, pp. 114, 115; and Bieber, ed., *Journal of a Soldier*, p. 40.

* Turney, ———. This passenger is unlisted by Reid and the *Missouri Republican*.

* Updyke, R. J. Updyke, or Updike, was from Fremont, Illinois, and belonged to Carriage No. 4. He was one of the few men Reid mentions who openly quarreled along the trail. He was in a "fray" with another man from Illinois, M. O. Andrews, on August 17.

* Upton, Sylvanda J. A former seafaring man from Belfast, Maine, Upton was a member of Carriage No. 8, whose nine passengers were all seafarers from Maine. Aged 32, he lived in El Dorado County in 1850. See U.S., *Bureau of the Census*, 1850 (California).

* Van Wight, P. S. A member of Carriage No. 1, he is unlisted in the *Missouri Republican*. Bernard Reid lists him with the title of Major, but he was not a veteran of the Mexican War. One of his messmates was Lell H. Woolley.

Waldo, William. Dr. Thomas White and his family left the Pioneer Line to join "Waldo's train" on the Truckee route on September 9. Waldo

almost certainly is William Waldo of Osceola, Missouri, the captain of
a large ox train of Missourians. In 1850 he was called "an angel of
mercy" when he spent two months in the California relief effort to
aid that year's gold rush emigrants. In 1853 he ran as a Whig for governor of California. See Unruh, *The Plains Across*, pp. 373–75; Barry,
Beginning of the West, p. 835; and *Missouri Republican*, May 9, 1849.

* Ware, William. From Salem, New Jersey, Ware was a member of Carriage No. 15. On July 14 he transferred to Carriage No. 17 with his
friend Bearce or Bierce and became a messmate of Niles Searls. Ware
left the train at the Carson River to pack with his messmate Horace
Guth of Northampton, Pennsylvania. See Searls, July 14, Sept. 23.

* Waters, W. T. Listed only in the *Missouri Republican*, Waters or Watters
was from New York.

* Wattles, W. W. Listed only by Bernard Reid, his name could have been
confused in the *Missouri Republican* with Waters or Watters, but clearly
they were two different passengers. Wattles, whom Searls believed to
be from Massachusetts, was a messmate of Bernard Reid's in Carriage No. 12, moving to No. 18 on July 14 after the train reorganized
at the Sweetwater River. All of his baggage burned on August 27. He
died on the road over the Sierra from scurvy on October 3. See
Searls, p. 64; Hutchings, p. 193; and *Missouri Republican*, Dec. 24,
1849.

White, Fanny. The daughter of Dr. Thomas J. White of St. Louis,
Fanny in 1849 married Edward J. C. Kewen in Sacramento at the age
of seventeen. Reid called Fanny the belle of St. Louis and wrote that
though he knew Kewen was a suitor, he did not expect Kewen to em-
bark on a "knight-errant" expedition across the plains to pursue her.
Douglass Perkins admired Fanny along the trail, writing in his diary
that she was "really very pretty but looked Entirely out of proper
place." See Reid to John Reid, May 30, 1850; Reid, journal, p. 84;
Paul, "My First Two Years in California," p. 38; Perkins, Sept. 3; and
U.S., *Bureau of the Census*, 1850 (Sacramento, Calif.).

White, Thomas J. A physician from St. Louis, Dr. White set out for
California with his family and three slaves; he planned to trade in
California and with a partner sent goods around Cape Horn. Many
observers commented on his progress along the trail. White served as
a civilian surgeon with the Mounted Riflemen after two army doctors
became sick with cholera. He settled in Sacramento and was elected
Speaker of the House in the first state election, in 1849, but resigned
in 1850 after the Sacramento flood. He had a thriving medical practice in Sacramento, became rich, and continued to dabble in politics.
See Bancroft, *Works*, V, 310; Cross, July 30; the article by Almaurin B. Paul (White's trading partner), "My First Two Years in California," pp. 25–26, 37–38; Barry, *Beginning of the West*, p. 825; *Missouri
Republican*, June 21, 1849; and the St. Joseph *Gazette*, Oct. 19, 1849.
White is incorrectly identified by Thomas D. Clark, the editor of

Perkins (Sept. 3), as Dr. Elijah White, the missionary and Indian agent.

Whitney, Asa. A merchant and railroad promoter, Whitney (1797–1872) agitated for years for a transcontinental railroad, and in 1844 unsuccessfully presented such a plan to Congress. He urged that the railroad, via South Pass, be paid for by the sale of land along the route. See *Dictionary of American Biography*, XX, 156–57; and U.S. House of Representatives, *Executive Document 72*.

Wilcox, ———. A guide for the Mounted Riflemen, who were marching across the plains in 1849, Wilcox apparently was murdered on the trail along the Bear River by an Indian scout he had known in Oregon. Niles Searls obtained this information from men in a division of the regiment who were traveling near the Pioneer Line. According to Searls, Wilcox, originally from New York, was murdered in revenge for some former deed. See Searls, June 27; and Cross, June 7.

*Winslow, E. D. From Charleston, South Carolina, Winslow was a member of Carriage No. 1; he was one of two men from the deep South who shared the mess with Northerners from Maine and Massachusetts. Lell H. Woolley was one of his messmates.

*Wolf, Peter. His name is spelled incorrectly as Wolfe in the *Missouri Republican*. From Washington, Pennsylvania, Wolf was one of five young men from the town who joined the train and messed together in Carriage No. 10. Searls wrote on July 5 that Wolf saved the life of a teamster, "Chihuahua Bob," thrown from a horse while swimming the Platte at the Deer Creek crossing. See Forrest, "Forty-Niners from Washington County, Pennsylvania," pp. 5–6.

*Woolley, Lell H. Born in Martinsburg, New York, in 1825, Woolley lived in Vermont before he left for California. He accompanied a friend, E. S. Gross of Boston, with whom he shared a mess in Carriage No. 1. Woolley left California for the East in 1852, married, and returned in 1854. He was a member of the 1856 San Francisco Vigilance Committee, as were two other Pioneers, Walter and Robert Hawxhurst. In 1861 Woolley owned a grocery business, and in 1868 he was a produce commission broker; from 1868 to 1884 he worked for the Southern Pacific Railroad. Woolley, a lifelong Mason, published his memoirs at the age of 88; writing was not his long suit. See Woolley, *California*; and Robert Hawxhurst to Bernard Reid, May 25, 1859.

Graves Recorded Along the Trail in 1849
by Bernard J. Reid

MAY

26 Capt. Ashley
26 Hagin, ———
28 Roush, ———
28 Woodson, ———
29 Ingraham, ———
29 James H. Marshall
30 Mrs. Keyes
31 B. F. Adams

JUNE

1 John Degnier
1 H. L. Dunlap
1 J. Landon
1 John Eathy
2 John Abbott
2 Sloan McMillen
4 Daniel Collins
4 Joseph Louis Wells
6 Alice Hibbard
6 Franklin Wilson
9 Joseph Hunter
9 John D. Bradshaw
15 Capt. Pleasant Gray
16 W. N. Goodwin
16 S. W. Moore
20 Rachel E. Patterson
21 John Hoover
22 William L. Stevens
22 E. Morse
23 Ellis Russel

JUNE (cont.)

23 Samuel P. Judsen
23 N. T. Phillips
24 Joseph Geser
25 M. Roby
25 F. Dunn
25 Joseph Blakely
25 Rufus Adams
29 W. More
29 J. M. Hay
29 Dr. McDermet
29 A. Hammond
29 W. Brimer

JULY

2 Thomas M. Rankin
3 C. B. Pratt
20 Robert Gilmore
20 Mary Gilmore
25 J. Merrill

AUGUST

1 John Clawson
25 Melinda Cain
26 Henry H. Robinson

SEPTEMBER

19 Daniel Brouett
19 Ezra Allen
19 Henderson Cox

Notes

EDITOR'S INTRODUCTION

1. Johnston, p. 79.

2. See, e.g., Potter's introduction to Geiger and Bryarly; Holliday, "Gold Rush Reconsidered," pp. 35–41; Mattes, *Great Platte River Road*; "Gen. Smith's Correspondence," in U.S. Senate, *Executive Document 52*, pp. 111, 112; Stewart, *California Trail*, chaps. 4–9; Unruh, *The Plains Across*, chaps. 2–5, 10. Quotation from McCall, p. 49. A recent book by J. S. Holliday, *The World Rushed In*, is a mine of information.

3. Cholera became a national scourge in 1849. On July 3 President Zachary Taylor appointed the following August 3 as a day of prayer to "stay the destroying hand." See the *Daily National Intelligencer* (Washington, D.C.), July 4, 1849; and Rosenberg, *Cholera Years*, chap. 6.

4. Potter's introduction to Geiger and Bryarly, p. 1.

5. Biographical information from sources such as family records, letters, genealogies, clippings of obituaries, wills, and biographical sketches, all in the Reid Papers. See also Reid, "California Gold Rush Letter"; and Reid, diary, 1846–47, Jan. 25, 1847. The Reids came from Carrickmacross, County Monaghan, in the northern province of Ulster, Ireland. Meredith Reid's father died in Youngstown in 1822 at about the age of seventy-four, and his mother in 1824 at sixty-eight. For references to Simon, who had some surveying experience, and to his comparative affluence, see Meredith Reid to Bernard Reid, July 12, 1842, Jan. 3, 1843; Bernard Reid to James V. Reid, Jan. 9, 1854; and Rev. James Reid to Bernard Reid, Jan. 9, 1854. A widower with two children, Simon Reid died in 1854. Henceforth letters from Bernard Reid will be cited as from Reid.

6. Meredith Reid to Bernard Reid, May 22, July 12, 1842, March 13, May 13, 1844; to children, Jan. 3, 1843; James V. Reid to Bernard Reid, Aug. 12, 21, 1844; and copy of Meredith Reid's will, Aug. 12, 1844, Reid Papers. The father bequeathed his real estate equally among his five children, and his surveying instruments to James, his watch to John,

and his staff to Bernard. The second house was in neighboring New Derry, Pennsylvania, where the Reids moved in 1826. Kate Reid's name is spelled variously, but her father spelled it Catharine.

7. Meredith Reid to Bernard Reid, April 10, May 5, 1840; to children, Jan. 3, 1843; Reid to Meredith Reid, Oct. 3, 1840; to Rev. E. F. Garland, May 13, 1841; newspaper clipping, Clarion *Democrat*, April 17, 1887, Reid Papers; and Reid, "California Gold Rush Letter," p. 218.

8. Reid, diary, 1846–47, Jan. 9, June 20, 1847; James V. Reid to Bernard Reid, March 26, 1841, Oct. 8, 1846; James Reid to Bernard Reid, April 28, 1847, Aug. 31, 1854. Rev. James Reid paid for the Reid daughters, including Ellen Findley, to continue their schooling at convents, and the children invariably consulted him before making important decisions. He appears to have been a stern man, respected rather than loved by his nieces and nephews, whose affection for their father had been much stronger. See also James V. Reid to Bernard Reid, June 17, 1849; Reid to James V. Reid, Nov. 11, 1850; and Kate Reid to Bernard Reid, March 29, 1860.

9. Levinson, *Seasons of a Man's Life*, pp. 57–58, 78–80. Since Levinson uses only a small sample, his categories and generalizations are open to question. But in his investigation of the lives of young men on the overland trail between 1843 and 1869, the historian Howard Lamar also finds Levinson's model useful. It fits the careers of scores of young men in a general way, he writes, and the careers of three diarists "with startling precision." See Lamar, "Rites of Passage," esp. p. 45. Cf. Faragher, *Women and Men on the Overland Trail*, p. 18.

10. Reid, manuscript journal based on the 1849 diary (henceforth cited as Reid, journal), pp. 1–2. See also Reid, diary, 1846–47, June 8, 1847.

11. Reid's "total abstinence" pledge card, No. 6849, signed by him at St. Paul's Cathedral, Pittsburgh, on August 16, 1840, is in the Reid Papers. Many middle-class Irish were active supporters of temperance and the so-called "Protestant" ethic. See Brown, *Irish-American Nationalism*, esp. pp. 23, 41, 46. Reid remained abstinent all his life. See also Henry Frew to Bernard Reid, Jan. 7, 1842; invitation to anniversary of the Henry Baldwin Literary Institute, Pittsburgh, Nov. 24, 1841, Reid Papers; Reid diary, 1846–47, April 7, 1847; and Reid's letter to editor, Pittsburgh *Post*, April 10, 1902, Reid Papers. Reid apparently learned their language from German priests at his local church of St. Vincent's, near Youngstown. See James V. Reid to Bernard Reid, March 26, 1841; and newspaper clipping of letter to editor, signed "B.J.R.," in the Pittsburgh *Vindicator*, Jan. 18, 1886, Reid Papers.

12. Quotation in Reid, diary, 1846–47, Jan. 9, 1847; see also Farran family records in the Reid Papers. There are frequent self-conscious references to Letitia Farran in Reid's diary accounts of his visits to Pittsburgh in January, April, and June 1847. Her father may well have been the owner of the dry goods store for whom Reid worked in 1840. Letitia Farran was born in 1827.

13. Quotation in Reid to Rev. Joseph Deane, Jan. 27, 1846. See also Reid, diary, 1846–47, Jan. 1, 3, 5, 6, 10, April 4–6, May 23, 30, June 20, 26, 1847.

14. Reid to Rev. Joseph Deane, Jan. 27, 1846. Reid gives no explanation for his aversion to the law.

15. Reid, diary, 1846–47, Jan. 7, 11, 1847. Material on Reid's method and lists of mnemonic symbols are included in the Reid Papers. Mnemonics was a useful tool in a period when schooling (including college) was based on rote learning, and when oratory was much prized.

16. *Ibid.*, Jan. 11–13, 23–25, Feb. 7–11, 14, 22, 25, March 3, 9–11, 18, April 3, 1847. On January 23, for example, Reid met a Miss Riggs with "brilliant black eyes, the prettiest I ever remember to have seen of that color."

17. *Ibid.*, Jan. 12, 16, 18, 24, 27, Feb. 4, 7–10, 14, March 3, 8, 18, April 3, 1847.

18. *Ibid.*, Jan. 27, Feb. 8, March 8, 1847. See also copy of letter in verse, Reid to Kate Reid, Feb. 26, 1847; and copies of Mrs. Hemans's verses, both in Reid Papers. For the popularity and influence of the poetry of Felicia Dorothy Hemans (1793–1835), see Douglas, *Feminization of American Culture*, pp. 72, 135, 253.

19. Reid, diary, 1846–47, Jan. 11, 12, Feb. 17, March 19, April 1, 1847. Reid's small profit, despite so few customers, is explained by his modest expenses. For example, his lodging for seven days, from January 31 to February 6, cost $3.75.

20. *Ibid.*, May 25, June 6, 11, 15, 24, 29, July 1–6, 1847. See also F. R. Conway to Bernard Reid, May 29, 1847. In this instance Reid did not inform his "Rev. Uncle" of his plans, but apparently received his approval. Nearly ten years later, Reid's brother James earned only 500 dollars a year working as a civil engineer for the B&O Railroad. James V. Reid to Bernard Reid, Jan. 6, 1856.

21. See, e.g., Bieber, "California Gold Mania," pp. 16–22; Billington, *Far Western Frontier*, chap. 10; and Paul, *California Gold Discovery*. Quotation in New York *Herald*, Dec. 11, 1848.

22. For the best description of the trail, see Paden, *Wake of the Prairie Schooner*. See also Mattes, *Great Platte River Road*, p. 52, for times of travel.

23. See, e.g., Stewart, *California Trail*, chap. 9; Potter's introduction to Geiger and Bryarly, pp. 7–32; Clark's introduction to Perkins, pp. ix–xviii; the introduction by Read and Gaines to Bruff, I, li–liii. For an exhaustive study of joint-stock companies, and varieties of partnerships, see John P. Reid, *Law for the Elephant*. The paramilitary organization of large wagon trains had long been the custom on the Santa Fe and Oregon trails. Officers were elected as in the militia, the elections frequently being held after some days of overland travel.

24. See, e.g., Kemble, *The Panama Route*, chap. 2; Mattes, "Jumping-Off Places on the Overland Trail," pp. 27–39; Unruh, *The Plains Across*, pp. 97–100, 401–2; Wyman, "Outfitting Posts"; *Missouri Republican*,

March 10, 1849; and the St. Joseph *Gazette*, April 20, 1849. The St. Louis *Missouri Republican* was known also as the *Daily Missouri Republican*.

25. Unruh, *The Plains Across*, pp. 260–66, esp. table 6, p. 265; Geiger and Bryarly, p. 133; John P. Reid, *Law for the Elephant*, chap. 5; and the series of articles entitled "The Ferries of the Forty-Niners" by Dale Morgan in *Annals of Wyoming*.

26. Gilman, "Pioneer Astronaut," p. 168; Watkins, "The Revoloidal Spindle and the Wondrous Avitor," pp. 24–27, 69–70; and the St. Joseph *Gazette*, Feb. 16, 1849.

27. *Missouri Republican*, Feb. 13, 22, 28, March 19, April 17, 23, and May 17, 1849, letter from Dr. S. M. E. Goheen; Unruh, *The Plains Across*, p. 101; and Wilkins, pp. 27–30. An Independence Company, Hansford and Peacock, for example, installed an agent in St. Louis and proposed sending out two trains, one an "express" expected to make the trip in the unrealistic time of 45–55 days. There is no record that either train ever left Independence.

28. See the Pioneer Line's daily advertisements in the *Missouri Republican*, appearing after Feb. 6, and editorials on Feb. 6, March 21, April 23, and June 1 and 21, 1849. See also New Orleans *Daily Picayune*, Feb. 12, 1849; New York *Herald*, March 8, 1849; and McCall, p. 35. Turner and Allen had been "in charge of a large number of wagons" transporting army supplies and sutler's stores in 1847 for the second expedition to the city of Chihuahua, Mexico (200 miles south of El Paso, Texas), during the Mexican War; the expedition was under the command of Col. Alexander Doniphan, who hired many civilian wagon masters. The Pioneer Line had its offices in St. Louis, and its references were impressive. Among the prominent citizens vouching for the company were bankers, the president of an insurance company, and Robert Campbell, the rich and respected merchant who, as a former fur trader, had joined William Sublette in founding Fort Laramie in 1834. Although the Pioneer Line required a deposit of half the fare when a passenger signed a contract, the custom-made carriages, described as "elegant" in the newspaper, were ready for inspection one month after the company first advertised, indicating that the company had advance capital. See *Missouri Republican*, Feb. 6, March 8, 1849; Bauer, *The Mexican War*, chap. 2; Lamar, ed., *Reader's Encyclopedia of the American West*, pp. 157–58; and Bieber, ed., *Journal of a Soldier under Kearny and Doniphan*, p. 40.

29. *Missouri Republican*, Feb. 6, March 8, 9, 21, April 23, 28, 1849. For the Pioneer Line's campground as Reid described it in 1904, see pp. 29–34; see also Searls, p. 8. For the Pioneer Line see also Gordon, "Overland to California in 1849."

30. Quotations from *Missouri Republican*, March 21, April 28, 1849; Perkins, Sept. 3; and *Gold Rush: Letters from the Wolverine Rangers*, p. 21. For "Black" Harris, a veteran guide for overland wagon trains, see pp. 28–29 and Appendix A.

31. Quotations from *Missouri Republican*, April 23, May 17, 1849,

letter from Dr. S. M. E. Goheen; Lyne to Henry Lyne, May 17; McCall, p. 35. See also Swain, May 3; and Perkins, Sept. 3.

32. *Missouri Republican*, April 5, May 17, June 21, 1849; Barry, *Beginning of the West*, p. 875; and Searls, who wrote on May 10 that the train was awaiting additional baggage wagons that would not be completed until May 12. The *Missouri Republican* had announced on May 17 that there were 18 baggage wagons; Reid's count of 22 is explained by the addition of others to carry food and baggage for the extra passengers. On May 8 Thomas Turner was in Lexington, Missouri, buying the extra wagons; see the *Missouri Republican*, May 13, 14, 1849.

33. See the *Missouri Republican*, May 17, 1849, for list giving the place of residence for most of the 125 passengers. The list is reasonably accurate, though some names are spelled phonetically, but a number of men in Reid's passenger list (Reid Papers), or mentioned by Reid and Niles Searls in their diaries, are unlisted, among them Searls himself. The majority of passengers gave their home towns as their residences. Reid, for example, gave Clarion, Pennsylvania, and several other passengers working in St. Louis (for example, John Brewster, Andrew Duhring, and John James) also gave their home towns in other states. Dr. Richard H. McDonald, however, gave Prairie du Rocher, Illinois, where he had lived most recently, as his address, though he was born and grew up in Kentucky, and Lell H. Woolley, born in New York, listed his home as Vermont, the state he had left to join the gold rush.

34. See, e.g., Bidlack, ed., *Letters Home*, pp. 13–15; Forrest, "Forty-Niners from Washington County, Pennsylvania," pp. 6–8; McDonald, *McDonald Overland Narrative*, *Missouri Republican*, July 6, 1849, letter from "Pawnee"; McCall, p. 35; Reid, journal, p. 11; and St. Louis *City Directory* for 1848. Quotation in Searls, p. 12

35. See Bidlack, ed., *Letters Home*, p. 13; McDonald, *McDonald Overland Narrative*, appendix; and Walter Hawxhurst's obituary (clipping), Reid Papers. See also Reid, journal, p. 101, for Robert Hawxhurst; and Wilkins, p. 74, n. 14, for Garrett's age.

36. See passenger lists in the *Missouri Republican*, May 17, 1849, and in the Reid Papers, for army ranks of six passengers. But only one (Captain Henry J. Reed) is listed in Heitman's *Historical Register* as serving in the Mexican War.

37. Searls, Aug. 12; cf. Woolley, p. 9.

38. Quotations in Reid to Thomas Sutton, Nov. 27, 1847. See also Socrates Newman to Bernard Reid, Dec. 15, 1848; S. P. Lalumière to Bernard Reid, June 28, 1849; and Conroy, *Arnold Damen, S.J.*, chap. 4. Blackstone's *Commentaries*, published in four volumes between 1765 and 1770, was a standard legal text in the United States.

39. For the importance of St. Louis as a base in the gold rush, see Unruh, *The Plains Across*, p. 98; and *Missouri Republican*, April 19, 1849. Other single male diarists who expressed a desire for adventure as well as gold include Ansel McCall, Isaac Wistar, William Johnston, Peter Decker, Charles Glass Gray, and Vincent Geiger and Wakeman Bryarly.

Through the writings of men like Washington Irving, Richard Henry Dana, Francis Parkman, and John C. Frémont, the West had become a beacon to the adventurous. For examinations of the West in the popular imagination, see Fender, *Plotting the Golden West*, chaps. 1, 2; Smith, *Virgin Land*; and Unruh, *The Plains Across*, chap. 1. For J. H. Tooke, the charlatan, see p. 26 and Appendix A.

40. Barry, *Beginning of the West*, pp. 193–94, 861–62; Bruff, I, 548–49; Mattes, *Great Platte River Road*, p. 33; Stewart, *California Trail*, pp. 234–35. The most detailed account is in Unruh, *The Plains Across*, pp. 101–4. Unruh relies chiefly on the typed copy of Reid's journal deposited in the Western Pennsylvania Historical Society Library, Pittsburgh.

41. David T. McCollum's two letters to J. H. Lund of Ann Arbor are included in Bidlack, ed., *Letters Home*. Woolley wrote his reminiscences, *California*, when he was eighty-eight years old; most of his facts are wrong, and he remembers only a few of the events along the trail. Dr. McDonald left the Pioneer Line on June 16 and packed the rest of the way. His son's biography of him (most likely a campaign biography) is useful for information about McDonald and his two companions, Dr. C. H. Swift and Louis Sloss; see McDonald, *McDonald Overland Narrative*. For Searls, see his autobiography, *Diary of a Pioneer*, pp. 65–70. Searls practiced law in Nevada City, and in 1887 was appointed chief justice. In their diaries Reid and Searls make no mention of one another. Searls and McCollum were messmates, and Reid mentions McCollum, McDonald, and Woolley. Only McCollum was middle-aged and married; Reid was twenty-six, Searls twenty-four, Woolley twenty-four, and McDonald twenty-nine.

42. Quotations from *Missouri Republican*, July 6, 1849, letter from "Pawnee." See also Gordon, "Overland to California in 1849," pp. 18, 19, 24.

43. Bryant, p. 49.

EDITOR'S AFTERWORD

1. Quotation from Searls, Aug. 12; see also under Aug. 12, above. For an overview of the Pioneer Line's journey, see Gordon, "Overland to California in 1849," pp. 17–36.

2. See Searls, May 11, for quotation.

3. *Missouri Republican*, Aug. 29, 1849, letter from "Joaquin"; see also under June 28, above.

4. *Missouri Republican*, Feb. 6, 1849; Searls, June 13.

5. The Pioneer Line expected to make the trip in sixty days but took provisions for 100 days. See the editorial in the *Missouri Republican*, March 8, 1849.

6. See Reid's diary entry for July 11, above.

7. John P. Reid, "Dividing the Elephant," pp. 81–87. See also Pot-

ter's introduction to Geiger and Bryarly, pp. 37–40; and Pritchard, June 4.

8. Reid to James V. Reid, Nov. 27, 1849.

9. John P. Reid, "Dividing the Elephant," p. 92; cf. John P. Reid, *Law for the Elephant*, introduction. John P. Reid is not alone (despite his claim to the contrary) in concluding that the overland experience was a conservative one. Historians of the westward emigration like John Faragher, Julie Roy Jeffrey, Howard Lamar, David Potter, and John Unruh emphasize the importance of social conditioning in determining the overlanders' essentially law-abiding responses to life on the trail.

10. Quotation from Searls, Aug. 12; see also under Aug. 12, 21, above. Reid's diary gives no indication that the hungry passengers attempted to live off the land like other emigrants who shot wild fowl and rabbits along the Humboldt. See, e.g., Gray, Aug. 11, 12; Hutchings, Sept. 16; Perkins, Aug. 26; and Pritchard, July 11, 21.

11. Quotation from Wilkins, Sept. 19; see also under Aug. 31, above.

12. See Potter's introduction to Geiger and Bryarly, p. 54.

13. See, e.g., Reid to James V. Reid, Nov. 27, 1849; Reid's diary entries above for May 29, June 13, July 4, 22, 23, Aug. 6, Sept. 7; Reid, "California Gold Rush Letter," pp. 225, 230; Reid Journal, p. 115; Searls, June 5, 13, Aug. 19; *Missouri Republican*, July 6, letter from "Pawnee" for the observation on Turner and Aug. 29, 1849, letter from "Joaquin"; St. Joseph *Gazette*, Oct. 19, 1849, letter from A. W. Babbitt; Perkins, Sept. 3; and Wilkins, June 26. Both the Reid and Searls diaries include other entries illustrating how the passengers depended on the crew to do the hard work. Reid's diary shows that he frequently rode ahead of the train to avoid tedious labor.

14. Compare the experiences of greenhorn members of the Charlestown Company, recounted in the Vincent Geiger and Wakeman Bryarly diary; the company of government clerks from Washington, D.C., in the Goldsborough Bruff diary; and diarists James Pritchard, Charles Glass Gray, and Elisha Douglass Perkins. Perkins, for example, a drug gist from Marietta, Ohio, became so proficient a jack of all trades that by July 2 he converted his wagon to a smaller, lighter conveyance. Gray, a clerk from New York City, and his companions became expert shots and unlike the Pioneers, lived off the land as they moved along the Humboldt; see esp. Gray's entries for Aug. 11 and 12.

15. Faragher, *Women and Men on the Overland Trail*, esp. chaps. 1, 2; Lamar, "Rites of Passage"; Potter's introduction to Geiger and Bryarly; and John P. Reid, *Law for the Elephant*, esp. introduction. The quotation is from Reid to James V. Reid, Nov. 27, 1849; also quoted under Aug. 30, above.

16. Although the majority of passengers undoubtedly were Protestant (e.g., Brewster, McCollum, McDonald, Searls, Woolley, and the two Hawxhursts), there were a number of probable Catholics (e.g., an O'Brien, two Flynns, a Turney, a McKaraher, and a Sloan) on the train,

in addition to Reid. McCollum was an abolitionist, close to Dr. Speer or Spears, a Virginian, and Dr. R. H. McDonald was a firm antislavery man whose closest friend was Dr. C. H. Swift from Alabama. McCollum and McDonald were temperance crusaders. The passenger list in the Reid Papers is divided into messes; in four (nos. 1, 7, 14, and 15) men from the deep South messed with Northerners from states like Maine, Massachusetts, New Jersey, and Ohio.

17. Lord, July 11; Reid, diary, above, June 7, July 26; Reid to James V. Reid, Nov. 27, 1849; Searls, July 4, 5, 25, Aug. 19; Faragher, *Women and Men on the Overland Trail*, p. 101.

18. See Reid, diary, above, Sept. 4, 8, 10, 11; quotations in Reid, journal, p. 102, and Searls, Sept. 23. See also Reid, "California Gold Rush Letter," pp. 225, 227; Reid to James V. Reid, Nov. 27, 1849; Searls, May 25–30, June 7, Aug. 19, Sept. 3; Woolley, p. 14; and Reid, journal, p. 114.

19. See correspondence between Reid and A. C. Bonnell, Reid and Walter and Robert Hawxhurst, and Reid and Dr. R. H. McDonald, all in Reid Papers; see esp. Robert Hawxhurst to Bernard Reid, July 14, 1860, for Hawxhurst's reference to the passengers as "our crowd." For ill-feeling on large wagon trains, see, e.g., Gray, July 2; McCall, p. 33; Staples, July 30; Faragher, *Women and Men on the Overland Trail*, pp. 101–3; and the introduction by Read and Gaines to Bruff, I, xxxvi.

20. *Missouri Republican*, June 21, 1849; Barry, *Beginning of the West*, pp. 875–76; Bruff, I, p. 548, n. 7; Dewolf, Sept. 3; Hutchings, Oct. 10; U.S. Senate *Executive Document* 52, 111, 112; Unruh, *The Plains Across*, p. 102. A remnant of the second train crossed the Sierra only ten days after the first, which was delayed for weeks at the Carson River.

21. *Missouri Republican*, Feb. 28, April 9, Nov. 18, 1850; St. Joseph *Gazette*, March 10, May 5, 1852; Barry, *Beginning of the West*, pp. 926, 1070–72, 1206; Price, p. 254; Stine to mother, June 3, 1850, and Stine, journal, July 23, 27, 30, Aug. 18, 22, 1850; Stout, *On the Mormon Trail*, II, 374–78; Moorman, June 6, 1850; and Unruh, *The Plains Across*, pp. 104–6.

22. Faragher, *Women and Men on the Overland Trail*, p. 36; Jeffrey, *Frontier Women*, pp. 28, 108.

23. *Missouri Republican*, Jan. 23, 1851, letter from Dr. S. M. E. Goheen; Stine, journal, July 22, 1850 (*"Deliver me* from a *passenger train"*). Dr. Goheen is the same physician mentioned by Reid in the prologue. After he had buried his brother in Independence, Dr. Goheen wrote a letter from his home in Belleville, Illinois, to the *Missouri Republican* (May 17, 1849) praising the Pioneer Line as a wagon train with "superior advantages" over other forms of conveyance; apparently he had not heard of the disastrous trip when he signed on as a passenger on a train in 1850.

24. Starr, *Americans and the California Dream*, p. 52; quotations in Reid to Kate Reid, March 12, 1852.

25. Quotation in Reid to James V. Reid, Nov. 27, 1849; see also Reid, "California Gold Rush Letter," pp. 229, 233.

26. For the primitive state of the hospitals, the number of incompetent doctors, and the unsatisfactory sanitary conditions in the city, see Groh, *Gold Fever*, esp. p. 41; and Muscatine, *Old San Francisco*, pp. 236–45.

27. Reid to James V. Reid, Nov. 27, 1849.

28. Reid to John Reid, May 30, 1850; and to his sisters, Jan. 28, 1851. See also another diary of Bernard Reid's, kept intermittently from January 1 to October 6, 1850, and published in 1937 under the title "Diary of Bernard J. Reid, 1850," by the *Pony Express Courier*, entries of Feb. 21–23, May 8, and June 11. The original 1850 diary is lost; a copy was sent to the paper by Reid's son Ambrose in 1937.

29. Reid, "Diary, 1850" (1937), entries of July 15–Aug. 11, Aug. 13–Sept. 11, 1850. See also Reid to John Reid, May 30, 1850; to Mary Reid, Aug. 23, 1850; and to James V. Reid, Nov. 11, 1850. Reid's note of indebtedness to Walter Hawxhurst, dated July 10, 1850, is in the Reid Papers. His St. Louis friend was O. M. Brown, an attorney, who had also boarded at Newman's. The southern mines were situated along the tributaries of the San Joaquin River, and Stockton was the port of supply; the northern mines were along the Feather, Yuba, Bear, and American rivers.

30. See Reid to John Reid, May 30, 1850; Lord, June 11, July 16, 1850; Paul, *Mining Frontiers of the Far West*, pp. 19–28; and Wyman, ed., *California Emigrant Letters*, pp. 85–88.

31. Reid to James V. Reid, Nov. 11, 1850, see also Reid to Mary Reid, Aug. 23, 1850; Reid to sisters, Jan. 28, 1851.

32. Reid to James V. Reid, Nov. 11, 1850. Reid's letters from the southern mines are being prepared for publication by the editor.

33. *Ibid.* See also Reid to sisters, Jan. 28, 1851.

34. Reid to James V. Reid, Nov. 11, 1850.

35. Reid to sisters, Jan. 28, 1851; Reid to Mary Reid, March 12, 1851.

36. Reid to sisters, Jan. 28, 1851.

37. *Ibid.* In referring to the "Sierras" (the correct term is sierra), Reid means both the coast range and the foothills of the Sierra Nevada. The Santa Clara valley later would be called the valley of Heart's Delight.

38. Quotations in Reid to Mary Reid, March 12, 1851; Reid, diary, 1851–52, Aug. 25, 1851. When he left for San Francisco on August 25, 1851, Reid owed Hawxhurst $345.46.

39. Reid, diary, 1851–52, Aug. 25, 30, 31, Sept. 2, 3, 13, 18, Oct. 28, 1851. See also George Doherty to John Nobili, Oct. 3, 1851, Doherty Correspondence; Doherty writes that Reid was "unable to procure a situation" and took the post at the school as "a *dernier resort*." The school had seventy scholars, and Reid boarded free at the rectory. In addition to his teaching duties Reid served as "procurator" in charge of household and school management, and taught English to the European

priests in residence. He also continued studying French and Spanish, and taught private classes in Spanish. The church, on Vallejo Street, conducted services in English, French, and Spanish, according to numerous church notices in the San Francisco *Herald* throughout the year 1851.

40. See Reid, diary, 1851–52, Sept. 18, 1851, to Jan. 3, 1852; and Reid, "Early Reminiscences of Santa Clara College" (May 1, 1901), p. 1 (cited henceforth as "Early Reminiscences"), Reid Papers.

41. For the college in 1851, see McKevitt, *University of Santa Clara*, pp. 12–40. Father Accolti was ordered back to Oregon by the Jesuit father general in Rome, but his leadership in the plan to establish a Jesuit college did not cease; Accolti was far more enthusiastic and confident than Nobili at that time. Mission Santa Clara, founded by Franciscans in 1777, had become the center of religious life in the valley. A decade after Mexico obtained its independence from Spain in 1823, the Mexican legislature secularized the mission system, and Mission Santa Clara became a parish church under Mexican padres. The last padre, José Suárez del Real, writes McKevitt (p. 11), was a dissolute friar whose interests "centered on horses, women, and local politics." He was dismissed by Alemany and sent back to Mexico in 1851, but not before he had sold church property for personal profit. He also had taken off for the goldfields in 1848 and acquired "a great deal of gold"; see Morgan's introduction in the William Perkins journal, p. 22.

42. See McKevitt, *University of Santa Clara*, pp. 25–37; Reid, diary, 1851–52, Nov. 30, Dec. 18, 19, 25, 1851; and Reid, "Early Reminiscences," p. 1. In 1851 both Father Accolti and Father Nobili visited the rectory, a haven for priests in San Francisco, and observed that Reid was a tower of strength to Langlois. Though more than half of the boarders were Protestant, and two Jewish, prayers and church services were compulsory for all pupils.

43. Reid, diary, 1851–52, Jan. 3, 1852. Father Langlois had a checkered career. A secular priest, he arrived at Santa Clara College in the spring of 1852 to enter the Jesuit order, but left to become a Dominican in 1854. He then left the Dominicans and was a parish priest in Half Moon Bay, California, in 1875, and chaplain at the Christian Brothers Novitiate in Martinez, California, in 1886. See Antoine Langlois to John Nobili, Oct. 1854, Nobili Presidential Papers; Langlois to Bernard Reid, April 30, 1886, Reid Papers.

44. Quotations in Reid to Kate Reid, March 12, 1852, and Reid, "Early Reminiscences," p. 5. See also the prospectus of Santa Clara College in the *Daily Evening Picayune* (San Francisco), Feb. 18, 1852, and draft written in Reid's hand, Nobili Presidential Papers; and McKevitt, *University of Santa Clara*, p. 45. Despite Nobili's qualms about his English, letters written by him in that language and preserved in the Presidential Papers are fluent and frequently elegant in expression.

45. Quotations in McKevitt, *University of Santa Clara*, p. 25; and Reid, "Early Reminiscences," p. 4.

46. Quotations in McKevitt, *University of Santa Clara*, pp. 26, 39, 44.
47. Quotations in Reid, "Early Reminiscences," p. 8; Reid to Mary Reid, March 12, 1851. The italics in the quotation about Judas are Reid's. The hanging and burning of the effigy of Judas Iscariot was a popular Mexican custom; see Hittell, *History of California*, III, 502. Father Nobili was equally impatient with Mexican customs; his purpose was to train young boys for entry into a predominantly Anglo-American culture, and he considered the "distractions" of a frontier society harmful to scholarship and "habits of regularity." See Reid, "Early Reminiscences," pp. 7–8; and McKevitt, *University of Santa Clara*, p. 45.
48. Reid, diary, 1851–52, June 2, 1852.
49. The cancelled note is in the Reid Papers; apparently Walter Hawxhurst forgave the 15 percent interest on it. See also Reid's record of payments, listed in the back of his diary, 1851–52; and Reid to Mary Reid, May 15, 1852. For Reid's salary see the ledger for 1852, Santa Clara College, Archives, University of Santa Clara. Reid taught his class in mnemonics at California Wesleyan (now the University of the Pacific in Stockton, California), established in Santa Clara in May 1852; see Reid to Kate Reid, July 14, 1852. Although Santa Clara College was the first to open in California, the Methodist school was the first chartered, in July 1851; Nobili did not acquire the 20,000 dollars required by the state for incorporation until 1855. Like Santa Clara, California Wesleyan was a preparatory school for some years.
50. Reid to sisters, Jan. 28, 1851; to Kate Reid, March 12, 1852; and to Letitia Farran, July 22, 1853.
51. Antoine Langlois to Bernard Reid, April 30, 1886.
52. Quotations in Reid to Mary Reid, May 15, 1852. See also poems to Jane Hawxhurst (called "Jeannie") in the Reid Papers; and notes in back of Reid's diary, 1851–52.
53. Reid to Kate Reid, July 14, 1852; Reid, diary, 1851–52, Sept. 1, 1852; Reid, "Early Reminiscences," p. 14. See also Reid to John Nobili, Aug. 31, 1852, Nobili Presidential Papers; Kemble, *The Panama Route*, p. 253; and the San Francisco *Herald*, Sept. 1, 1852, which reported that the *Winfield Scott* sailed with 627 passengers and twenty "on deck." The ship was built to carry 315 passengers.
54. Reid, diary, 1851–52, Sept. 6–19, 1852. Conditions on the overcrowded ships to Panamá were wretched, and most returning emigrants complained bitterly about the high cost of passage and the unsatisfactory quarters and bad food, which contributed to the spread of diseases. Cf. Batchelder, Nov. 1850; Lord, Feb. 15, 16, March 4, 1851; and Tiffany, Feb. 1851.
55. Reid, diary, 1851–52, Sept. 20–23, 1852. Reid's cryptic notes are scribbled in pencil on this stage of the journey home. The Reid Papers also contain a page of a letter from Reid to an unknown addressee, describing his passage across the Isthmus. He shared a mule to carry his baggage at a cost of twelve dollars; on reaching Cruces he was "muddy from head to foot—clothes torn—soaking with perspiration." In the

letter he wrote of the trip to Cruces, "For 'badness' it beats all I had ever seen before." On the Isthmus passage cf. Bruff, July 5, 1857; Lord, March 6, 1851; Kemble, *The Panama Route*, chap. 7; Marryat, *Mountains and Molehills*, chap. 24; and William Perkins, pp. 366–72.

56. Reid, diary, 1851–52, Sept. 23 to Oct. 3, 1852; see also a page of a letter in the Reid Papers describing part of the journey home. The railroad across the Isthmus was completed in 1855. Aspinwall (now Colón) was its terminus on the Atlantic side, and by 1852 ships had begun to use this port as well as the port of Chagres. Reid wrote that the passengers on board the ship were so greedy and "hoggish" that he "said a cross word to a man" for the first time in years. The *United States* was Reid's connecting ship; he had paid for through passage to New York, and the ship left thirty minutes after Reid hastened aboard. Like the *Winfield Scott*, the *United States* was a wooden side-wheel steamer; both were owned by the New York and San Francisco Steamship Line. See Kemble, *The Panama Route*, p. 62.

57. Reid, diary, 1851–52, Oct. 3–11, 1852, and list of names of families of California friends in the back of the diary. Reid also stopped off in Philadelphia for a day on his return to Pittsburgh by rail, to visit other families; one visit was to the mother and sister of a fellow Pioneer Line passenger, John McKaraher.

58. Quotations in John Reid to Bernard Reid, Feb. 22, 1851; Reid to Letitia Farran, July 22, 1853; to Rev. George Reid, Oct. 14, 1902. See also Reid to Letitia Farran, Sept. 24, Nov. 13, 1853; Kate Reid to Bernard Reid, May 27, 1850; and family records in the Reid Papers.

59. Reid to James V. Reid, Nov. 1, 1854, July 1, 1855; Walter Hawxhurst to Bernard Reid, Jan. 15, 1855. The height of Know-Nothingism occurred in the 1850's. Anti-Catholicism was deep-rooted in American society, having arrived with the Puritans. It took political form in 1854 with the organization of the American, or Know-Nothing, party. The party achieved "spectacular" political victories in 1854 and 1855, chiefly in the northeast, but it had collapsed by 1856. For the complex ramifications of this third party, see Billington, *Protestant Crusade*, chap. 15; Holt, *Political Crisis of the 1850's*, chaps. 6, 7.

60. See Reid to James V. Reid, May 29, 1859; and family records in the Reid Papers.

61. See, e.g., scrapbook of clippings on the 1856 Democratic party national convention, Reid Papers; Reid's letter to the Pittsburgh *Post*, May 9, 1860; and Reid to Letitia Reid, Oct. 6, 1861. Reid was no abolitionist but a Douglas Democrat, pinning his free soil hopes on popular sovereignty. As the Civil War progressed he became a firm supporter of emancipation. In supporting Lincoln and emancipation, Reid again was no stereotypical Irish Catholic. For the opposition of ethnic Catholics to emancipation, see McPherson, *Ordeal by Fire*, pp. 272–75.

62. See in the Reid Papers the voluminous correspondence on Reid's recruiting efforts for the Union army; Bishop I. M. Young (of Erie, Pennsylvania) to Bernard Reid, July 22, 1861, commending Reid's "pa-

triotic ardor"; and Reid's first letter to his wife from Camp Hays, Sept. 22, 1861.

63. Reid to Letitia Reid, July 17, 29, Aug. 2, 5, Dec. 1, 8, 29, 1861; Rev. Robert Sutton to Ambrose Reid, Dec. 9, 1904; and letter of commendation to the Clarion *Democrat* from Reid's noncommissioned officers, Aug. 10, 1862, Reid Papers. Reid left the battlefield in early August, but his resignation was accepted officially in October; see S. Williams (Army of the Potomac Headquarters) to Bernard Reid, Oct. 17, 1862.

64. See, e.g., Reid to Letitia Reid, Oct. 30, Nov. 4, 24, 1861, July 22, 1862.

65. Reid to Letitia Reid, Sept. 22, 29, Oct. 6, 20, Nov. 4, Dec. 22, 1861.

66. Reid to Letitia Reid, April 6–8, 13, May 4, 12, 16, 31, June 1, 4, 15, July 1, 1862. Reid wrote to his wife on November 4, 1861, that a tour of picket duty had been his first realization of the state of war, and on November 12 that he had engaged in his first "hostile march" against the enemy. Reid's company took part in the siege of Yorktown in April 1862, and in the Battle of Williamsburg on May 6. But the terrible fighting and severe casualties came with the Battle of Fair Oaks or Seven Pines on May 31 and June 1, 1862. His company was under steady fire during the Seven Days battles in the final week of June, and it supported Gen. FitzJohn Porter at the Battle of Gaines' Mill, June 27. The company was in the vanguard of troops, "more dead than alive," retreating under General McClellan's orders to Harrison's Landing on the James River in Virginia. On July 1 Reid heard the "cannonading" of the Battle of Malvern Hill from Harrison's Landing. For the Peninsula Campaign, see Catton, *Terrible Swift Sword*, pp. 312–14, 325–38; and Commager, ed., *The Blue and the Gray*, I, 119–47, 310–13, 770–77. For a history of the 63rd Regiment, Pennsylvania Volunteers, see Hays, comp., *Under the Red Patch*.

67. Reid to Letitia Reid, July 10, 21, Aug. 6, 1862. See also Lt. I. N. Fenstermaker to Bernard Reid, Sept. 29, 1862; Bishop I. M. Young to Bernard Reid, Nov. 25, 1862; and Lt. G. W. Fox to Bernard Reid, June 18, Oct. 5, 1863. Apparently family members criticized Reid for reenlisting, since his infant son, John James, had died on February 2, 1863, and Letitia was pregnant; another son, George, was born during Reid's absence on July 8, 1863. On August 5, 1863, Reid wrote to his wife about her understanding attitude, saying that only extreme danger to state and country had "called him from home."

68. Reid to Letitia Reid, July 25–27, Aug. 6, 9, 1863. See also Reid, "California Gold Rush Letter," p. 219. On July 27 Reid learned that General Morgan had been captured the day before by the cavalry near New Lisbon, Ohio. Morgan later escaped and was killed at Greenville, Tennessee, on September 4, 1864. Reid's regiment mustered out on August 9, 1863. For John Hunt Morgan, see the *Dictionary of American Biography*, XIII, 174.

69. Family records, Reid Papers. Reid formed a new law firm, Reid and Patrick, after his return to Clarion in 1863.

70. See, e.g., copy of letter from Reid to Peter Burnett, Feb. 18, 1883; Reid to Charles Vincent Reid, March 8, 1873; and to Ambrose Reid, Oct. 5, 1873; obituaries of Bernard Reid; clipping from the Pittsburgh *Times*, Dec. 10, 1903, on the celebration of the fiftieth anniversary of Reid's admission to the Bar, all in Reid Papers. See also Reid, "California Gold Rush Letter," pp. 219–20. Bernard Reid's most important legal work was his role as resident counsel for John D. Rockefeller in 1879, when the Standard Oil Company was prosecuted for conspiracy; see Clarion *Democrat*, clipping, Dec. 18, 1879, Reid Papers.

71. See, e.g., Ambrose Reid to Bernard Reid, March 4, 1889; copy of letter from Judge Galbraith to Governor Patterson, Dec. 25, 1884; copy of letter, Judge James Campbell to Governor Patterson, Nov. 25, 1891; and correspondence between Reid and his sisters, all in Reid Papers. See also correspondence between the three Reid aunts and Ambrose Reid, Ambrose B. Reid Papers. Reid's foster sister, Ellen Findley, was always considered a full member of the family. His three sisters kept house for their uncle, Rev. James Reid, from 1848 until his death in 1867; they then returned to Clarion. John Reid, though the most successful of the brothers financially, became known as one of Clarion's eccentrics, remembered as "a shriveled up, little old man in an old, rusty, black frock coat." See Alfred D. Reid, Jr., to this editor, for a copy of the recollection by an aged Clarion resident, Oct. 10, 1980, in my possession.

72. The Reid Papers contain abundant materials on Reid's lifelong religious activities. He belonged to Catholic societies, attended congresses of Catholic laymen, wrote letters to newspapers defending Catholicism, and belonged to the Catholic International Truth Society, formed to combat anti-Catholicism. But at a time when Catholicism was defensive and culturally isolated, Reid urged greater understanding among different faiths, and he cultivated friendships with Protestants like the Hawxhursts, his law partner, and Rev. Joseph Twichell, a Civil War padre. Although Reid's belief that his faith was the "true religion" prevented real ecumenicism, Rev. Joseph Twichell, who held Reid in "uncommon affection," wrote: "Though we were not of the same religious communion outwardly we were, as regards the truths of the Christian faith that are most vital, in deep accord." See Rev. Joseph Twichell to Ambrose Reid, Oct. 5, 1904, Reid Papers. Reid, however, was never an "Irish-American." There is no evidence that he joined Irish associations or gave support to Ireland in its troubles.

73. Copy of letter from Reid to Peter Burnett, Feb. 18, 1883. In that year the Reids added a wing to their house in Clarion. See Reid to Ambrose Reid, Sept. 30, 1883.

74. Ambrose chafed at the limitations of his life in Clarion and experienced at a later age (thirty-two) the restlessness his father had demon-

strated in 1846. See the remarkable letter from Ambrose Reid to Bernard Reid, March 4, 1889, telling his father of his decision to leave Clarion. George became a Professor at St. Paul's Seminary in St.Paul, Minnesota, after some years of parish duty in Texas. Mary Agnes became Mother Superior at St. Joseph's Academy in Titusville, Pennsylvania, and Letta a nurse, eventually a pharmacist, at Mercy Hospital in Pittsburgh. Charles Vincent (known as Vincent or "C. V.") lived in Fairhaven, Washington, from 1890 to around 1894, where he opened a typing and shorthand school and engaged in real estate ventures. See family records and obituaries, Reid Papers; Reid to Letitia Reid, June 27, July 5, 1891; and to Rev. George Reid, July 22, 1892. After Ambrose Reid moved to Pittsburgh in 1889, Bernard Reid's law firm became Reid and Maffett, with F. J. Maffett as his partner.

75. Copy of letter, Reid to Peter Burnett, Feb. 18, 1883; Reid to Rev. George Reid, May 26, June 6, July 22, 1892; copy of letter to Rev. Joseph Twichell, July 18, 1895; Genevieve Reid to Letitia Reid, July 30, 1892; and family records in Reid Papers. Reid became friendly with Peter Burnett in 1850, and taught his two sons at Santa Clara in 1852; see Reid-Burnett correspondence, Reid Papers.

76. Copy of letter, Reid to Peter Burnett, Feb. 18, 1883; Reid to Rev. George Reid, Sept. 3, 1895; Ambrose Reid to Bernard Reid, March 4, 1899; Anna Reid to Letitia Reid, July 7, 1877; to Bernard Reid, Oct. 26, 1877. In 1895 Reid assumed payment of the interest on Norbert's share of an $18,000 debt he had incurred in business with two partners (Reid wrote to his son George that Norbert was "not a good manager"). At the time of his death in the influenza epidemic of 1918, Norbert owned a men's clothing store in Pittsburgh. Vincent was unemployed for a time after he returned from Fairhaven in the 1890's but eventually found work with the Salvage Security Company in Pittsburgh. Vincent became the black sheep of the family, apparently because of his misuse of family funds in real-estate ventures. Estranged from his family, he left Pittsburgh and was living in Oklahoma in 1911. Vincent was buried in Pittsburgh in 1935. In his will Bernard Reid forgave Vincent's debts, but excluded him from a share in his estate. See legal documents in the Reid Papers; a letter in my possession from Alfred D. Reid, Jr., Jan. 6, 1983; and B. J. Reid's will, Nov. 13, 1904, in the Reid Papers.

77. Reid to Letitia Reid, July 22, 1899; to Rev. George Reid, Sept. 4, 1900; Ambrose Reid to parents, Feb. 20, 1900; copy of letter from Reid to Rev. Joseph Twichell, Oct. 11, 1902; Reid to Ambrose Reid, July 1903; and family records in Reid Papers.

78. See voluminous correspondence with former officers and men of Company F, officers of the Sixty-third Pennsylvania Regiment, and officials of the Society of the Potomac and the GAR, Reid Papers. See also Reid, "History of Company 'F'"; and Folder 18, containing speeches Reid made to schools and civic groups on patriotism and the Civil War,

both in Reid Papers. For the GAR, the "most powerful patriotic society of the day," see Higham, *Strangers in the Land*, esp. pp. 29–32, 60–63, 77–87.

79. Quotations in Starr, *Americans and the California Dream*, p. 61.

80. Reid to Mary Reid, Aug. 23, 1850; and to Letitia Reid, Aug. 18, 1886. Reid and Walter Hawxhurst were particularly faithful correspondents. The two men never met again after Reid left California; Hawxhurst died in 1883 at the age of eighty-nine. After Walter Hawxhurst's death Reid corresponded with his son, Robert Hawxhurst, and saw him frequently during his later visits to San Francisco. See esp. Robert Hawxhurst to Bernard Reid, April 7, 1883; and Walter Hawxhurst's obituary, clipping, n.d., Reid Papers. See also Reid to James V. Reid, April 12, 1856; copy of letter, Reid to Peter Burnett, Feb. 18, 1883; and William Bulkley to Bernard Reid, April 11, 1856.

81. Reid to Genevieve Reid, July 11, 1886; to Letitia Reid, July 14, 1886; and to Letta Reid, July 8, 1886.

82. Reid to Genevieve Reid, July 18, 1886; to Letitia Reid, July 22, 1886; and to Ambrose Reid, July 26, 1886.

83. Reid to Letitia Reid, Aug. 18, 1886; and to Ambrose Reid, July 26, 1886. For the college in 1886, see McKevitt, *University of Santa Clara*, chap. 9. The mission church had been renovated "almost beyond recognition," writes McKevitt (p. 117), the adobe walls having been replaced with wooden ones; but the church's interior remained much the same.

84. Reid also went west in 1891, but did not visit California; he went to Fairhaven, Washington, to visit his son Vincent, and to buy land for himself and his brother John. In 1892 Reid took his daughter Genevieve to California to spend the summer with John Burnett (once a student of Reid's at Santa Clara, and a son of Peter Burnett, former governor of the state) and his family, in a desperate effort to prolong her life. Reid's most touching reunions were with the Hawxhurst family, to whom he remained devoted, as they to him. He saw Jane again; she had married happily in 1853. On her death in 1889, her sister Eliza sent Jane's photograph to Reid, in recognition of the special fondness they once had had for one another. See Reid to Letitia Reid, Nov. 23, 1890, June 27, 1891; to Letta Reid, June 27, July 5, 1891; Genevieve Reid to Letitia Reid, July 30, 1892; to Bernard Reid, Aug. 16, Dec. 18, 26, 1892; and Eliza Hawxhurst to Bernard Reid, April 14, 1889.

85. Reid to Letitia Reid, Nov. 23, 1890.

86. Copies of letters from Reid to R. E. Kenna, S.J., Sept. 4, 1886, Jan. 6, 1894; M. A. Key, S.J., to Bernard Reid, Dec. 22, 1893, Jan. 14, 1894. See also Reid, "Early Reminiscences"; copy of letter, Reid to R. E. Kenna, S.J., May 25, 1901; *Golden Jubilee and Souvenir*, Santa Clara College, 1901, Archives, University of Santa Clara. All the material sent by Reid to the college, with the exception of a letter to the president, June 6, 1894 (Kenna Presidential Papers), has been lost. His invaluable "Early Reminiscences" was thus unavailable to Gerald Mc-

Kevitt when he prepared his history of the University in 1979. Reid's copies were discovered only when a collection of Reid Papers arrived at the University's archives in 1980.

87. Reid to Letitia Reid, Oct. 25, 1890. See also Reid to Ambrose Reid, July 21, 1886, Aug. 8, 14, 1903; to Letitia Reid, Nov. 23, 1890; R. H. McDonald to Bernard Reid, Feb. 26, 1891; card from A. C. Bonnell (1890); and membership certificate (1886) in the Society of California Pioneers, Reid Papers. Dr. R. H. McDonald's brother made the overland trip in 1850.

88. Reid wrote to Rev. Joseph Twichell, a Congregational minister and Civil War comrade, that "we, as Catholics, find a special consolation in the doctrine of Communion of Saints. . . . Our prayers follow our loved ones beyond the grave, and they in turn are intercessors for us who wait." But he and his wife suffered intense anguish during the long illness of their daughter, the child of their middle age. See copy of letter, Reid to Rev. Joseph Twichell, July 18, 1895; and Reid to Rev. George Reid, June 6, 1895. For Reid's distress over his wife's poor health and the change in her personality, see Reid to Rev. George Reid, Sept. 4, 1900.

89. Reid most likely began the journal based on the diary sometime after he received replies about the Goheens in late January 1904. Apparently he wrote some of it during a stay in Mercy Hospital, Pittsburgh; he was not seriously ill, and may have been hospitalized for a recurrence of a carbuncle that had sent him to the hospital in 1902. The manuscript is written on foolscap and on the back of legal calendars, some for March 1904. See Reid, "California Gold Rush Letter," p. 221, for evidence that Reid wrote part of the journal in the hospital; and Reid to Rev. George Reid, May 1, 1902, for his sickness in 1902. Quotation in clipping from the Pittsburgh *Times*, Dec. 10, 1903, Reid Papers.

90. See Lucy Reid to Ambrose Reid, July 21, 24, 1904, for Bernard Reid's "revival" after his trip east, similar to the salutary effect of his trip to California in 1903; Reid to Rev. George Reid, June 2, Oct. 24, 1904; to Ambrose Reid, Oct. 30, 1904; and one page from Ambrose's pocket diary, Nov. 13–15, 1904, with notes on Bernard Reid's last days in Mercy Hospital, Pittsburgh, in Reid Papers. Ambrose, who was very close to his father, and clearly Reid's favorite son, wrote on November 15, "He died at 9 minutes to one."

Bibliography

The following abbreviations are used in the Bibliography:

AUSC Archives, University of Santa Clara, Santa Clara, Calif.
BRBL Beinecke Rare Book and Manuscript Library, Yale University, New Haven, Conn.
CSmH Henry E. Huntington Library, San Marino, Calif.
CU-BANC Bancroft Library, University of California, Berkeley, Calif.

Overland records—diaries, guides, narrative journals, letters, and memoirs—are designated by an asterisk.

Appleton's Cyclopaedia of American Biography. New York, 1888–89.
* Austin, Henry. Diary, 1849. TS: CU-BANC.
* Backus, Gurdon. Diary, 1849–51. MS: BRBL.
* Badman, Philip. Diary, 1849. MS: BRBL.
Bancroft, Hubert Howe. Works. 39 vols. San Francisco, 1888.
* Banks, John Edwin. Diary, 1849. In Howard E. Scamerhorn, ed., The Buckeye Rovers in the Gold Rush. Athens, Ohio, 1965.
Barry, Louise. The Beginning of the West: Annals of the Kansas Gateway to the American West, 1540–1854. Topeka, Kan., 1972.
* Batchelder, Amos. Diary, 1849–50. MS: CU-BANC.
Bauer, K. Jack. The Mexican War, 1846–1848. New York, 1974.
Bean, Walton. California: An Interpretive History. New York, 1968.
* Berrien, Joseph W. Ted and Caryl Hinckley, eds. "Overland from St. Louis to the California Gold Fields in 1849: The Diary of Joseph Waring Berrien." Indiana Magazine of History, LVI (Dec. 1960), 273–352.
* Bidlack, Russell E., ed. Letters Home: The Story of Ann Arbor's Forty Niners. Ann Arbor, Mich., 1960.
Bieber, Ralph P. "California Gold Mania." Mississippi Valley Historical Review, XXXV (June 1948), 3–28.
———, ed. [George Rutledge Gibson's] Journal of a Soldier under Kearny and Doniphan, 1846–47. Glendale, Calif., 1935.

Billington, Ray A. The Far Western Frontier, 1830–1860. New York, 1956.

———. The Protestant Crusade, 1800–1860: A Study of the Origins of American Nativism. New York, 1938.

* Bond, Robert. Diary, 1849. MS: BRBL.

* Brown, John Evans. "Memoirs of an American Gold Seeker." *Journal of American History*, II (Jan.–March 1908), 129–54.

Brown, Thomas N. Irish-American Nationalism, 1870–1890. Philadelphia, 1966.

* Bruff, Goldsborough. Georgia Willis Read and Ruth P. Gaines, eds. Gold Rush: The Journals, Drawings, and Other Papers of Goldsborough Bruff, Captain, Washington City and California Mining Association, April 2, 1849–July 20, 1851. 2 vols. New York, 1944.

* Bryant, Edwin. What I Saw in California. New York, 1848.

* Bryarly, Wakeman. See Geiger and Bryarly.

Buffum, Edward Gould. Six Months in the Gold Mines. Philadelphia, 1850.

* Buffum, Joseph C. Diary, 1847–55. TS: CU-BANC.

* Burbank, Augustus R. Diary, 1849–51. Microfilm of MS: CU-BANC.

Burnett, Peter. Recollections and Opinions of an Old Pioneer. New York, 1880.

* Castleman, P. F. Diary, 1849–51. TS: CU-BANC.

Catton, Bruce. Terrible Swift Sword. New York, 1963.

* Chamberlain, William E. Diary, 1849. Microfilm of MS: CU-BANC.

* Churchill, Stillman. Diary, 1849. Microfilm of MS: CU-BANC.

* Clark, Bennett C. Ralph P. Bieber, ed. "Diary of a Journey from Missouri to California in 1849." *Mississippi Valley Historical Review*, XXIII (Oct. 1928), 3–43.

* Clayton, W. The Latter-day Saints' Emigrants Guide: Being a Table of Distances from Council Bluffs to the Valley of the Great Salt Lake. St. Louis, 1848.

Cline, Gloria Griffith. Exploring the Great Basin. Norman, Okla., 1963.

Commager, Henry S., ed. The Blue and the Gray: The Story of the Civil War as Told by Participants. 2 vols. New York, 1950.

Connelley, William Elsey. "The Prairie Band of Pottawatomie Indians." *Collections*, Kansas Historical Society, XIV (1915–18), 488–570.

Conroy, Joseph P. Arnold Damen, S.J.: A Chapter in the Making of Chicago. New York, 1930.

* Cosad, David. Diary, 1849–50. Photocopy of MS: CU-BANC.

* Cross, Osborne. "The Journal of Major Osborne Cross." In Raymond W. Settle, ed., The March of the Mounted Riflemen. Glendale, Calif., 1940.

Cullum, George W. Biographical Register of the Officers and Graduates of the U.S. Military Academy at West Point. 2 vols. New York, 1868.

* Darwin, Charles B. Diary, 1849. MS: CSmH.

* Decker, Peter. Helen S. Giffen, ed. The Diaries of Peter Decker: Over-

land to California in 1849 and Life in the Mines, 1850–1851. Georgetown, Calif., 1966.
* Delano, Alonzo. Across the Plains and Among the Diggings. Auburn, N.Y., 1854.
———. Old Block's Sketch Book: Or, Tales of California Life. Sacramento, 1850.
De Voto, Bernard. The Year of Decision: 1846. Boston, 1943.
* Dewolf, David. Edwin E. Cox, ed. "Diary of the Overland Trail, 1849, and Letters, 1849–1850, of David Dewolf." *Transactions*, Illinois Historical Society, 1925, pp. 183–222.
* Dickensen, Luella. Reminiscences of a Trip Across the Plains in 1846. San Francisco, 1904.
Dictionary of American Biography. Allen Johnson and Dumas Malone, eds. 20 vols. New York, 1928–36.
Doherty, George, Correspondence. MS Collection: AUSC.
Donnelly, Joseph P., ed. Wilderness Kingdom, Indian Life in the Rocky Mountains, 1840–47: The Journals and Paintings of Nicolas Point. New York, 1967.
Douglas, Ann. The Feminization of American Culture. Reprint, New York, 1978.
* Doyle, Simon, Diary, 1849. MS: BRBL.
Encyclopedia of the History of St. Louis. 3 vols. New York, 1899.
* Everts, F. D. Diary, 1849. MS: BRBL.
Faherty, Wiliam B. Better the Dream: Saint Louis: University and Community, 1818–1968. St. Louis, 1968.
Faragher, John M. Women and Men on the Overland Trail. New Haven, Conn., 1979.
* Farnham, Elijah B. Merrill J. Mattes and Elsey J. Kirk, eds. "From Ohio to California in 1849: The Gold Rush Journal of Elijah Bryan Farnham." *Indiana Magazine of History*, XLVI (Sept. and Dec. 1950), 297–318, 403–20.
Fender, Stephen. Plotting the Golden West: American Literature and the Rhetoric of the California Trail. New York, 1981.
Ferrier, William Warren. Ninety Years of Education in California, 1846–1931. Berkeley, Calif., 1937.
Filler, Louis. The Crusade Against Slavery, 1830–1860. New York, 1960.
Forrest, Earle R. "Forty-Niners from Washington County, Pennsylvania." *Pony Express*, XII (Sept. 1944), 5–8.
* Foster, Isaac. Diary, 1849–50. TS: CSmH.
* Frémont, John C. Report of the Exploring Expedition to the Rocky Mountains in the Year 1842, and to Oregon and North California in the Years 1843–44. Washington, D.C., 1845.
Gardiner, Howard C. Dale L. Morgan, ed. In Pursuit of the Golden Dream: Reminiscences of San Francisco and the Northern and Southern Mines, 1849–1857. Stoughton, Mass., 1970.
Garraghan, Gilbert J. The Jesuits in the Middle United States, 3 vols. New York, 1938.

* Geiger, Vincent E., and Wakeman Bryarly. David M. Potter, ed. Trail to California: The Overland Journal of Vincent Geiger and Wakeman Bryarly. Reprint, New Haven, 1962.
* Gelwicks, Daniel W. Diary, 1849. TS: CU-BANC.
* Gibbs, George. "The Diary of George Gibbs." In Raymond W. Settle, ed., The March of the Mounted Riflemen. Glendale, Calif., 1940.
  Gilman, Rhoda R. "Pioneer Astronaut: William Markoe and His Balloon." *Minnesota History*, XXXVIII (Dec. 1962), 166–76.
* The Gold Rush: Letters from the Wolverine Rangers to the Marshall, Michigan, Statesman, 1849–1851. Mt. Pleasant, Mich., 1974.
* Goldsmith, Oliver. Overland in Forty-Nine: Recollections of a Wolverine Ranger After a Lapse of Forty-seven Years. Detroit, 1896.
  Gordon, Mary McDougall. "Overland to California in 1849: A Neglected Commercial Enterprise." *Pacific Historical Review*, LII (Feb. 1983), 17–36.
* Gould, Charles. Diary, 1849. TS: CU-BANC.
* Gray, Charles G. Thomas D. Clark, ed. Off at Sunrise: The Overland Journey of Charles Glass Gray. San Marino, Calif., 1976.
  Groh, George W. Gold Fever: Being a True Account, Both Horrifying and Hilarious, of the Art of Healing (So-Called) During the California Gold Rush. New York, 1966.
  Gusfield, Joseph. Symbolic Crusade: Status, Politics and the American Temperance Movement. Urbana, Ill., 1963.
* Hackney, Joseph. Diary, 1849. In Elizabeth Page, ed., Wagons West: A Story of the Oregon Trail. New York, 1930.
  Hafen, Leroy R., ed. The Mountain Men and the Fur Trade of the Far West. 10 vols. Glendale, Calif. 1965–72.
* Hale, Israel F. "Diary of a Trip to California in 1849." *Society of California Pioneers Quarterly*, II (June 1925), 61–130.
* Hall, O. J. Diary, 1849. TS: CU-BANC.
* Hamelin, Joseph P. Diary, 1849–50. MS: BRBL.
  Hanchett, William F., Jr. "The Question of Religion and the Taming of California, 1849–54." *California Historical Society Quarterly*, XXXII (June 1953), 49–56.
* Harker, George Mifflin. "Morgan Street to Old Dry Diggings, 1849." In Stella Drumm, ed., *Glimpses of the Past* (Missouri Historical Society), VI (1939), 35–76.
  Hart, James A. A Companion to California. New York, 1978.
* Haun, Catherine Margaret. Recollections of a Trip Across the Plains, 1849. TS: CSmH.
  Hays, Gilbert Adams, comp. Under the Red Patch: The Story of the 63rd Regiment Pennsylvania Volunteers. Pittsburgh, 1908.
  Heitman, Francis B. Historical Register and Dictionary of the United States Army, 1789–1925. 2 vols. Washington, D.C., 1903.
  Higham, John. Strangers in the Land: Patterns of American Nativism, 1860–1925. New York, 1965.

Hittell, Theodore H. History of California, 4 vols. San Francisco, 1885.

* Hixson, Jasper M. Diary, 1849. Photocopy of TS: CU-BANC.

Holland, Dorothy Garesché. "Saint Louis Families from the French West Indies." In J. F. McDermott, ed., The French in the Mississippi Valley. Urbana, Ill., 1965.

Holliday, J. S. "The Gold Rush Reconsidered." In K. Ross Toole, John Alexander Carroll, Robert M. Utley, and A. R. Mortensen, eds., Probing the American West: Papers from the Santa Fe Conference. Santa Fe, 1962.

* ———. The World Rushed In: The California Gold Rush Experience. New York, 1981. (Based on the William Swain diary.)

Holt, Michael F. The Political Crisis of the 1850's. New York, 1978.

* Hoover, Vincent A. Diary, 1849. MS: CSmH.

Howe, Daniel Walker, ed. Victorian America. Philadelphia, 1976.

Howe, Octavius T. Argonauts of '49: History and Adventures of the Emigrant Companies from Massachusetts, 1849–1850 . Cambridge, Mass., 1923.

* Howell, Elijah P. Diary, 1849. Photocopy of MS: CU-BANC.

Hunt, Rockwell D. "Pioneer Protestant Preachers of Early California." *Pacific Historical Review*, XVIII (Feb. 1849), 84–95.

* Hutchings, James M. Shirley Sargent, ed. Seeking the Elephant, 1849: James Mason Hutchings' Journal of His Overland Trek to California. Glendale, Calif., 1980.

* Ingalls, Eleazar S. Journal of a Trip to California by the Overland Route Across the Plains in 1850–1851. Waukegan, Ill., 1852.

* Jagger, D. Diary, 1849–59. Microfilm of MS: CU-BANC.

Jeffrey, Julie R. Frontier Women: The Trans-Mississippi West, 1840–1880. New York, 1979.

* Johnson, John A. Notebook, 1849. MS: BRBL.

* Johnston, William G. Experiences of a Forty-Niner. Pittsburgh, 1892.

Kemble, John H. The Panama Route, 1848–1860. Berkeley, Calif., 1943.

Kenna, R. E., Presidential Papers. MS Collection: AUSC.

* Kirkpatrick, Charles A. Diary, 1849–50. MS: CU-BANC.

Lamar, Howard R. "Rites of Passage: Young Men and Their Families in the Overland Trail Experience, 1843–1869." In Thomas E. Alexander, ed., Soul Butter and Hog Wash and Other Essays on the American West. Provo, Utah, 1978.

———, ed. The Reader's Encyclopedia of the American West. New York, 1977.

* Leeper, David R. The Argonauts of 'Forty-Nine: Some Recollection of the Plains and Diggings. South Bend, Ind., 1894.

Levinson, Daniel J. The Seasons of a Man's Life. New York, 1978.

* Lewis, John F. Diary, 1849. MS: BRBL.

* Lindsey, Tipton. Diary, 1849. MS: CU-BANC.

* Long, Charles L'H. Diary, 1849. MS: BRBL.

*Lord, Israel S. P. Diary, 1849–51. MS and newspaper clippings: CSmH. (In a number of bibliographies, Lord is identified incorrectly as Isaac S. P. Lord.)

*Loring, William W. "Report of Colonel Loring, October 15, 1849." In Raymond W. Settle, ed., The March of the Mounted Riflemen. Glendale, Calif., 1940.

*Love, Alexander. Diary, 1849–52. MS: BRBL.

*Lyne, James. Letters, 1849–50. MS: Thomas E. Eastin Collection, BRBL.

*Mann, Henry R. Diary, 1849. TS: CU-BANC.

Marryat, Frank. Mountains and Molehills, or, Recollections of a Burnt Journal. 1853. Reprint, New York, 1962.

Mattes, Merrill J. The Great Platte River Road: The Covered Wagon Mainline via Fort Kearny to Fort Laramie. Lincoln, Neb., 1969.

———. "The Jumping-Off Places on the Overland Trail." In John F. McDermott, ed., The Frontier Re-Examined. Urbana, Ill., 1967.

Mattison, Ray H. "Alexander Harvey." In LeRoy R. Hafen, ed., The Mountain Men and the Fur Trade of the Far West. Glendale, Calif., 1965–72. IV, 119–23.

*McCall, Ansel J. The Great California Trail in 1849. Bath, N.Y., 1882.

*McCoy, Samuel F. Pioneering on the Plains. Kaukauna, Wisc., 1924.

McDermott, John F. "De Smet's Illustrator: Father Nicolas Point." Nebraska History, XXXIII (March 1952), 35–40.

———, ed. The Frontier Re-examined. Urbana, Ill., 1967.

*McDonald, Richard Hayes. Frank V. McDonald, comp. The McDonald Overland Narrative and Biography: Notes Preparatory to a Biography of Richard Hayes McDonald. Cambridge, Mass., 1881.

*McIlhany, Edward W. Recollections of a '49er. Kansas City, Mo., 1908.

McKevitt, Gerald. The University of Santa Clara: A History, 1851–1977. Stanford, Calif., 1979.

*McKinstry, Byron N. Bruce L. McKinstry, ed. The California Gold Rush Overland Diary of Byron N. McKinstry, 1850–1852. Glendale, Calif., 1975.

McPherson, James M. Ordeal by Fire: The Civil War and Reconstruction. New York, 1982.

*Middleton, Joseph. Diary, 1849–51. MS: BRBL.

*Moorman, Madison B. Irene D. Paden, ed. The Journal of Madison Berryman Moorman, 1850–1851. San Francisco, 1948.

Morgan, Dale L. "The Ferries of the Forty-Niners." Annals of Wyoming, XXXI (April 1959), 5–31; XXXI (Oct. 1959), 145–89; XXXII (April 1960), 51–69; XXXII (Oct. 1960), 167–203.

*Morse, E. W. Diary, 1849–50. MS: CSmH.

Murphy, Celeste G. The People of the Pueblo, or, The Story of Sonoma. Sonoma, 1937.

Muscatine, Doris. Old San Francisco: The Biography of a City from Early Days to the Earthquake. New York, 1975.

New Orleans Daily Picayune, 1849.

New York *Herald*, 1848–49.

Nobili, John, Presidential Papers. MS Collection: AUSC.

* Orvis, Andrew M. Diary, 1849–50. MS: BRBL.

The Pacific (San Francisco), 1852–53.

Paden, Irene D. The Wake of the Prairie Schooner. New York, 1943.

* Parke, Charles R. Diary, 1849–52. MS: CSmH.

Paul, Almaurin B. "My First Two Years in California." *Society of California Pioneers Quarterly*, IV (March 1927), 25–54.

Paul, Rodman W. The California Gold Discovery: Sources, Documents, Accounts and Memoirs. Georgetown, Calif., 1967.

———. Mining Frontiers of the Far West, 1848–1880. New York, 1963.

Peltier, Jerome. "Moses 'Black' Harris." In LeRoy R. Hafen, ed., The Mountain Men and the Fur Trade of the Far West. Glendale, Calif., 1965–72. IV, 103–17.

* Perkins, Elisha Douglass. Thomas D. Clark, ed. Gold Rush Diary: Being the Journal of Elisha Douglass Perkins on the Overland Trail in the Spring and Summer of 1849. Lexington, Ky., 1967.

Perkins, William. Dale L. Morgan and James R. Scobie, eds. Three Years in California: William Perkins' Journal of Life at Sonora, 1849–1852. Berkeley, Calif., 1964.

A "Pile," or, A Glance at the Wealth of the Monied Men of San Francisco and Sacramento City; also, An Accurate List of the Lawyers, Their Former Places of Residence, and Date of Their Arrival in San Francisco. San Francisco, 1851.

* Pleasants, W. J. Twice Across the Plains, 1849 to 1856. San Francisco, 1906.

* Pond, A. R. Diary, 1849–52. MS: CSmH.

Potter, David M. The Impending Crisis: 1848–1861. New York, 1976.

———, ed. See Geiger and Bryarly.

* Price, Joseph. Thomas M. Marshall, ed. "The Road to California: Letters of Joseph Price." *Mississippi Valley Historical Review*, XI (Sept. 1924), 237–57.

* Pritchard, James A. Dale L. Morgan, ed. The Overland Diary of James A. Pritchard from Kentucky to California in 1849. Denver, 1959.

Reid, Ambrose B., Papers. MS Collection: AUSC.

Reid, Bernard J., Papers. MS Collection: AUSC. (Cited as Reid Papers.)

* Reid, Bernard J. "A California Gold Rush Letter from Bernard J. Reid." James D. Van Trump and Alfred D. Reid, Jr., eds. *Western Pennsylvania Historical Magazine*, XLIV (Sept. 1961), 217–35. (Ambrose B. Reid included a typed copy of this letter in the copy he made in 1931 of Reid's journal, cited below. The original letter is lost.)

———. Diary, 1846–47. MS: Reid Papers, AUSC. (Cited as Reid, diary, 1846–47.)

* ———. Diary, 1849. MS: Reid Papers, AUSC.

———. Diary, 1851–52. MS: Reid Papers, AUSC. (Cited as Reid, diary, 1851–52.)

————. "Diary of Bernard J. Reid, 1850." *Pony Express Courier*, Oct. 1937, pp. 9–10, 13–14. (The original diary is lost.)

————. "Early Reminiscences of Santa Clara College." May 1, 1901. TS: Reid Papers, AUSC. (Cited as "Early Reminiscences.")

*————. Journal, 1849, written in 1904. MS: Reid Papers, AUSC. (Cited as Reid, journal. An inexact copy of the journal, edited and typed by Ambrose B. Reid in 1931, is also in the Reid Papers.)

————. Letters, 1840–1904. MS: Reid Papers, AUSC.

Reid, John P. "Dividing the Elephant: The Separation of Mess and Joint Property on the Overland Trail." *Hastings Law Journal*, XXVIII (Sept. 1976), 72–92.

————. Law for the Elephant: Property and Social Behavior on the Overland Trail. San Marino, Calif., 1980.

————. "Sharing the Elephant: Property and Social Behavior on the Overland Trail." *University of Missouri–Kansas City Law Review*, XLV (Winter 1976), 207–22.

Root, George A. "Ferries in Kansas." *Kansas Historical Quarterly*, II (Nov. 1933), 343–76; III (Feb. 1934), 15–42.

Rosenberg, Charles E. The Cholera Years: The United States in 1832, 1849 and 1866. Chicago, 1962.

Sacramento *Transcript*, 1850.

San Francisco *Alta California*, 1849–52, 1854.

San Francisco *City Directory* for 1850, 1852, 1854, 1856.

San Francisco *Daily Evening Picayune*, 1851–52.

San Francisco *Herald*, 1850–52.

*Searls, Niles. Diary, 1849. MS: CU-BANC.

*————. The Diary of a Pioneer and Other Papers. San Francisco, 1940. (Searls's published 1849 diary, which includes an introduction, lists of deaths, and an autobiography, should be read in conjunction with the manuscript diary, since there are many errors in the transcription from the manuscript diary.)

*Sedgley, Joseph. Overland to California in 1849. Oakland, Calif., 1877.

*Settle, Raymond W., ed. The March of the Mounted Riflemen. Glendale, Calif., 1940.

*Shaw, Reuben C. Milo Milton Quaife, ed. Across the Plains in Forty-Nine. Chicago, 1948.

Smith, Henry Nash. Virgin Land: The American West as Symbol and Myth. New York, 1950.

Soulé, Frank, John H. Gihon, and James Nisbet. The Annals of San Francisco. New York, 1855.

*Stansbury, Howard. Explorations and Surveys of the Valley of the Great Salt Lake of Utah, Including a Reconnaisance of a New Route Through the Rocky Mountains. Philadelphia, 1852.

*Staples, David J. Diary, 1849. MS: CU-BANC.

Starr, Kevin. Americans and the California Dream, 1850–1915. New York, 1973.

Stewart, George R. The California Trail: An Epic with Many Heroes. New York, 1962.

―――. Committee of Vigilance: Revolution in San Francisco, 1851. Boston, 1964.

*Stine, Henry A. Journal and Letters, 1850. TS: CU-BANC.

St. Joseph (Mo.) *Gazette*, 1849–56.

St. Louis *City Directory* for 1848.

St. Louis *Missouri Republican*, 1847–56.

Stout, Hosea. Juanita Brooks, ed. On the Mormon Frontier: The Diary of Hosea Stout, 1844–1861. 2 vols. Salt Lake City, 1964.

*Swain, William. Diary and Letters, 1849–51. MS: BRBL. (For the published diary see Holliday, *World Rushed In*.)

Tamony, Peter. "'To See the Elephant.'" *Pacific Historian*, XII (Winter 1968), 23–29.

Taylor, Bayard. Eldorado, Or, Adventures in the Path of Empire. 1850. Reprint, New York, 1949.

*Tiffany, P. C. Diary, 1849–51. MS: BRBL.

*Tinker, Charles. Eugene H. Roseboom, ed. "Charles Tinker's Journal: A Trip to California in 1849." *Ohio State Archaeological and Historical Quarterly*, LXI (Jan. 1952), 64–85.

Toole, K. Ross, Robert M. Utley, John Alexander Carroll, and A. R. Mortensen, eds. Probing the American West: Papers from the Santa Fe Conference. Santa Fe, 1962.

Unruh, John. The Plains Across: The Overland Emigrants and the Trans-Mississippi West, 1840–60. Urbana, Ill., 1979.

U.S. Bureau of the Census. Population Schedule. 6th Census, 1840; 7th Census, 1850; 8th Census, 1860.

U.S. *Congressional Globe*. 30th Congress, 2d session, Senate, 580, Feb. 22, 1849.

U.S. House of Representatives. Executive Document 72. 28th Congress, 2d session, 1844.

U.S. Senate. Executive Document 52. 31st Congress, 1st session, 1850.

*Van Dorn, T. J. Diary, 1849. MS: BRBL.

Walsh, Victor A. "'A Fanatic Heart': The Cause of Irish-American Nationalism in Pittsburgh During the Gilded Age." *Journal of Social History*, XVIII (Winter 1982), 187–204.

The War of the Rebellion: A Compilation of the Official Records of the Union and the Confederate Armies. Vol. X. Washington, D.C., 1887.

*Ware, Joseph E. John Caughey, ed. The Emigrants' Guide to California, 1849. Reprint, Princeton, N.J., 1932.

Washington, D.C., *Daily National Intelligencer*, 1849.

Watkins, T. H. "The Revoloidal Spindle and the Wondrous Avitor." *American West*, IV (Feb. 1967), 24–70.

Webb, Todd. The Gold Rush Trail and the Road to Oregon. New York, 1963.

*Webster, Kimball. The Gold Seekers of '49: A Personal Narrative of the

Overland Trail and Adventures in California. Manchester, N.H., 1917.

Webster's American Military Biographies. Springfield, Mass., 1978.

* Wilkins, James F. John Francis McDermott, ed. An Artist on the Overland Trail: The 1849 Diary and Sketches of James F. Wilkins. San Marino, Calif., 1968.

* Willis, Edward J. Diary, 1849. MS: BRBL.

* Willis, Ira J. Irene Paden, ed. "The Ira J. Willis Guide to the Gold Mines." *California Historical Society Quarterly*, XXXII (Sept. 1953), 193–207.

* Wilson, William. Letters and Daybooks, 1850–51. MS: BRBL.

* Wistar, Isaac J. Diary, 1849. Autobiography of Isaac Jones Wistar, 1827–1905. New York, 1937.

* Wood, Joseph W. Diary, 1849–53. MS: CSmH.

* Woolley, Lell H. California, 1849–1913. Oakland, Calif., 1913.

Wright, Louis B. Culture on the Moving Frontier. New York, 1961.

Wyman, Walker D. "The Outfitting Posts." *Pacific Historical Review*, XVIII (Feb. 1949), 14–23.

* ———, ed. California Emigrant Letters. New York, 1952.

Index